SHRAPNEL

SHRAPNEL
CONTEMPLATIONS

LANCE OLSEN

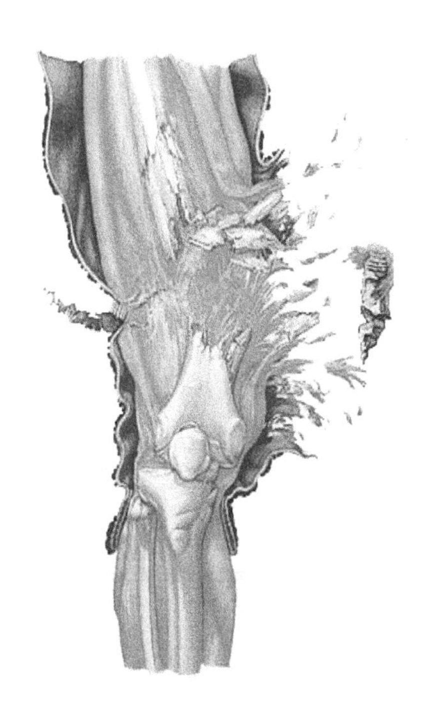

Shrapnel: Contemplations

ISBN: 979-8-98-654792-3
Library of Congress Number: 9798986547916

First Anti-Oedipal Paperback Edition: February 2024

Published in the United States by Anti-Oedipus Press, an imprint of
Raw Dog Screaming Press.

www.rawdogscreaming.com

Interior Design by D. Harlan Wilson
www.dharlanwilson.com

Cover Design by Matthew Revert
www.mathewrevert.com

Anti-Oedipus Press
Grand Rapids, MI

@AntiOedipusP
@antioedipuspress

www.anti-oedipuspress.com

ALSO BY LANCE OLSEN

NOVELS

Live from Earth
Tonguing the Zeitgeist
Burnt
Time Famine
Freaknest
Girl Imagined by Chance
10:01
Nietzsche's Kisses
Anxious Pleasures
Head in Flames
Calendar of Regrets
Theories of Forgetting
There's No Place Like Time
Dreamlives of Debris
My Red Heaven
Skin Elegies
Always Crashing in the Same Car
Absolute Away

FICTION COLLECTIONS

My Dates with Franz
Scherzi, I Believe
Sewing Shut My Eyes
Hideous Beauties
How to Unfeel the Dead

NONFICTION

Ellipse of Uncertainty
Circus of the Mind in Motion
William Gibson
Lolita: A Janus Text
Rebel Yell: A Short Guide to Writing Fiction
Architectures of Possibility: After Innovative Writing
[[there.]]

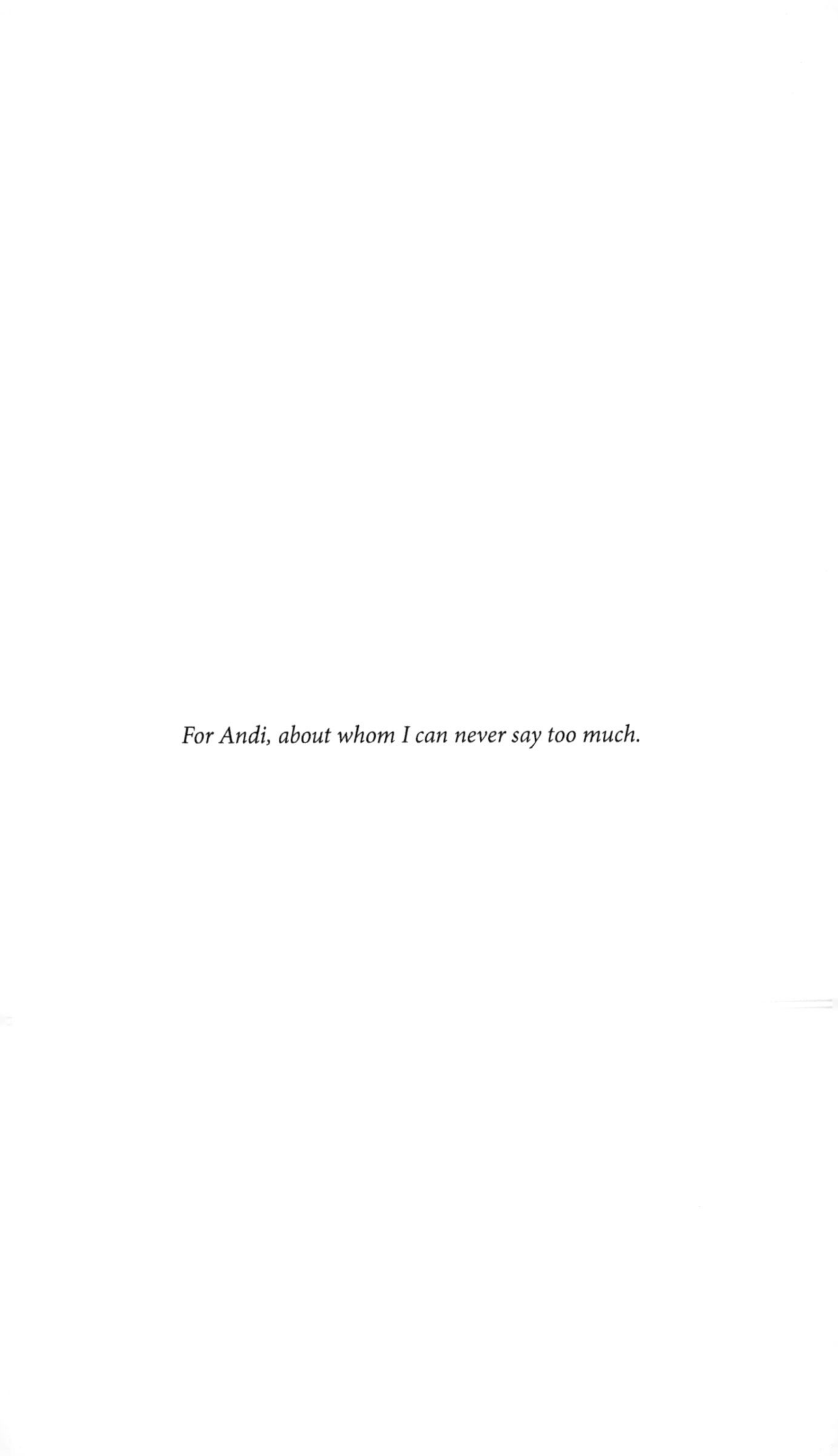

For Andi, about whom I can never say too much.

"The pleasure of realizing that one may have to undergo the same realizations, write the same notes in the margin, return to the same themes in one's work, relearn the same emotional truths, write the same book over and over again—not because one is stupid or obstinate or incapable of change, but because such revisitations constitute a life."

—Maggie Nelson, *The Argonauts*

"Nobody writes about anything but themselves."

—Tom Ford, *Nocturnal Animals*

CONTENTS

1

LIMIT SITUATIONS

CARNAGE CARNIVAL: (TRANS)FORMS AS PHILOSOPHY

AFTER YESTERDAY'S CRASH

Let me begin with a quote:

> The American writer in the middle of the twentieth century has his hands full in trying to understand, describe and then make credible much of American reality. It stupefies, it sickens, it infuriates and finally it is even a kind of embarrassment to one's own meager imagination. The actuality is continually outdoing our talents, and the culture tosses up figures almost daily that are the envy of any novelist.

Except for the mention of the mid-twentieth century in the first sentence, doesn't that sound like it might have been uttered this morning? Probably *was* uttered this morning as we doom-scrolled through today's news over our first cup of coffee? In fact, though, it appeared more than sixty years ago—in March, 1961—in an essay by Philip Roth published in *Commentary*, the leading postwar journal committed to constructing Jewish identity in the US following the Holocaust—appeared before, that is, the assassination of John F. Kennedy, Bobby Kennedy, and Martin Luther King, Jr.; before the social convulsions of the sixties, Vietnam, and Watergate; before the moon landing and the advent of the PC, the World Wide Web, Amazon, the cellphone, Facebook, YouTube, Twitter, Instagram, TikTok, video games, and virtual reality; before AIDS, 9/11, the US debacles in Iraq and Afghanistan, and the deciphering of the human genome; before the resignation of Richard Nixon, the inauguration of Barack Obama, the emergence of Donald Trump and his Trumpniks, the resurgence of the far right (with its magnification of the racist, sexist, despotic, and violent impulses innate to American culture); before the exponential growth of income and health-care inequality, the weaponization of disinformation on social media and off, and the intrinsic dysfunction of our political and academic systems.

And now look at us.

We might be tempted to say much of what I just listed strikes us as a little quaint in its ability to shock, befuddle, and enrage, even as we find ourselves weathering a pandemic that, according to the World Health Organization, has already claimed more than 15,000,000 lives worldwide; in the midst of a redefinition of geopolitics (with a renewed spotlight on the grim realities of refugeeism) in response to Russia's brutal invasion of Ukraine; and on the brink of a climate catastrophe, which may well be too late to stop, and which has prompted some think tanks to begin pondering the question: *How can we learn to adapt to our own extinction?*

For the past twenty-two years, the American West, where I have lived and worked for three decades, has suffered a megadrought sparked by that catastrophe. In California, the result has been the eruption of massive wildfires that have burned millions of acres while pumping more than 112 million tons of greenhouse gasses into the atmosphere, making the air toxic for months on end. A byproduct of that nightmare has been the disappearance of lakes. The Great Salt Lake in Utah, for example, which has been shrinking for decades, has now reached an historic low. If the trend continues—and there is no reason to suspect it won't—scientists predict it will evaporate entirely within the next decade or so. If that happens, clouds of arsenic dust concentrated in the dry lakebed will blow into Salt Lake City on a regular basis. Prolonged exposure will lead to greatly increased rates of lung cancer.

Another way of saying this: things will get a lot worse before they get a lot worse.

WRITE AS IF YOU WERE DYING

The scale implicit in Roth's observation, in short, has changed spectacularly. What once seemed huge has been recalibrated by the events of the last, say, quarter century. Richard Powers's 2018 eco-novel, *The Overstory*, about nine Americans whose relationship with trees invites its readers to contemplate the destruction of our forests and the implications of that loss, is emblematic of this transformation. The novel's first of three sections, "Roots," is initially told on the timespan of trees rather than human beings—an exceptional move. Powers thereby recasts a calcified narrative arc to emphasize the insignificance of the individual within earth's 4.5-billion-year (and the universe's 14-billion-year) history. His bleak hope in the opening section relocates itself in the endurance, not of homo sapiens, but those other species that might survive murder at our hands. Tellingly, that relocation undoes itself in the second and third sections of the novel as it re-focalizes on human protagonists, re-privileging our timescale and troubling its own argument by returning to narrative business more or less as usual. Nonetheless, *The Overstory* teaches us something important about narrativity: telling from an unanticipated angle opens onto drastically new comprehension.

The Overstory underscores a vital pair of aesthetic and existential questions: What is the contemporary novelist, the contemporary literary citizen, supposed to do in view of our current situation, one an author of Roth's generation simply couldn't begin to fathom? How do we proceed in light of a challenge Annie Dillard posed decades ago—"Write as if you were dying. At the same time, assume you write for an audience consisting solely of terminal patients. That is, after all, the case … What could you say to a dying person that would not enrage by its triviality?"—how do we proceed now that we have grasped that our mortality is taking place on a planetary scale? How do we proceed knowing in the heart of our anxious hearts that novels don't change the world, never have, and never will, that we are fiddling while Rome burns? Do we damn ourselves with yet more faint optimism, trying to persuade ourselves that living in history has always been savage, and today is no exception? Perhaps settle for maintaining armchair-outrage from inside our bougie retreats?

I don't think so. Or at least I hope not. And what I want to think about is the why of that. Let me start by proposing what I think most of us here already intuit: that while novels don't change the world, never have, and never will, they continuously change individuals, change us, within the world, so long as we allow ourselves to become fully present in their presence. In other words, their function has never been global, but rather local; never been external, but rather internal. Perhaps that's why we experience such cognitive dissonance when we come across the proposition that novels don't transfigure anything at all. Every one of us who reads them is a walking example of how untrue such a proposition is. We each remember the hour a novel changed the worlds within us, and by doing so changed our relationship to the worlds outside us.

I recall two texts—one a novella, one a novel—which I encountered in high school that shocked me into the writing, reading, and thinking life. Before I tell you about them, however, you have to envision what a terrible student I was. I confess I was that annoyingly apathetic one who sat in the back of the classroom, staring out the window, daydreaming, biding my time until the period I was suffering through was done. I wore my D average as a badge of courage and apostasy, believing unwaveringly—along with high school students everywhere—that I had it all figured out.

For some inexplicable reason, my eleventh-grade English teacher took exception with my premises. Her name was Joyce Garvin. She stood barely five feet tall, was almost eerily slight, and sported forehead-slappingly red hair and unreasonably large green turtle-shell glasses. One day after class, as I was trying to escape without notice, she caught me and handed me a copy of Kafka's *Metamorphosis*. She said I should read it.

We could then get together and talk about it if I was interested. That first sentence we all know so well—"As Gregor Samsa awoke one morning from uneasy dreams, he found himself transformed in his bed into a gigantic insect"—both turned me into an author and lured me far into the German language. The stunning labor it accomplishes in so few words and with such mathematical grace; the abrupt blossoming of its unhinged vision and complex tone; its literalization of a metaphor that both critiques capitalism's dehumanization of the working subject and unlocks an exploration into existential alienation and disability—how could I possibly be the same person after reading it as before?

When we finished talking about the *Metamorphosis*, Joyce Garvin offered me a full-blown novel: Faulkner's *As I Lay Dying*. Although there were whole galaxies I didn't understand about it, what blew me away were its reimagining of the sentence in a rural southern register, its use of interior monologue and stream of consciousness (which I had never met before), and, most momentous for me, its embrace of Nietzsche's notion of perspectivism (a notion which, I later learned, arrived by way of Faulkner's own mentor: his friend Phil Stone, an attorney in Oxford, Mississippi, who had graduated Yale and introduced the young wannabe outrider of overwrought Romantic poetry to Marx, Joyce, and Modernist art, thereby helping him become the Faulkner we recognize today), which suggests that a polyphony of voices means a multiplicity of contradictory realities, a refusal to welcome any single absolute epistemological or ethical point of view.

Like many of us, I imagine, in graduate school I experienced the same kind of adventure Joyce Garvin introduced me to, only now several times a day. I was never the same person Friday that I had been Monday. I recall opening Stein's *Tender Buttons* for the first time, and confronting passages like this:

> In the inside there is sleeping, in the outside there is reddening, in the morning there is meaning, in the evening

> there is feeling. In the evening there is feeling. In feeling anything is resting, in feeling anything is mounting, in feeling there is resignation, in feeling there is recognition, in feeling there is recurrence and entirely mistaken there is pinching. All the standards have steamers and all the curtains have bed linen and all the yellow has discrimination and all the circle has circling. This makes sand.

It's that sort of encounter which taught me how to realize I was standing before the experimental: a sparking provocation up and down my spine to invent a new discourse with which to discuss this new event. In Stein's case that had to do, in part, with how she deployed linguistic illegibility to create the impression of micro-arguments (here the last sentence indicates by its form it has arrived at a conclusion that obviously doesn't exist) while undoing logic (the essence of argument, which is to say the essence of Enlightenment thought) through the use of a para-grammar, where word clusters look like sentences, engage with the syntax and the other trappings of sentences (verbs, nouns, and so on), yet refuse to function as units of unambiguous meaning. To put it otherwise: trying to navigate a line by Stein is to enter an anti-teleological activity, a zone of perpetual suspension, a process of unlearning everything I once took for granted about language and literature.

I recently attended a talk by Azar Nafisi, during which she spoke about Alice's experiences in Wonderland as an extended metaphor for reading. All readers, like Alice, Nafisi said, don't know what they will find when they plunge down the rabbit hole of a new book. That's where our excitement and perhaps vague apprehension resides. And somewhere along the journey those readers will encounter the caterpillar. They may ask him, along with Alice: Who are you? But in the end the caterpillar poses the final question for us all: Who are *you*? That's the query waiting for us at the center of every text, but, I would suggest, that query, those feelings, are amplified in those texts we have come to call innovative.

HOMELESSNESS

What was it that I responded to so deeply in such distinct Modernists? And how does that commence addressing at least one corner of the question I posed at the outset of this essay? Last semester, I taught, as I regularly do, a course on Modernist intellectual and aesthetic history, in part to thank literary, theoretical, musical, filmic, dance, and artistic texts that have meant so much to me over the decades. The first book we read, perhaps unexpectedly, was *The Odyssey*, and the first large question I posed to my students was why so many Modernists, from James Joyce to Virginia Woolf and William Faulkner, gravitate toward it.

One reason, I offered, has to do with its deep-structure assertion that rhymes with one aspect of Heidegger's thinking. Heidegger argues that, while many of us want to believe being-at-home is the fundamental human condition, living proves furiously otherwise: not-being-at-home is the much more fundamental one. *The Odyssey* isn't, as we usually tell ourselves, about Odysseus reaching the Ithaca of the mind. Rather, it is about how the Ithaca of the mind can never be reached. Settling down is just a rumor in Odysseus's rented world. Rather, *The Odyssey* is about the two decades Odysseus fights in the Trojan war and wanders around southern Europe and northern Africa. Even when he returns home, he doesn't, in any essential sense, return home: the suitors have overrun the place; Penelope doesn't recognize him; Odysseus is no longer the young man who set out all those years—all those bodies, all those beliefs—ago.

Kafka, Faulkner, and Stein searched for fresh narrative modes to tell what they perceived as a chaotic, cruel, bewildering present in which not-being-at-home was a heart-slamming given. The mythic journey underpinning the Bundren family's odyssey through flood and flame from their farm to Jefferson to bury their matriarch, Addie, is straightforward to track. In Kafka, though, that sense of not-being-at-home moves from the landscape of the natural environment into the landscape of an unnatural body through Gregor's transformation. There the corporeal becomes an estranged horrorshow, a haunted house, Odysseus's helter-skelter Mediterranean basin where the real teratoids turn out to be our own ever-shifting flesh, even as the domestic space of the Samsa apartment blurs into precarious fever dream. In Stein, the terms change again, placing the reader into the role of nomad among a language that rejects the domestic coordinates of signification completely. The Modernist project, that is, was an attempt to invent ways to narrativize an uncertain contemporary without fully abandoning or fully perpetuating the past.

It goes without saying that that project isn't unique to them. It has been the most important undertaking for those of us invested in challenging writing practices since (let us say by way of approximation) the late-nineteenth century. The question that serves as its engine is one succinctly voiced by Jean-François Lyotard in 1979: *How do we present the unpresentable?* While Lyotard frames his reasoning around the Kantian sublime, I'd like to go somewhere else by rephrasing it—posing Lyotard sans Lyotard: *How do we present a contemporary that feels beyond presentation itself?*

EVERY FORM SUGGESTS A PHILOSOPHY

By way of a tentative answer, let me bring to the surface what has so far remained my mostly subtextual argument: *Every form suggests a philosophy.* If so, then writing doesn't simply embody its thematics at the level of character, dialogue, setting, leitmotif, symbol, and so forth, the textual loci we have become habituated to uncover and explicate, but also at the level of structure itself, which is to say, among the architectonics of everything from story organization to page design, image layout, sentence construction, font choice, and other cultural/interpretative invisibles.

It seems to be untenable to repeat ossified forms as much as it does to repeat ossified conceptions of character (i.e., ossified conceptions of selfhood), arrangement (i.e., ossified conceptions of epistemology and telos), setting (i.e., ossified conceptions of the world), and the rest, whose deep assumptions have led us to the calamity called now. Doing so strikes me at best as a reactionary reflex, at worst as an exemplar of a kind of willed blindness. The danger intrinsic in that move is that it consciously or unconsciously sustains received narratives, which is to say, it consciously or unconsciously sustains received systems of knowing, and, as Trump and his Trumpniks fathom only too well (to paraphrase a quote often inaccurately attributed to Goebbels), if you tell a lie big enough and keep repeating it, people will eventually come to believe it. If we structure our narratives familiarly enough, reproduce them frequently enough, people will eventually come to assume those structures tell us something true about how our universe works—that complexity and conflict can unravel (as romantic comedy instructs us) into easy resolution; or that (as detective novels instruct us) reason and the careful collection of evidence can lead to certitude; or that the plot arc of life (as many memoirs instruct us) is fundamentally fundamentalist Christian in nature: a fall from innocence into sin that leads through tribulation to redemption.

Yet don't the cataclysms I mention above, this carnage carnival in which we are complicit, imply that our cosmos arrives as shrapnel, not logic or illumination, and that the only telos we can be sure of is a continuous anti-teleological condition of flux, uncertainty, and question till death do us part? The feeling is akin to the sense you sometimes get when rapidly surfing the web: an ongoing disorientation followed by orientation followed by disorientation in a data hurricane. *Information sickness*, Ted Mooney termed it prophetically in his 1981 novel, *Easy Travel to Other Planets*, where overwhelmed pedestrians now and then drop in place along New York streets and curl into fetal balls, bleeding from the nose, when it all becomes too real.

We disrupt narrative structure, not because it's fun (though it most definitely is that), and not because it's gimmicky (it most definitely isn't that), but instead because, as the protagonist of Lidia Yuknavitch's novel, *Thrust*, knows: "Stories are quantum." Serious, self-reflective stories written here, now, are the antithesis of Newtonian. They exist in multiple, in simultaneity, from manifold perspectives, shot through with skepticism, active interrogation, and fierce doubt, set in relentless resistance to the received complacency, the received whistling in the dark, that has made the world this world. Through the constant act of disturbance as a way of being—a passionate, permanent incarnation of the examined life—extreme narrativity asks us to envision the text of the text, the text of our lives, and the text of the world other than they are, and thus asks us to contemplate the idea of fundamental change in all three. It acts as a portal for transformation while foregrounding marginalized subjectivities, alternative positions, unique ways of experiencing experience, past and present, of envisioning all tomorrow's parties and our own funerals. As Saul Bellow once wrote: Freedom is an ordeal.

I was asked recently by an interviewer why exploring the dark spaces doesn't lead me to give in to despair. I suppose I see what I'm doing through a different optic. First, talking about *giving in to despair* strikes me as the wrong way to put it. That metaphor connotes losing a struggle. But why should entering a state of despair be conceptualized as failure? It is simply (and complexly) an emotion we embrace among the myriad others that make humans human. I don't get why at this turn in history we would want to repress, distract, or self-medicate ourselves away from a frantic sense of helplessness. This, after all, is who we have become. This is what we have done to ourselves. We reside in the city of extremis among a flood of antidepressants, conspiracy theories, and New Age quackery and superstitions (another assortment of conspiracy theories), a consequence of our society's choices that feels bewildering and dismal. Examining and articulating our despair—not "working through it," as our pop psychologists recommend, but embracing it, these personal and social traumas without end—is an essential part of what it means not to "heal" but to be a thoughtful, full-feeling intersectional individual.

Second—and this may sound paradoxical in light of what I just said—engaging in defiant narrativity, in reminding ourselves that trying to maneuver through the world using someone else's choreography is both dangerous and deadening. We should remind our students in the classroom and our readers outside its doors that we don't have to live this way, that we can continually *imagine* the act of rewriting our scripts, despite the evidence, despite the untellables, at least locally. Engaging in defiant narrativity is the precise inverse of despair, a further complication of despair's complications. (I often wonder if it is syntax and grammatical encumbrance that are to blame for our belief that we can only experience one category of emotion at a time.) This puts me in mind of how searingly Carole Maso expresses a related idea in her essay "World Book":

> We write now into our extinction with surprising reserves of energy, perversely embracing the motion toward our disappearance. From the erasures, from the negations, from the violence and assaults and trespasses and betrayal, from the love for all that passes, the novel in new forms will persist; it alone has the potential of coming closer than any other human document to the poignancy and terror of the moment.

As I recite those lines, I'm thinking of Melanie Rae Thon's postgenre work *As If Fire Could Hide Us*, part lamentation, part desperate love song to our species' sightlessness and demise, part post-Christian neo-mysticism inflected by a transcendental pantheism evinced in a boiling oceanic consciousness that wants very much to believe time (despite time's piercing arrow) and space (in a sense) don't exist, creating a narrative timelessness and wherelessness. She wants very much to believe that all people, all things, all atoms are connected, rich with the opportunity for love among the ruins, afflictions, bodily and spiritual pains and longings that make us who we are, all held together in the form of the exploded page, a performative precinct, which sometimes looks and reads like poetry or sacred chant, sometimes like what we used to call prose, sometimes like some both-and. The narraticules comprising it are reminiscent of the young woman in one of the book's episodes whose body after death is taken apart and donated to others so that they can continue living through her, even as they remain unaware of her. The largest venture is the detonation, however, not of the page, but of the everyday, the already-told, through its magnificent rhythms, lush lyricism, the headlong drive toward salvation and oblivion. *As If Fire Could Hide Us* thereby considers what a postmodern holy book might look like that can no longer wholly acquiesce to the meaning of any of its constituent modifiers.

I'm thinking, as well, of Steve Tomasula's eco-horror novel, *Ascension*. Typical of his explorations, it is an act of lavish research and penetrating critical thought, a report sent back from the library of tomorrow—in this case about how humans invent "nature" even as their conception of "nature" invents their thinking and thus their "reality." The first chapter portrays that instant on the cusp of Darwin remaking the natural world; the second, that instant in the eighties when the nature of "nature" translates from analog to digital; and the third and final, that instant of our contemporary condition, when humans are devolving into anachronisms. *Ascension* thereby tackles the convulsions of colonization, digitization, and our encroaching extinction by examining how "nature" occurs as a substantiation of species Rorschach Test rather than some sort of objective out-there. At the same time, *Ascension* tackles what history feels like at a scale where homo sapiens are gradually becoming the size of stray thoughts. As with most of Tomasula's work, *Ascension* merges text and images, each page of the first chapter seeded with nineteenth-century illustrations of "nature," the third with QR codes to access various databases documenting our decline, from mass shootings to the Extinction Clock. A modified interactive version of chapter three also appears online.

And I'm thinking of one of the most intriguing postgenre texts I've encountered lately: the Canadian poet/novelist/performance artist M. NourbeSe Philip's *Zong!*, which dwells in a literary space committed to extreme innovation in the service of social justice. *Zong!* untells the narrative of the eponymous merchant ship that in 1781 sailed from the west coast of Africa with 442 slaves and seventeen crewmembers on board. Due to poor navigation, the usually nine-week voyage ended up taking twice that long. Water ran short and sickness proliferated. To preserve some of what the captain referred to as its African "cargo," the crew began to throw ill slaves overboard. Many of those still in good health, witnessing the massacre before them, committed suicide by leaping into the sea. Somewhere between 130 and 150 drowned. Upon the ship's arrival in Jamaica, its owners made a claim to its British insurers for a loss of "cargo." The insurers refused to pay, the case went to trial, and the judgement came back that the deliberate killing of slaves was legal. Consequently, the insurers were obliged to pay out.

"There is no telling this story," Philip launches her essay on how she came to write *Zong!* How, she asks, does one go about narrativizing the unimaginable? Her answer is to take on the legal document from the trial—the judicial, institutional, so-called rational version of what transpired—and to detonate it across *Zong!*'s pages, dismantling its language and presuppositions at the levels of thematics and form as she burns forward into a text comprised of six smaller ones, a glossary, the ship's fictitious manifest, and Philip's own notes about her unwriting process. The outcome is in "equal parts song, moan, shout, oath, ululation, curse, and chant," mourning as archival undoing, an enraged ghost story that emulates the thoughts and experiences of the slaves whose thoughts and experiences cannot be emulated, thus generating a fugal counter-narrative, a documentary poetics, that chronicles America's cruel forensic landscape, fully acknowledging the contradictions inherent in such a gesture. Having completed the book rendition of *Zong!*, Philip extended its text beyond its covers by means of days-long collaborative performances begun on each anniversary of the massacre. Her activity is a work, then, of historiographic metafiction, a narratological mode close to my own heart, whose goal is to trouble the very idea of yesterday, what is told, from what angle, how, and from what centers of power in order to explore how history is always about the impossibility of truth recovery.

Here we might recall Vladimir Nabokov's remark: "Curiosity is insubordination in its purest form." The texts I have been discussing are indicative of (trans)forms that transfigure—philosophies that adopt a Heraclitean transitivity by refusing to settle. One might propose, in light of this, that they are, from a certain perspective, radically democratic texts that understand democracy is never designed to make the individual comfortable. Just the opposite. Comfort is the job of late-stage capitalism's spectacular despotisms. Democracy, on the other hand, is precisely about an unstable state of perpetual inconvenience. Back for a moment to Saul Bellow and Azar Nafisi, the latter of whom said about the former: "He not only critiqued totalitarian systems but correctly predicted the dilemmas of democracy, and the dangers threatening it, not least our sleeping consciousness, atrophy of feeling, and our desire to forget."

EMPATHY TECHNOLOGY

I want to conclude by talking about something else going on in these texts. The cognitive psychologist and psycholinguist Steven Pinker calls fiction "empathy technology," a magnificent phrase intimating that one reason we read is to inhabit—in ways other arts don't allow—the consciousness of other human beings for extended periods; to live among their thoughts, feelings, and experiences; and to appreciate again and again that reading can be an act of overt political resistance as well as human compassion, which, after all, is another kind of political resistance.

Yet I don't think that's exactly how things work. The texts I've been discussing do something different. They teach us that unproblematized empathy—a word that tracks back through the German *Einfühlung* (meaning *feeling at one with*) coined in 1858 by the philosopher Rudolf Lotze as a translation of the Greek *empatheia* (meaning *to suffer with another*)—is an impossibility. After all, how can we possibly gain deep knowledge of somebody else when such a goal stands outside our reach even when talking about ourselves? We spend our lives having the epiphany that the idea of gaining full self-understanding amounts to a utopian venture. How in the world could we possibly attempt to understand—let alone share the feelings of—another human being whose gender, race, geopolitical and economic position, education, sociohistorical moment, and so on are utterly removed from our own?

My point, naturally, isn't that we should give up trying. Rather, the texts I've been discussing contend through their (trans)forms as well as their content that, as we wander deeper and deeper into our culture's atrocity exhibition, we should attempt to situate radical empathy inside our classrooms and out, in our innovative writing practices and the practices comprising our daily existences … even as we know we absolutely cannot, even as we know we absolutely must, even as we know chasing empathy will unremittingly usher us from conflicted and confounding educations into the pith of failure, which are simultaneously the most beautiful educations imaginable, these countless instants of fleeting, fraught, desperately inadequate instants of hope.

RENEWING THE DIFFICULT IMAGINATION

THE MIDDLE MIND

I was sitting in a 727 a couple of weeks ago on a flight from somewhere to somewhere else, laptop open in front of me, trying to get a little writing done, when I began inadvertently tuning into the conversation of the two passengers in front of me. They were grayish guys, probably in their mid-fifties, apparently businessmen, and they were talking about the novel the one on the left was reading. Almost nobody talks about fiction in public anymore, except in maybe two or three university departments, the odd independent bookstore, and a diminishing handful of smart podcast and review outlets, so I wanted to hear what they had to say. I leaned forward and snuck a peek between their seatbacks to see what they were discussing. It was the latest by one of those corporate authors whose books are seen less as books than as rough drafts for screenplays.

"Pretty good?" asked the guy on the right, indicating with his thumb the hardcover the guy on the left was holding up.

"Yeah," said the guy on the left. "I guess."

"How so?" asked the guy on the right.

"Um," said the guy on the left. "It's got three-page chapters. I love novels with three-page chapters."

BARBARA CARTLAND & LIFTING WEIGHTS

That exchange, it seems to me, helps form a larger sociohistorical context in which to comment on narrative and politics.

That exchange and the results cited in the NEA's controversial *Reading at Risk: A Survey of Literary Reading in*

America. The study questioned 17,000 adults about their literary preferences and habits. It defines "literature," I should mention, as "any type of fiction, poetry, and plays [sic] that ... respondents felt should be included and not just what literary critics might consider literature." Consequently, opening one of the 723 novels Barbara Cartland wrote during her lifetime (which have sold more than a billion copies worldwide) or the hardcover those two guys in front of me were conversing about is equivalent in the minds of those conducting the survey to opening Virginia Woolf's *Mrs. Dalloway*.

Even so, the survey discovered that since 1982 there has been a loss of roughly 20,000,000 readers in the US (a number representing a ten percent drop in readership), and that reading rates are declining among all demographic groups regardless of gender, ethnicity, education, age, or income level, with the steepest drop in the youngest groups—i.e., those between 18-to-24 and 25-to-34, respectively. Although annual sales for all types of books are predicted to top $44 billion this year, up 58 percent from last, only 46.7 percent of adults say they are reading "literature" compared with 56.9 percent two decades ago.

Of those surveyed, 95.7 percent said they preferred watching television to reading, 60 percent attending a movie, and 55 percent lifting weights. "At the current rate of loss," the NEA concludes, "literary reading as a leisure activity will virtually disappear in half a century."

PAYING FOR BOREDOM

What happened to us? (And when I say *us*, I mean *them*.) *Reading at Risk* points to the rise of electronic media—especially television, movies, and the internet—as the primary culprits for drawing our culture's attention away from fiction, poetry, and drama to varieties of the spectacle.

Yet it strikes me that the problem isn't simply that people are reading less. It is also that they are reading easier, more naively. I'm talking about the nature of the narratives people experience daily, both inside and outside books. In *The Middle Mind*, Curtis White contends that the stories generated and sustained by the American political system, entertainment industry, and academic trade have helped teach us over the last half century or so by their insidious simplicity, plainness, and ubiquity how not to think for ourselves. Given the current global economic and political disasters, I doubt much needs to be said about how the political narratives of the United States have led to the "starkest and most deadly" poverty of imagination, nor about how, "on the whole, our entertainment … is a testament to our ability and willingness to endure boredom … and pay for it."

A little probably should be said, though, about White's take on the consequences of this dissemination of corporate consciousness throughout academia. For him, the contemporary university "shares with the entertainment industry its simple institutional inertia"; "so-called dominant 'critical paradigms' tend to stabilize in much the same way that assumptions about 'consumer demand' make television programming predictable." If, in other words, our student-shoppers want to talk about video games, fan fiction, and S&S in the classroom, well, that's just what they're going to get to talk about, since that's how English departments fill seats, and filling seats is how they make money, and making money is what it's all about … isn't it?

Who needs Dante or Milton, Wallace Stevens or Claudia Rankine?

Unfortunately the result, particularly in the wake of Cultural Studies, has been the impulse to eschew close, meticulous engagement with the page; to search texts "for symptoms supporting the sociopolitical or theoretical template of the critic"; to flatten out distinctions between, say, the value of studying Ezra Pound and Lydia Davis, on the one hand, and Taylor Swift's oeuvre, YA novels, or *Minecraft*, on the other—and therefore unknowingly to embrace and maintain the very globalized corporate culture that Cultural Studies claims to critique.

THE DIFFICULT IMAGINATION

What we are left with is the death of what I think of as the Difficult Imagination—that textured mode of discourse that often comes with charges of exclusiveness, snobbery, and elitism leveled by frustrated, faintly anxious readers of disruptive, transgressive, nuanced, intricate texts dedicated in myriad heterodox ways to confronting, complicating, interrogating, and even short-circuiting the user-friendly narratives produced by late-stage capitalism that would like to see such narratives told and retold until they begin to pass for something like verities about aesthetics and the human condition.

I have to confess that I'm not at all sure what we really mean by "accessibility," since it's one of those highly subjective words that, as Nabokov cautioned about "reality," should always appear between quotation marks. Nor am I clear about to whom a narrative should be "accessible"—the two guys in front of me on the plane, a typical MFA student, a bus driver, an associate professor of biology? Nor do I understand why many people seem to believe texts in general should be more than less "accessible." But what I want to offer here is that, whatever we may think of when we use that pregnant word, texts in general should be just the opposite. They should be less accessible, not more. They should demand greater labor on the part of readers, even a good degree of uneasiness, rather than effortlessness.

Why?

Because texts that make us work, think, and feel in unusual ways attempt to wake us in the midst of our dreaming, are more valuable epistemologically, ontologically, and sociopolitically than texts that make us feel warm, fuzzy, and forgetful.

So when I speak of renewing the Difficult Imagination, I am not referring to the renewal of a series of vanguard theoretical constraints, doctrines, or trends, so much as to the renewal of a narratological interzone in which we are asked to envision thoroughgoing alterity. This interzone of impeded accessibility is an essential one for human freedom. In it, everything can and should be considered, attempted, and troubled. What is important about its products is not whether they ultimately "succeed" (whatever we may mean when we say *that* word) or "fail" (ditto—although I do possess a special fondness for Beckett's Icarian dictum: "Try again. Fail again. Fail better."). What is important is that they come into being often and widely, because in them we discover the perpetual manifestation of Nietzsche's notion of the unconditional, Derrida's of a privileged instability, Viktor Shklovsky's ambition for art and Martin Heidegger's for philosophy: the return, through entanglement and provocation (not predictability and ease) to perception and contemplation.

J. M. COETZEE & READING BAFFLED

Writing of the Difficult Imagination will always make you feel a little foolish, a little tongue-tied, a little excluded before an example of it. You will find yourself standing there in a kind of disconcerted wonder that will insist upon a faintly new manner of perceiving, of speaking, to capture what it is you just met.

I remembered, as I typed that last line, how I felt upon reaching the end of J. M. Coetzee's *Elizabeth Costello*, which commences by telling the life and obsessions of a contemporary writer in her late sixties by means of a series of lectures she gives and attends. It begins, that is to say, in the realm of psychological realism, but a psychological realism tweaked, askew, both by its structuring principle of those lectures as well as by a disquietingly flat prose style and odd narratorial insertions (the passage of weeks, months, or even years, for example, is covered by the abrupt, self-reflexive phrase: "We skip."). In the seventh of eight chapters, as the reader settles into these conventions, the novel unexpectedly leaves the universes of logical mimesis and Freudian depth-psychology behind and veers first into a highly textured meditation, still from the protagonist's point of view (although her presence drops back decidedly from it, and symbol starts swamping personhood) about the relationship between gods and mortals in a variety of mythological iterations. Then, in the final chapter, the novel retells Kafka's parable "Before the Law," in which Elizabeth rather than Kafka's man from the country seeks entrance in vain, not from the quotidian world into the law, but from a purgatorial in-between place into some beyond-region—possibly heaven itself. The book ends with a short, cryptic postscript that takes the form of an epistle from another (or is it somehow the same?) "Elizabeth C." (Elizabeth, Lady Chandos). This one is quite possibly on the verge of madness, written on 9/11—not in 2001, as we might expect, but in 1603, the year the English Renaissance begins its conclusion with the demise of Elizabeth I.

With that, everything we have just read stutters into suspension. Is the narrative supposed to add up to the hallucinations of a seventeenth-century woman? A twentieth-century woman imagining from beyond the grave or on her way to it? A serious postulation of cyclical rebirth or eternal recurrence? An ironic one? Or, more likely, a text that denies character and mimesis in favor of a series of philosophical dilemmas, an investigation into a novel ripped open as unpredictably as our planet was on that glistery blue September day, a cosmic universe and a universe of discourse exploring the conditions of their own self-perplexing unmaking?

HESITATION AS HOPE

Writing of the Difficult Imagination reminds us that language, ideas, and experience are profoundly tricky things. As Brian Evenson comments in "Notes on Fiction and Philosophy":

> Good fiction, I would argue, always poses problems—ethical, linguistic, epistemological, ontological—and writers and readers, I believe, should be willing to draw on everything around them to pose tentative answers to these problems and, by way of them, pose problems of their own … It is our ability as writers to stay curious, to borrow, to bricoler, to adapt and move on, that keeps us from becoming stale.

But such talk may seem to beg the central question implied by that back-and-forth between those two guys sitting in front of me on the plane, not to mention the sobering results of the NEA's survey: can the Difficult Imagination's project ever aspire to something resembling hope, however we may define it? The answer is no. And maybe. Only not really. Staging the inaccessible is an inevitably futile scheme. And an indispensable one. Its purpose is never a change, but rather a changing—an unending profiting from the impossible, a viewpoint from which we can re-involve ourselves with history and technique, present ourselves as a constant (if, admittedly, embarrassingly minor) prompt that things can always be, should always be, various.

THERE'S NO PLACE LIKE TIME

THE GENERATIVE BACKSTORY OF WASTE

My wife and collaborator Andi Olsen and I move to Salt Lake City in 2007, a month before I begin teaching at the University of Utah after a six-year intermission at a little cabin in central Idaho away from increasingly corporatized, bland, and parroty academia. Almost from the day I arrive, my new colleagues urge us to take the two-and-a-half-hour drive to the northeastern shore of the Great Salt Lake near Rozel Point to see (better: be a part of) Robert Smithson's *Spiral Jetty*, his most well-known and vital earthwork. They know, my new colleagues say, we will love it. Still, those initial pedagogical and administrative responsibilities that bog one as one launches into a new academic position bog me in spades. It isn't until 27 September, 2008, just over a year after my arrival, that Stephanie Strickland flies into town for a week as our university's Visiting Poet in Residence, and Andi and I realize we have finally collected the needed excuse to make our sojourn. Seven months later Susan Howe—also in Salt Lake for a week as Visiting Poet in Residence—asks if we might make an outing with her to Smithson's work.

Andi and I return several more times over the course of the next few years, drawn to the earthwork's dazzling ways of being in the landscape, being with the landscape, being the landscape. On April 16, 2011, while teaching Mark Z. Danielewski's *House of Leaves* in my Experimental Forms graduate seminar, it occurs to me that talking about that novel's deep-structure metaphor of the labyrinth will be ever so much richer if undertaken in the presence of a version of a three-dimensional one. So the students, Andi, and I fieldtrip to Smithson's amazement. What strikes me upon stepping out of our Jeep is the students' immediate rapt attention to everything around them—how, within breaths, they have scattered, some walking the earthwork, which appears as a 1500-foot black vertebrae curled in the shallow pink water of the Great Salt Lake, some wandering out half a mile, a mile, in rubber boots into the shallow water, some photographing, some sitting on boulders on the shoreline, taking notes. Andi has begun videoing the scene.

I am taken by how this singular space dedicated in so many ways to dispersal, disintegration, a wasting away into salt mush, is also stunningly generative, prolific in its stillness.

GRENZSITUATIONEN

Throughout his work, Karl Jaspers explores what he calls *Grenzsituationen* or Limit Situations, those moments in which a human must confront the restrictions of his or her own existence, abandon the solace of her or his everydayness, and thereby enter a new realm of self-awareness.

One thinks, by way of example, of the death of a close friend or beloved.

Such experiences wrench us, compel us to come alive and reenter the diurnal re-thought. Translate Jasper's notion from existential into aesthetic terms, and we have what I think of as Limit Texts—those designed to set us adrift, make us feel interpretive arrival is ever elsewhere, give rise to a set of reading practices that urges us to confront the restrictions of existing forms and those forms' assumptions about how and why we tell. Once we open such texts—exactly which constitute this category will be different for each of us, and for each stage of our lives—we will never be able to close them and slip them back on the shelf again.

They ask us to envision our writing practices and ourselves differently, what elemental change in each might look like, and why it might look that way.

THE TOXIC SUBLIME

Smithson constructs *The Spiral Jetty* over the course of six days in April 1970 near the site of an abandoned oil rig littered with dented, rusting oil drums, spilled pools of black sludge, and remnants of a wooden jetty that slant rhymes with his own. I imagine he is drawn to the anti-pastoral beauty of the place, a holdover from his childhood in Passaic, New Jersey, a gritty swatch of the state about twelve miles from where I grew up in River Edge, and to what I think of as an aesthetics of waste in the service of a toxic sublimity.

From the moment it is completed, *The Spiral Jetty* begins undoing itself. Smithson miscalculates the average water level in the lake, which quickly rises and covers his construction, which subsequently remains submerged for decades. It doesn't become visible again for a prolonged period of time until the megadrought in the early 2000s sets in. Meanwhile, salt encrusts it as it slowly sinks into the world with which it is in losing conversation.

Unless "salvaged" on a regular basis, it will be gone in another decade, just like Smithson would have wanted it.

The site itself is remote, the drive out a species of pilgrimage, an act of faith and devotion to an unhurriedly ephemeral art. If you're leaving from Salt Lake City, the first sixty-five miles are on I-15 north. You exit onto Route 13, a winding two-lane road, to Corrine, a tiny town with the last gas station you'll encounter before *The Jetty*, then twenty miles or so beyond. The last ten or twelve is an unpaved, deteriorating dirt track with poor signage. Although DIA, current owner and custodian of the earthwork, not long ago improved that final approach a little, when Andi and I first tried it in 2008, four-wheel drive was a necessity, we rarely encountered anybody throughout the course of a day, and getting lost seemed like the norm. *The Spiral Jetty* begins long before one encounters it, redefining the concept of the museum/gallery even as it dismantles contemporary art's obsession with commodification every mile one travels into the barren, hilly, alien scrubland.

At certain times of the year, the microbes in the water, which thrive in the extreme twenty-seven percent salinity of the lake's north arm, turn the color of rosé or watery blood. This is what clenched the site for Smithson during his first recon flyover. The stark area on the shores of the usually boatless lake doesn't feel like it should exist on this planet except, perhaps, as it might be dehabituated in a speculative fiction by J. G. Ballard. That rosé hue comes and goes, the light remains in constant flux, the water level rises and falls. As I write this, the lake has pulled back, completely exposing *The Spiral Jetty*. Now the waterline is more than half a mile away as a result of the slow violence of climate change, and desiccated animal carcasses—birds, mostly, but also the odd snake and deer—appear, disappear, and reappear in the surrounding mush alive with brine shrimp and flies. What may at first seem a static environment—and a splendid minimalist one, according to the famous photographs one comes across on the web—is actually in a state of continuous, frenetic flux. It is out of the question to visit the same spot twice.

To write about this sense of unceasing, uncanny transition and dissipation in a multitude of modes, Smithson borrows Lévi-Strauss's neologism *entropology*, a portmanteau of *entropy* and *anthropology*. Entropology, Lévi-Strauss postulates in *A World on the Wane*, "should be the word for the discipline that devotes itself to the study of [the] process of disintegration in its most highly evolved forms." For Smithson, entropology embodies structures in dissolution, yes, but not in a negative sense, not with a sense of sadness or loss. For him, entropology embodies the astonishing allure inherent in the process of wearing down, wearing out, continuous de-creation at the level of geology, thermodynamics, civilizations, and the bodies and minds within them.

THEORIES OF FORGETTING

Thoughts about entropology bother me in the wake of that fieldtrip in 2011, and I can sense the first wisps of my novel

Theories of Forgetting starting to accumulate around the disturbances. An experimental speculative fiction, it turns out after many starts and stops to consist of three narratives. The first involves a middle-aged filmmaker, Alana Olsen, at work on a short innovative documentary about *The Spiral Jetty*. She falls prey to a pandemic called The Frost, whose symptoms include an increasing sensation of coldness and growing amnesia. The second involves Alana's husband, Hugh, and his slow dispersal (for want of a better word) throughout Europe and across Jordan while on a trip there both to remember and to forget in the aftermath of Alana's death. His vanishing is linked in part to the Sleeping Beauties, a rising global religious cult that worships barbiturates for their ability to bring about another kind of mnemonic oblivion in the face of the present. The third involves Alana and Hugh's daughter, Aila, an art critic and conceptual artist living in Berlin, and the parasitic marginalia she scribbles in the manuscript by her father (which may be a novel, although it is equally feasible it is a third-person autobiographical account of the end of his life) she discovers after his disappearance. Through that marginalia, Aila attempts to establish a conversation with him in order to remember, re-member, and dis-member him. She chooses what strikes her as textured words—words that carry significance for her, if not necessarily anyone else—and riffs on them paratextually in a longhand the color of the Great Salt Lake on a sunny day. These three narratives are edited and made into the book that the reader encounters by Alana's estranged brother, Lance.

Each narrative manifests its own form and texture. Alana's takes the shape of a diary/collage containing photographs, drawings, quotations, newspaper clippings, medical reports, and meditations on Smithson's work, with which she becomes increasingly obsessed. As her cognitive abilities decline, suggestive misspellings/typos reveal another sort of entropological charge, this time in language. Hugh's narrative is more normative—save that he may be telling himself in the third person—its voice numbed, bewildered, in the wake of Alana's unexpected death. The phrases and/or images making up both Alana's and Hugh's narratives gradually fade into the page (and into each other). The last and first words of these chapters seem to be parts of the same sentence, dovetailing. Aila's narrative is condensed, fragmented, associative, cerebral.

Each page of the novel is divided in half. One of the two main narratives—either Alana's or Hugh's, depending upon which the reader opens to first (the "front" and "back" covers of the novel are identical, thereby privileging neither)—runs across the "top" from "front" to "back," while the other runs "upside down" across the "bottom" of the page from "back" to "front." One could thereby say the novel's physical structure brings to mind a spiral. The reader must physically manipulate the book in a spiraling gesture in order to move through the text fruitfully. The main narratives are faintly contradictory, so what the reader chooses to engage with initially will put pressure on their interpretative strategies.

In some measure, then, I was also interested in estranging the reading process, making the oddness of reading (and hence the oddness of meaning-making) odd again. Too, at the very moment the book is undergoing dematerialization in our culture by way of Kindles, iPads, smartphone screens, and the rest, I was interested in rematerializing it, investigating what it can do that other modes of data delivery cannot. (Indeed, a Kindle or iPad version of *Theories of Forgetting* is an impossibility, since those devices, no matter which way one turns them, "right" the page. This knowledge gives me great pleasure.) Finally, readers often talk about politics occurring at the stratum of the written text (character, thematics, and so on), but I was interested in thinking about the politics of structuration. I wanted to recount that we can always alter the forms of the scripts that try to govern us—the ones that have been written onto us, around us, into us.

Change our narrative structures, and we can start to change our lives.

Change our narrative structures, and we can start to change our worlds.

LABYRINTH & MAZE

The spiral design was of essential significance to Smithson's task, intrigued as he was by how ubiquitous that shape is—from megalithic art in the Newgrange Tomb in County Meath, Ireland; to the petroglyphs in Gila Bend, Arizona; to our fingerprints, hurricanes, florets in a sunflower, snail shells, the path of draining water, the 200 billion stars that comprise the Milky Way. The counterclockwise one constituting Smithson's basalt creation is a visual relative of the labyrinthine, archaic symbol for meditation and spiritual evolution, a journey from this world to the next, while its formal relative, the maze, is the structure that snags my curiosity as *Theories of Forgetting* grows into itself.

While the labyrinth is unicursal, featuring one entrance and one pathway leading to a center evocative of enlightenment, it is the maze I fell for, a centerless configuration (on which I will also base my next novel, *Dreamlives of Debris*, a rethinking of the Minotaur myth) with many entrances and exits evocative not so much of contemplation as disorientation, not so much of spiritual evolution as perplexity, not so much of a journey toward enlightenment as one toward unlearning and ignorance as rich methods of existence.

The labyrinth and maze are likewise metaphors for two ways of reading the text of the text and the text of our universe—the labyrinth an emblem of Barthes's notion of the *lisible*, the maze with his notion of the *scriptible*.

I wanted to literalize that metaphor.

I wanted to build a book that embodied it.

Building rather than writing, as I moved from Microsoft Word to InDesign in order to achieve the effects for which I was aiming, I noticed, is the term I've come to use when describing what I am doing these days. I am *building* as much as, if not more than, writing a novel. From *Theories of Forgetting* forward, my work will first arrive in my mind not as plot, or character, or even a particularly powerful sentence or phrase or image, but rather as an architecture whose implications want to be teased out.

MULTIMODAL SPILLAGE

Tucked into a corner of *Theories of Forgetting* (page 146, Hugh's side) appears a URL. Type it into a browser and you are taken to the experimental video Alana Olsen makes about *The Spiral Jetty* as she succumbs to The Frost. The voiceover is lifted from Hugh's narrative, a queer occurrence since that narrative could only have been composed after Alana's death. It describes a man who may or may not be Hugh watching a video in the Istanbul Modern Art Museum, mildly hallucinating after popping pills throughout the day about whose contents he is clueless. The video involves a female performance artist in a skimpy maid's costume and red lipstick kissing—and thereby marking—all the objects in her apartment. The voiceover (female) in the second half of the video involves an erasure of the voiceover (male) in the first half, disordering point of view and gender roles. With that erasure, another sort of entropologic ghosting creeps into the novel's machinery, even as the novel releases itself from the codex.

One afternoon, with the manuscript of *Theories of Forgetting* moving into production, Andi and I begin wondering if it might be possible to help the book spill yet farther into the world. In the midst of our conversation, the concept for *There's No Place Like Time*, our multimodal installation, emerges: a three-dimensional novel you can walk through. The idea is to create a retrospective of my character Alana's work curated by her daughter, Aila, show it in galleries, and give talks about it in those galleries and assorted universities across the US and Europe. While we launch the exhibit in Berlin in November, 2015, we envision it as an ongoing project, one that continues to expand and metamorphose over the years, so that, like *The Spiral Jetty* itself, one cannot experience the same show twice.

It turns out Alana produces a modest oeuvre—fewer than twenty relatively short videos that span roughly four decades—and yet, despite the paucity of those numbers, they exert a strong influence on such important artists as Lars von Trier,

Douglas Gordon, and Martin Arnold. Some pieces, Andi and I learn, have already gone missing. Others surface from time to time in unexpected cultural corners. (Although Andi creates those videos via Final Cut, she takes pains to mimic the visual look of earlier technologies.) From 1985 the viewer is offered, for example, *Where the Smiling Ends*, an anthropology of loneliness shot in front of the Trevi Fountain in Rome that captures the moment just after a photograph is snapped, when tourists—when we all—return once again from the staged public to the unstaged private. From 1989 comes the eponymous video, an Avant-Pop appropriation and manipulation of one of the most famous Merrie Melodies cartoons, *Duck Amuck* (1953), a metafiction featuring Daffy Duck struggling to free himself from his malicious cartoonist, Bugs Bunny, and failing repeatedly. The soundtrack splices together bits of Judy Garland's voice from *The Wizard of Oz* (1939) to form the sentence: "There's no place like time." Those words cycle the entire two minutes and nineteen seconds the video lasts. From 2006 arrives a very different piece: *Denkmal* (German for *monument* or *memorial*) for which Alana grafts over 1200 photographs taken while a guest at The American Academy in Berlin; they all show one of the manors tucked into woods across Lake Wannsee from the Academy—the Wannsee Conference Center, where the goals of Final Solution were set out—every day through five months. The soundtrack undoes Adolf Eichmann's (one of the participants at the Conference) testimony during his 1961 trial in Israel, turning his words into stuttery jibberish. Alana thus steals Eichmann's language even as he stole that of the Jews whose extermination he oversaw. The video lasts four minutes and thirty-three seconds, an allusion to John Cage's famous non-musical illumination about the unattainability of silence.

The installation is accompanied by a catalogue of critical and biographical essays about Alana's body of work; an interview with her; and stills from her videos, her life, and of objects that appeared in one of the lost works (those objects also appear on podiums throughout the exhibit). The installation's curator,

Alana's daughter Aila, writes the catalogue's introduction. A number of critics and theorists, many of whom exist in our world (Larry McCaffery, Christina Milletti, Davis Schneiderman) and many of whom don't (although I take the liberty of composing all their essays for them), as do a number of former friends. A timeline of Alana's life and descriptions of lost videos are included. Further, the catalogue provides a URL for the Zweifel und Zweifel Galerie (zweifelundzweifel.org), the real website for the nonexistent gallery in Berlin handling Alana's work. (*Zweifel*, one might remember, is the German word for *doubt*.) In addition to general information about the gallery, its (fictional) address, hours, and contact information, the website offers up a short essay by Aila and five of Alana's videos from *There's No Place Like Time* for those who might not be able to visit one of the three-dimensional manifestations.

Like the reader in a codical novel, the audience is invited to infer the protagonist's development, obsessions, evolving aesthetics, and relationship with her daughter, not to mention her curator-daughter's relationship with her. Yet almost immediately, difficulties arise for those participants paying attention to the text they inhabit. One learns from dates mentioned in passing in the catalogue and around the installation that the exhibit always takes place a few months in the future, not the present. To step into the gallery space is to step into a speculative fiction. It is possible, as well, given several suggestions Aila makes in her marginalia in *Theories of Forgetting*, that in fact this is not—or not primarily—a retrospective at all, but one of Aila's conceptual undertakings. If so, participants are actually moving through a third- or perhaps fourth-order fiction.

Another interpretive question emerges: Where should one begin to experience the installation, and where finish? That is, one is welcome to take in *There's No Place Like Time* in any order one likes, for as long as one likes. Some audience members stay a few minutes, others hours, presumably to radically different effects; some start interacting with the work at the gallery's entrance and track through the installation chronologically, while others wander as the mood strikes them, perhaps only viewing one or two videos before leaving. Whatever the case, one can expend as much or as little concentration and inquisitiveness as one likes, all along distracted by the voices and observations of other participants, injecting significant noise into the interpretive system. Each gallery housing the installation is of course laid out differently from all the others and, depending on its size and resources, displays more or less of the installation and provides new navigational coordinates. Andi and I envision someday planting actors in the vernissage Q&A to pose as artists, reviewers, and Alana's friends. They would share their memories of Alana with the general public, thereby adding another, corporeal stratum of fabrication.

In our post-truth landscape, the texts we inhabit seem to have turned into maze all the way down—ways of knowing and unknowing simultaneously, an extended and dense metaphor for our current sense of lived experience, a game whose rules we can no longer resolve—that sense we often have of being awash in massive, contradictory, networked, centerless, clamor-jammed data fields that may lead everywhere and nowhere at once.

YESTERDAY'S NEVERLAND

Andi and I want to raise questions about what an aesthetics of obscurity looks like, how it takes shape in our culture, about the relationship between quality and quantity in an art world where celebrity, media saturation, sales, and the like have become equated with talent and success—where, that is, the simulation of talent and success reifies into the things themselves for no particular reason.

Perhaps more than anything, however, we want to open a room for various hypotheses and interventions that do not simply seek to replicate, replace, or stand in for a past that never happened, a future that never will, but rather to aggravate the very idea of temporality. In other words, we want to create a three-dimensional novel that partakes in Linda Hutcheon's notion of historiographic metafiction—an aesthetic zone revealing a theoretical self-awareness that asks one to consider how both history and fiction are human constructs that are by nature highly artificial, manipulated modes of comprehension, where "there are only truths in the plural, and never one Truth; and there is rarely falseness per se, just others' truths." We want to create a space of synchronic and diachronic mutability.

There's No Place Like Time is thus meant to encourage the participant to invent his or her own choreography, to rediscover and contemplate those complications known as textuality, genre, identity, and historical knowledge.

NARRATIVE FALLACY

In addition to maze, the texts humans inhabit become multilayered fictions within multilayered fictions, an idea that recalls Nassim Nicolas Taleb's notion of narrative fallacy.

Humans are nothing if not pattern-recognition machines. From conspiracy theorists to scholars, we delight in connecting the dots, as David Clark says at the opening of his hypermedial work *88 Constellations for Wittgenstein*—whether or not the connections are indeed there in the first place. *There's No Place Like Time* is an expedition into that profound and profoundly revealing impulse. The human needs to explain, make cosmos out of chaos, make coherent narrative out of what often is little more than incoherent and/or incompatible data points. In *The Black Swan*, Taleb argues: "The narrative fallacy addresses our limited ability to look at sequences of facts without weaving an explanation into them, or, equivalently, forcing a logical link, an arrow of relationship, upon them … [I]t increases our impression of understanding."

Yet our *impression* of understanding isn't the thing itself, and that, precisely, is Taleb's point.

Our impression of understanding is a kind of willed misunderstanding.

To walk into *There's No Place Like Time* is to walk into a quandary that instigates a journey into subjective exegesis as well as an exegesis of the idea of exegesis—and one that is multiple, palimpsestic, and profitably conflicted. This presumes a relatively inquisitive, sophisticated reader. Uncurious, unsophisticated readers will exit the installation believing they have experienced precisely what the installation appears to be: a retrospective of Alana Olsen's work.

FORMATIVE FICTION

Each instance of what Joshua Landy refers to as *formative fiction* "contains within itself a manual for reading, a set of implicit instructions on how it may best be used ... [T]he more we are capable of, the more demanding our challenges can be, and the more demanding the challenges, the greater the impact on our abilities."

Another way of saying this: every formative fiction—if we are willing, patient, and dedicated readers—teaches us how to read it (and thereby read ourselves) in a protracted, reciprocal dance; the experience changes us as we change it, and vice versa. This is a space, Landy continues, that constitutes "a special variant of the 'hermeneutic circle.' We cannot understand a text as a whole without understanding its various parts ... but neither can we understand the parts without understanding the text as a whole."

In the long run, *There's No Place Like Time* is about the perplexing, frustrating, boring (in both senses of the word), fascinating, fumbling, joyous, revelatory activity termed reading—about, namely, trying to make seen and self-conscious that which our culture has made unseen and insipid by its ubiquity and uniformity. Our multimodal installation is an act of reconnaissance into the consequences of choosing to read one way in favor of another, adjusting and adapting as one puzzles through the material, which is to say, *There's No Place Like Time* is about choosing to pilot experience this way instead of asking ourselves where fiction ends—if we can say it really ends anywhere at all—and something else begins.

READING/WRITING AS TANGLE: METAFICTION AS MOTION

WHAT IS READING?

I wonder if it might be useful to think about metafiction, reflexivity, and self-consciousness as having less to do with a given category or categories of text than with the kind of imagination a reader brings to bear on textuality itself. That is, I wonder in what ways it might be beneficial to consider texts as holding within themselves a potential self-awareness activated by a certain sort of reader who cares about them in a certain way—a reader who approaches any semiotic system as an unfinished, dynamic, indeterminate, collaborative, transactional space rather than a space confined by limited and limiting conceptual categories. Isn't it perhaps the case that one mode of imagination might engage with Proust's *Swann's Way* to little or no illuminating end, while another mode—inquisitive, fully *there*, focused, culturally and politically and textually informed, nuanced, playful, restless, even self-parodic—might open up a scrawl of graffiti in a restroom stall into a constellation of compelling interpretive opportunities?

WHAT IS UNFINALIZABILITY?

I am reminded of what happens when Barthes reads restaurant menus or Derrida conjectures about the single line Nietzsche scribbled on a scrap of paper and unintentionally left behind among his writings: "I have forgotten my umbrella." I am reminded of Bakhtin reminding readers that novels are by nature flexible, unconfinable forms that exhibit self-awareness and are analogous to human beings who can never be fully circumscribed or categorically understood.

WHAT IS A FIRST PAGE?

Once upon a time, Martin Buber recounts in *Tales of the Hasidim*, one of Rabbi Levi Yitzchak of Berditchev's students asked him why the first page number is missing in all the tractates of the Babylonian Talmud. "However much a man may learn," the rabbi replied, "he should always remember that he has not even gotten to the first page."

WHAT IS NEULAND?

Innovative writing practices pose reading itself as a problem. Reading is *the* problem. We know we are in the presence of such work because without warning we sense we are on a quest for a first page that will never show up. We feel the need to devise a new set of semiotic coordinates to describe and discuss where we have just discovered ourselves. German has a word that approximates that feeling: *Neuland*—new territory, unfamiliar locale, unexplored terrain. *Ich kenne mich das noch nicht aus. Das ist Neuland für mich.* I don't know my way around here. That's new country for me.

WHAT IS READING?

In my mind, Nietzsche, Bataille, and Deleuze aren't philosophers—those readers committed to establishing coherent systems that account for and manage various realms of experience—but rather thinkers. They represent the kind of readers about whom I'm talking, exemplify procedures of deliberate reflexive misreading, over-reading, hyper-idiosyncratic associative reading that reveals a caricature of New Criticism's earnest emphasis on close textual analysis backed by the naïve belief that a work of literature functions as a self-contained aesthetic entity.

WHAT IS WRITING?

Nietzsche, Bataille, Deleuze, and others are emblematic of the appreciation that texts don't exist in any meaningful way until the event of reading occurs, and that that event is a form of writing and unwriting. Reading is less dependent on the text itself than on the quality of the reader's mind that engages with it, writes it in an (un)certain way. Anyone can attempt to read Balzac's story "Sarrasine." Barthes's circus of the mind in motion on display in *S/Z*, however, can take for granted in its encounter that all theory is spiritual autobiography and move forward from that assumption to (mis)mine Balzac's work into a volatilely edifying instant about Barthes's critico-creative ingenuity. Anyone can attempt reading Hegel and/or Genet. Derrida's *Glas*, however, understands it can understand that philosopher and author only by (mis)eventing and (re)inventing them, denarrating them into material metaphors that turn text into self-conscious performance art.

WHAT IS UNFINALIZABILITY?

Joshua Landy remarks that formative fictions' function "is to fine-tune our mental capacities … They present themselves as spiritual exercises (whether sacred or profane), spaces for prolonged and active encounters that serve, over time, to hone our abilities and thus, in the end, to help us become who we are." True enough, but, given what I've just said, it may also be instructive to contemplate the opposite assertion: Readers train texts how to be read—although "train" is far too loaded a term in this context, connoting as it does a kind of discipline, even domination (isn't all interpretation an act of intellectual and emotional colonization?), that may be at odds with what I'm proposing. Readers fine-tune texts (bringing to bear the readers' selves-as-other upon them) as they actively create areas for prolonged and active meetings. From this angle, all texts may be considered formative texts—metafictional, reflexive, self-conscious—to the extent that experimental readers approaching them do so with a robust, sometimes contradictory, ever developing/revising/adapting self-reflexive activity. Beckett's Unnamable: "The thing to avoid (I don't know why) is the spirit of system."

WHAT IS A WRITER?

When I read as a writer, I'm keenly aware of elements many lay readers aren't: the shape of individual paragraphs, of individual sentences, white space, alignment, density, layout, the page itself (whether in normative or difficult fiction) as an arena of action and as a material correlative for what's happening at the strata of plot, character, and thematics.

WHAT IS A BEGINNING?

"Forgive me for all this philosophy," Matthew Goulish apologizes in *39 Microlectures: In Proximity of Performance*, "but what I'm trying to say is, in reaching the end of our road of beginnings, we now realize that beginnings are all there are."

WHAT ARE MY EYES?

They are always my eyes. They are never my eyes. How they read/write depends on my own imagination, education, age, where I live, how I live, socioeconomic context, gender, race, awareness of my body, comprehension of language structures and functions and slippage, what interpretive communities I intuit myself part of, how I have complicated those terms, how those terms have complicated me, how many times I have run into a particular text and how many times I have studied and unstudied to see it, how many times and how deeply I have been in love, how many things and people and ideas and hopes I have lost, how many I have gained, how deeply I have experienced hurt and hope and trauma and sheer joy, how capable I am of feeling, how capable I am of contemplation, how many family resemblances I can use the pattern-recognition machine of my brain to recognize between the text at hand and all those I have ever read/written before (and some I haven't), my relationship to the other arts, to social relations, to the world of accidents, my transactions with other beings, other things, other places, in addition to where and when and how I am situated in history.

WHAT IS TIME?

One can never read the same *Tristram Shandy* twice, let alone once, let alone read it as Sterne wrote it, or his contemporaries (if we could convince ourselves such a collective noun meant something) read and understood it. In the first half of the twenty-first century, one can only read Sterne's marvel through the lens of Pynchon's *Gravity's Rainbow* and William Gass's *The Tunnel*, perhaps Vanessa Place's *Dies: A Sentence*—whether or not, of course, one has ever actually read those novels (if they are in fact novels) or not. One can only read through one's own now, however one might begin to define and bewilder that word.

WHAT IS NOW?

How do you write/read today in a way that (mis)understands, consumes, and thinkfeels through the past in energetic and generative ways?

How do we beyond yesterday when *beyond* exists solely as a transitive verb?

How do we forge writing realms in which everything can be mindfully attempted, challenged, undone, rethought, re-felt, and failed at in absorbing, incandescent gestures for a purpose, even if that purpose remains a mystery to us, comes into being only during the event of reading/writing, when an Other animates our work in ways we can't fathom?

WHAT IS SLOW THINKING?

One difference between reading/writing art and reading/writing entertainment has to do with the speed of perception. Art willfully slows and complicates writing/reading, hearing, and/or viewing so we are provoked to reconceive form and experience. Entertainment willfully accelerates and simplifies reading/writing, hearing, and/or viewing so we don't have to think about or feel very much of anything at all except, perhaps, the adrenalin rush of the spectacle erupting before us. Experimental writing/reading practices are a method of imagination intensified, pointedly made more difficult and reflexive, in order to create a Thinking Text, or better, a Thinkfeeling Text.

WHAT IS DIFFICULTY?

Donald Barthelme: "Art is not difficult because it wishes to be difficult, but because it wishes to be art. However much the writer might long to be, in his work, simple, honest, and straightforward, these virtues are no longer available to him. He discovers that in being simple, honest, and straightforward, nothing much happens: he speaks the speakable, whereas what we are looking for is the as-yet unspeakable, the as-yet unspoken."

WHAT IS READING?

N. Katharine Hayles makes a helpful distinction between two cognitive modes, deep attention and hyper attention. Deep attention, usually associated with normative writing/reading, is the sort able to concentrate on a single object thoroughly for an extended period of time. Recollect your experience reading a novel by Orhan Pamuk or Doris Lessing. Hyper attention switches focus rapidly and often. It is attention with the jitters. Recollect your experience navigating a video game. Perhaps oddly, I would offer that challenging writing/reading practices use both cognitive modes concurrently: an intense, extended concentration coupled with a quick-scanning function in order to discern both the deep-structure rules and the limits of serious play. Such reading/writing practices are designed to increase our experience of life through a network of surprises, exercising our ability for problem-solving and sensation.

WHAT IS THINKFEELING?

To slow thinkfeel a text is to begin to raise elemental, sensual questions that otherwise remain invisible about reading: Where does a book exist? In what ways does how-a-page-matters matter? How do we read with our hands? How is the ideology of characterization not a psychological but sociocultural exercise? How is reading/writing the opposite of a fixed habit? All of which is to announce the obvious: innovative writing/reading practices don't comprise a laundry list of techniques, a wheel continuously reinventing itself, a tool box, fashion's flavor of the week, but rather an approach to existing in the world. It foregrounds radical interest, heresy, reflection, embroilment, adaptability, risk, heterogeneity, acute attendance in the whirled of words and whirled of the world, a natural rebelliousness against thanatos in all its manifestations, unpredictability, unfamiliarity, astonishment, disruption, self-consciousness, passion, compassion, contention, shock, resistance, the pleasures of collapse, thrill, self-irony, bliss, literate rather than fiscal economies, collective ecologies rather than competitive ones, the replacement of the Romantic myth of the gifted solitary artist/critic with rhizomatic interrelationships of support, vigorous independent literary activism as the dominant means of production and dissemination.

WHAT IS NOW?

Behind questions about slow thinkfeeling is not only a poststructuralist web of assumptions—an echo of Barthes's assertions that texts only exist as intertexts—but also the relatively sudden material proliferation of art books in the nineties (with a hypothetical trajectory that extends at least back to 1789 and Blake's *Songs of Innocence and Experience*, if not to the ninth century and such illuminated manuscripts as Book of Kells, if not long before), and the exchange between them and the conventional codex, on the one hand, and hypermedial creation, on the other. In Danielewski's *House of Leaves*, by way of illustration, one sees how intersemiotic forms display reverse remediation: as computers become more like books in such delivery systems as iPad and Kindle, books become more like computers. *House of Leaves* is a hypermedial project about our culture of data excess that asks through its maximalist page layout: What constitutes vital data, what trivial, what is the difference, and how can we tell? We find ourselves in an aesthetic Neuland where the book's relentless disembodiment via digital reading devices and other screens heralds a moment that inquires: What can a book do that other media can't, and what can other media do that a book can't?

WHAT IS THE FUTURE?

In writing what I have just written, in thinking about the kind of writerly/readerly consciousness about which I am thinking, I am reminded of Borges, who tells us in "Kafka and His Precursors" that we are in the ongoing process of inventing our artistic and existential antecedents. After discussing how he can hear Kafka's voice in the works of Zeno, Han Yu, Kierkegaard, Léon Bloy, and Lord Dunsany, Borges famously concludes: "In each of these texts we find Kafka's idiosyncrasy to a greater or lesser degree, but if Kafka had never written a line, we would not perceive this quality; in other words, it would not exist … The fact is every writer creates his own precursors. His work modifies our conception of the past, as it will modify the future."

WHAT IS POLITICAL HETERODOXY?

Young-Hae Chang and Heavy Industries' text-films, which can be accessed for free via one's laptop, but which also appear frequently as large installations in gallery spaces, use Flash animation techniques to make words fly across screens at speeds the viewer/reader can't control. *Traveling to Utopia: With a Brief History of Technology* takes the form of multiple black and green texts in old-computer font simultaneously racing across the top, middle, and bottom of bright whiteness. The reader/viewer often needs five or more sittings (one circuit through *Traveling to Utopia* takes about three minutes), each shot through with anxiety in the face of the film-text's evasive meaning and speed, before being able to assemble enough information to generate something like a narrative to account for what s/he is watching. Along the top runs a fiction in Korean characters, indecipherable to most English speakers. Along the bottom runs one in English that recounts the Kafkaesque dream of a nameless (and ambiguously gendered) narrator stopped by three policemen at a subway station that may be in Seoul, but may instead be in Paris, questioned, and allowed to go on his/her way. Along the middle runs the story of a (probably) different nameless female narrator's experience with technology from her first encounter with a computer in her father's office to her own first laptop and beyond. Walking through a metal detector at an airport one day, she sets off the alarm. A visit to the doctor reveals a chip implanted in her abdomen used to track endangered species. Her story concludes inconclusively with the narrator reporting that she has taken to living in airports, which for her represent atemporal, non-spatial territories that make her feel safe. All three narratives are interrupted, once, by an unnervingly out-of-place screen-sized smiley face clock, while a comically upbeat jazz score at odds with the narratives' content plays throughout. Chang's text-film could not have been conceived except as a reaction to and conversation with conventional linear narrativity, the history of digital arts (including the Flash technologies which once enabled it), and the ubiquity of movies and video games. *Traveling* situates the viewer/reader in the same place as the narrator(s) with respect to technology: unable to manage it, even as it broadcasts both from inside and outside our bodies, dematerializing the self even as it relentlessly tracks the subject position. Chang's work thereby not only writes about but performs its thematics through a troubled interface with its reader/viewer, who in many ways becomes the piece's protagonist, suggesting that the new flesh (in this case the female abdomen, site of bio-reproduction) has become impregnated with media (the site of semiotic and economic reproduction) that knows more about "us" than we do about "ourselves." The "characters" in her work, such as they are, exist superficially, erratically, illogically, like flows of unconnected data streams.

WHAT IS UNFINALIZABILITY?

Anne Carson's *Nox*, an elegy for her outrider older brother, whom she didn't know well and who died unexpectedly while on the run from the law in Europe, arrives in a box that simulates a thick book from one perspective, and, from another, the brother's coffin and/or tombstone. Open it, and inside one discovers an accordioned series of "pages" that folds out into an arrangement connoting an ancient scroll (Carson was trained as a classicist) made up of shards of her brother's letters, old photographs, tickets, the author's observations and memories, Catullus' poem 101 (the one addressed to the Roman poet's dead brother, a doubling of Carson's situation), and extensive dictionary entries on all the words that make up that poem, which Carson spends the length of the text trying and failing to translate accurately. The material manifestation of *Nox* is, like Chang's text-films, difficult to control, but for different reasons: it wants to sprawl, slide off one's lap or desk, be as hard to manage as the poet's brother, as memory itself. Carson's dilemmas in translating Catullus' poem—in managing it—mirrors her dilemmas in translating her brother into finalizable meaning. The aggregate produces a collage about the impossibilities of aggregates, full comprehension, capturing the absences and overdeterminations that are language, which continually means more and less than what it means to mean.

WHAT IS A WRITER?

Christian Bök's *The Xenotext* literalizes and inverts William S. Burroughs's apocryphal claim that language is a virus from outer space by encoding a short verse into a sequence of DNA and then implanting that sequence into a bacterium to observe its mutations, thereby making said bacterium into a reading/writing machine. His long-term goal is to rocket the organic result into outer space, sending language back to where it came from while creating an ever-changing poem that would outlive the works of Homer, Chaucer, Shakespeare, Pound, and Dr. Seuss as well as the earth, the solar system, and the galaxy. If Chang's project is concerned with art's ephemerality, Bök's is concerned with its immortality.

WHAT IS A FIRST PAGE?

I'm happy to say I don't know. Nobody does. That's precisely why I'm faithfully, unfaithfully, futilely, gratefully, vitally, painfully, provisionally, clumsily, determinedly, joyfully doing and undoing what I do.

14 NOTES TOWARD THE MUSICALITY OF CREATIVE DISJUNCTION

1. CONCLUSION: AMPHIBIOUS AESTHETICS

If we are witnessing at the creative peripheries of our culture the proliferation of a postgenre composition that questions the need for discussing such apparently singular species as science fiction and what we once dubbed the postmodern (but now simply call our lives), we are also witnessing the proliferation of a postcritical writing that questions the need for discriminating between such apparently singular species as theory and fiction. We are witnessing—and have been for at least the last thirty or forty years—what Steven Connor addresses as the slow "collapse of criticism into its object." We are witnessing, that is, the advent of performative critifictions dedicated to effacing, or at least deeply and richly complicating, the accepted boundaries between privileged and subordinate discourses.

2. CONTAMINATION METAPHYSICS

The collage imagination at the core of that gesture is one committed to liberating juxtaposition, mosaic, conflation, fusion and confusion, collaboration, Frankensteinian formations, cyborg scripts, centaur texts.

A poetics of beautiful monstrosity.

3. RONALD SUKENICK, 1972

We have to learn how to look at fiction as lines of print on a page and we have to ask whether it is always the best arrangement to have a solid block of print from one margin to the other running down the page from top to bottom, except for an occasional paragraph indentation. We have to learn to think about a novel as a concrete structure rather than as an allegory, existing in the realm of experience rather than in the realm of discursive meaning, and available to multiple interpretation or none, depending on how you feel about it.

4. FRIEDRICH NIETZSCHE, 1874

One day sitting at his writing desk in his Basel flat Friedrich Nietzsche will look at the pages of the manuscript on which is working and grasp with resounding disappointment the design of every phrase is wrong his house of signs a ruin not the what of saying but the how. He will look at the sheet of paper before him and all he will see is how every blocky paragraph is the color of ashes just another sentence in a language messy with them because every writer in his country has become a journalist wearing a blend-in essence and in the next breath it will come to him writing isn't expansion but compression a texturing into fragment saying in seven sentences what everyone else says in a book saying in seven sentences what everyone else doesn't say in a book employing the figure of aphorism and the form of collage to construct a particle philosophy for a particulate world bringing together what is shard and riddle and chance engineering with flesh.

5. RONALD SUKENICK, 1975

This novel is based on the Mosaic Law the law of mosaics or how to deal with parts in the absence of wholes.

6. QUOTATION AS CHANCE

Both the structuring and the reading of collage involves an aleatoric component that calls to mind the Cubist work of Braque and Picasso alongside the Dada and Surrealist of Duchamp and

Breton: occupation with the found object, the readymade, the chance encounter. Calls up Lévi-Strauss's notion of bricolage, as Gregory L. Ulmer points out, foregrounding concepts of already-extant messages, severing, discontinuity, multifariousness. Ulmer goes on: collage is a form of citation *carried to an extreme … collage being the "limit case" of citation*, while Derrida underscores that *every sign, linguistic or non-linguistic … can be cited, put between quotation marks; in so doing it can break with every given context, engendering an infinity of new contexts in a manner which is absolutely illimitable.*

Collage, then, opens up and opens out through the very process of cutting up and cutting off. By quoting away from context, the form releases new and unexpected interpretive environments, reconstitutions and recontextualizations that can surprise the author as much as the reader.

7. LITERAL & METAPHORIC COLLAGE

The notion of collage can be used literally or metaphorically in composition. That is to say, collage fiction can be deeply appropriative in nature, cutting up previous texts to create new ones, as in the work of Eliot or William Burroughs. But it can also be used as a constitutional principle for new textual units—not only as a juxtapositional combination of readymades, but of just-mades, as in Julio Cortázar's *Hopscotch* or Renata Adler's *Speedboat.*

8. RONALD SUKENICK, 1994

You need to understand that understanding is an interruption. Understanding is always an interruption of which you understand in the form of the cryptic. You need to interrupt yourself.

9. PATCHWORK BODY

Collage writing attends to the sensuality of the page, to the physicality of the book, to writing as a post-biological body of text.

Imagine Steve Tomasula's novel *VAS: An Opera in Flatland*. Replete with three-color graphics, foldout pages, wild typographic play, diagrams, doodles, drawings, and disparate citations, the former involves an expansive comic plot about a man named Square living in a (literally) two-dimensional suburb with his wife, Circle, and their daughter, Oval, and Square's struggle over whether or not to undergo a vasectomy. But it is the structure of that plot—that is, the body of the text about the text of the body—that makes Tomasula's collage fiction a unique reading experience.

Imagine Shelley Jackson's hypermedial work *My Body*, where the reader chooses which parts of her critifictional autobiography to read by clicking on various parts of her body in a schematic sketch, the sound of lungs inhaling and exhaling in the background.

10. SHELLEY JACKSON, 2003

In collage, writing is stripped of the pretense of originality, and appears as a practice of mediation, of selection and contextualization, a practice, almost, of reading. In which one can be surprised by what one has to say, in the forced intercourse between texts or the recombinant potential in one text ... Writers court the sideways glances of sentences mostly bent on other things. They solicit bad behavior, collusion, conspiracies. Hypertext just makes explicit what everyone does already. After all, we are all collage artists.

11. COLLAGE AS CONTINUUM: A

Just as there are many modes of realism, there are also many modes of collage writing. If we imagine a narratological continuum of textual possibilities, we discover at one end scholarly works with their will toward intellectual authority through collaged citation, or, slightly farther on, my critifiction *Girl Imagined by Chance* that blends authentic citation with false, questionable, and purely fictional ones to generate a lyrical structure whose intent, among other things, is to investigate notions of cultural memory and textual prerogative.

12. COLLAGE AS CONTINUUM: B

Near the middle of our hypothetical continuum, we discover particulate writings that assume but don't require a reading strategy that arcs from beginning to end. Here I am thinking of Robert Coover's short story "The Baby Sitter," with its interlacing of multiple suburban realities in tiny prose blocks, or Joe Wenderoth's epistolary novel *Letters to Wendy's*, in which an unstable narrator composes a series of easily interchangeable prose-poem missives to the fast-food chain. Farther on appear writings that employ both text and graphics in collaged arrangements, like Kathy Acker's avant-punk *Blood and Guts in High School*, Eckhard Gerdes' avant-samizdat *Cistern Tawdry*, and Eduardo Galeano's politico-surrealist *The Book of Embraces*, whose narraticules (most only a few lines long, none more than two pages of prose) are sometimes political in nature, sometimes philosophical, sometimes fictional, and almost always highly metaphorical, meditative, and elusive; none contributes to an overarching plot, but each speaks with and adds to the rest.

13. COLLAGE AS CONTINUUM: C

Beyond these are events like Max Ernst's *Hundred-Headed Woman* that employ no (or virtually no) text whatever, and, at the far end of our continuum, we discover bookless do-it-yourself collage texts like Marc Saporta's *Composition #1* that comes to us as a bundle of loose pages in a box along with instructions to shuffle and read, or web-based hypermedial compositions requiring a reading strategy uninterested in or even actively antagonistic to notions of beginning, middle, and end, like Stuart Moulthrop's *Reagan Library* and Talan Memmott's *Lexia to Perplexia*.

All these modes share, to one degree or another, a belief in the musicality of creative disjunction because:

14. VICTOR SCHKLOVSKY, 1917

The purpose of art is to impart the sensation of things as they are perceived and not as they are known. The technique of art is to make objects "unfamiliar," to make forms difficult, to increase the difficulty and length of perception because the process of perception is an aesthetic end in itself and must be prolonged.

LESSNESS

A little less of us every day.

Seven words, nine syllables, twenty-three letters.

That's all that is the case, precisely what we really know about ourselves, sans irony, wit, posturing, desperate belief: how it is useless to reason with our own bodies.

There is hope, Franz Kafka once wrote, but not for us.

Blessed is he who expects nothing, Alexander Pope once wrote, for he shall never be disappointed.

An email from a friend, her lung cancer having recently metastasized to her brain: They have me on this experimental chemo pill, long-term, which is supposed to reduce the risk of recurrence greatly. The problem is it made my face break out in this horrendous acne-like rash. So I've cut back to half a dose and begun taking antibiotics as well as using all sorts of creams. My dermatologist's assistant spent nearly an hour with me showing me how to use makeup to cover the rash. I've never used makeup in my life, and really hadn't planned on starting now, but it does seem to make a difference.

We seem to believe it possible to ward off death by following rules of good grooming, Don DeLillo once observed.

How we keep writing anyway.

How we keep writing anyway until we don't keep writing anyway.

The bioengineered replicant Roy Batty to his creator, Tyrell, in *Blade Runner*, a moment before Roy crushes Tyrell's skull, drives his thumbs into Tyrell's eyes: I want more life, fucker.

How I saw the writer Ronald Sukenick for the last time one humid rainy April afternoon in his Battery Park City apartment two months before he died of inclusion body myositis, a muscle-wasting disease that eventually makes it impossible for one to swallow, then to breathe.

Jaspers's philosophy being an extended effort to prove and describe the margins of human experience, an effort to confront what he thought of, beautifully, as The Unconditioned.

Death is so terrifying, Susan Cheever once wrote, because it is so ordinary.

Ron couldn't use his fingers anymore, so he bought a voice-recognition program and wrote by means of that.

Ridley Scott re-editing the scene so that in the final cut Batty says: I want more life, father—thereby draining the life out of the line, making it into mere Oedipal cliché.

How my wife and I strolled along the banks of the Bagmati river in Kathmandu among myriad cloth-wrapped bodies burning on funeral pyres.

How Ron and I both knew this was it, how there would be no future meetings. How we both understood there were no social conventions to cover such an event. How the unsettling result was that each of our simple declarative sentences seemed anything but.

When we speak of "seriousness" in art, Thomas Pynchon penned, ultimately we are talking about an attitude toward death.

How, shortly before his death in 1631, John Donne obtained an urn, his own burial shroud, and the services of an artist. He wrapped himself in said shroud, posed atop said urn, and had said artist render a charcoal sketch of him, which the poet kept by his bedside throughout his final illness.

In his early fifties, David Bowie visited a funeral home, picked out an unadorned coffin, and asked to lie in it for an hour in a vacant room.

The distance between the real and the ideal.

Two large-framed photographs hang on the walls of my writing studio, both by Joel-Peter Witkin. They are the only ones by an established artist my wife and I have ever felt a necessity to purchase. Each is a still life, a *nature morte*, constructed from corpse parts the photographer found and posed in morgues in Mexico and France.

Families of the dead in severe circles around the pyres along the river.

Holy men spattering butter on the fires to help them burn faster.

How, to pass time on the Paris metro once between stops, I asked my sister, with whom I was riding, how old she wanted to live to be, and, instead of answering, she began to cry.

Jaspers referred to the ultimate boundaries of being as *Das Umgreifende*—The Encompassing: the indefinite horizon in which all subjective and objective experience is possible, but which can itself never be apprehended rationally.

Eighty-three, less than a year before he died, Kurt Vonnegut: I've written books. Lots of them. Please, I've done everything I'm supposed to do. Can I go home now?

One only becoming authentically human, in other words, according to Jaspers, at the instant one allows oneself awareness of The Encompassing by confronting such unimaginables as contingency and the loss of the human, which is to say the loss of the what we used to separate into body and mind.

Everything else refusal, fear, repression.

How the last words Roy Batty speaks, huddled on a dark rainy L.A. rooftop in a 2019 that never occurred, are some of the saddest, most powerful, in the entire film: All the things I have seen; these shall be lost in time.

How it is the case, precisely, that life can be defined as a slow dying.

A terminal illness.

Birth, Beckett once wrote, was the death of him.

The goal of all life, Freud once wrote, is death.

How it is the case that death is a protracted amnesia visited upon those who live beyond the lost one's passing.

Ernest Becker: The irony of man's condition is that the deepest need is to be free of the anxiety of death and annihilation; but it is life itself which awakens it, and so we must shrink from being fully alive.

Remembering, Milan Kundera once wrote, is a formula for forgetting.

My dying friend: A lot of the brain motor difficulties that I was expecting after the first surgery seem to be appearing now. My left hand feels more or less like a stroke patient's, unable to do very much except spill a glass of water on a computer keyboard or leave A. walking two blocks behind me because I had no sensation that I let go of his hand. For about two weeks there I was having some real palsy tremors, what they're calling mini-seizures.

On a large enough timeline, Chuck Palahniuk writing, the survival rate for everyone will drop to zero.

That's it. That's all.

How, as I was working on my novel about Friedrich Nietzsche's last mad night on earth, I couldn't shake the eerie realization that inside always becomes outside in the end.

The simple, brutal notion: how that which separates us from the world—our sphincterial control, our skin, our biological deep-sea suit—gradually goes away.

We are always becoming something other than we are, something other than we want to be.

Like it or not, we are always traveling away from ourselves.

Every once in a while Ron Sukenick stopped talking, shifted in his electric wheelchair, looked out his picture window at the Hudson, then drifted back to what we were saying, and we would pick up where we had left off. I drank bourbon, Ron tea through a straw. He was having trouble swallowing. He was becoming tired very quickly.

Every parting gives a foretaste of death, Schopenhauer noting.

How I could hear steam building inside the skulls of the corpses as I moved along the banks of the Bagmati.

Then the pops.

How Hemingway turned himself into a character in one of his books and shot himself in the head. How Hunter Thompson turned himself into a character in one of his books and shot himself in the head. How Yukio Mishima turned himself into a character in one of his books and committed seppuku. Publicly. In 1970.

Outside, people not cheering Mishima on, but rather heckling him, jeering, as he disemboweled himself.

Gradually, or not so gradually. It depends.

I lost all my hair two weeks ago, my dying friend emailing. One of the things they talked about was the need to keep the head covered at all times and I ended up buying a large assortment of what they call chemo turbans, some of them reasonably stylish, to wear around the house. I mean, it's a perfectly good wig, and I'm sure was once a very nice beaver or groundhog or whatever it was, but I hate it. The hair of my nightmares.

"The head." Not "My head."

As if she had already begun to become something other than her own body.

My sister-in-law was in town, my dying friend wrote, and her comment was it looks okay, it just looks nothing like me. I'll use it for teaching, since it still masks hair loss, and there's no need to impose my limitations on the students. Then I decided to say screw the chemo turbans and looked at some hats. I ended up buying three outrageously exquisite retro-style felt fedoras which cover the whole head and are marvelously comfortable. You won't believe these. I've never been so stylish in my life.

Roy Batty, a replicant, virtually identical to humans in every way—except for the fact that the memories he believes are his own are really someone else's implanted within him, except for the fact that he has a four-year lifespan—is more human than the other so-called humans around him.

A ball will bounce, Richard Wilbur once wrote, but less and less.

How the sadhus, Hindi holy men who live by begging, cooked bread by burying it among shards of smoking human bones.

I want to enjoy my death, Beckett commenting.

Presumably with some irony.

In that race which daily hastens us towards death, Camus observing, the body maintains its irreparable lead.

How Tennessee Williams accidentally swallowed the cap of his nasal spray and suffocated alone in his hotel room.

How Sherwood Anderson choked on a toothpick at a party in Panama.

How Maupassant tried killing himself by slicing his own throat, failed, was declared insane, spent the last eighteen months of his life in an asylum, dying from syphilis he contracted in his youth, as did Manet, as did Gaugin, as did Schubert, as did Nietzsche, as did Scott Joplin.

How, after a little more than an hour, I realized I should take my leave of Ron. How I don't believe I've ever experienced more difficulty closing a door behind me.

How that door both shut and remained wide open.

How the only real closures come in regulated fiction and memoir, redemption and faux wisdom hardened into commodity, like an order of Arby's Cheesecake Poppers.

How a group of children stood knee-deep in the river, oblivious, in the black oily water that used to be strangers, throwing a red rubber ball through gusts of coppery haze.

Charles Sanders Pierce: If man were immortal he could be perfectly sure of seeing the day when everything in which he had trusted should betray his trust, and, in short, of coming eventually to hopeless misery. He would break down, at last, as every good fortune, as every dynasty, as every civilization does. In place of this we have death.

The graveyards are full of indispensable men, Charles de Gaulle remarking.

Death is not an event in life, Wittgenstein noted. We do not live to experience death.

Yes, I want to say, and no.

My mother waiting primly in her living room in suburban Dallas, also dying, also of cancer, this time breast metastasized to the spine, liver, brain, inventorying the clutter that took her nearly 77 years to quilt around herself, announcing out of the blue, almost casually, to no one in particular: All these things will forget their stories the moment I'm gone.

A little less, and then a little less.

The first Witkin photograph on my wall: a plump old woman, the top of her head missing, her skin blotched, her body supported by wires, sitting at a chair next to a table in a sparse room. On the table is a book. Her finger holds her place, although the arm to which the finger is attached isn't itself attached to her torso. *Interrupted Reading*, the photograph is entitled.

Anna Karenina throws herself under a train.

His books are questions of survival of personality, Carole Maso commented about the narrator's former lover in *Ava*.

Yes, and no.

My cousin entered the hospital for routine hip-replacement surgery to fix his fullback years in college. The operation went off without a hitch—until an infection flowered within him, one of those virulent bacterial strains that chew through a patient's every prospect. One week my cousin was perfectly fine, minus the limp and a certain throbby stiffness. The next he was on a ventilator. The next his wife was emailing what amounted to acquaintances like me in an attempt to drum up something that looked like an acceptable audience for the memorial service, dubbed "a celebration," which I had absolutely no intention of attending.

Emma Bovary eats arsenic, Eva Braun cyanide, Alan Turing cyanide, Abbie Hoffman phenobarbital.

There is no boat in Hades, no ferryman Charon,
No caretaker Aiakos, no dog Cerberus.
All we who are dead below
Have become bones and ashes, but nothing else.
    Someone carved on a Roman tombstone 2000 years ago.

The second Witkin photograph: a woman's untorsoed head, eyes closed, atilt on some dark surface (let's call it a table), next to which a stuffed monkey is posed.

Patrik Ouredník recounts how, during the first months Buchenwald was open for business, those in charge gave the inmates postcards that said: Accommodation is wonderful, we are working here, we receive decent treatment and are well looked after. The inmates were made to sign them and address them to relatives, some of whom apparently believed what they read. One Greek prisoner mailed his postcard to his father in Pyrgos. Three months later, his father arrived for a visit.

At the railroad platform, the son leapt upon him, strangling him to death before the Germans could get their hands on him.

My wife Andi's grandmother refused to be buried, insisting on being entombed in a mausoleum instead because, she said, she didn't want to get dirty.

Whatever opinion we may be pleased to hold on the subject of death, Proust providing, we may be sure that it is meaningless and valueless.

How it would be a perfect misreading of his work to suggest that Witkin's intent is to shock, disgust, exploit his subjects, his viewer's vision.

My uncle had a heart attack on a beach while feeding pigeons. A good Scandinavian, he was too embarrassed to draw attention to himself, reported his wife, who had been sitting beside him at the time, and so he expired, sotto voce, on the spot.

Diane Arbus swallows barbiturates and slashes her wrists, as does Mark Rothko.

The living being is only a species of the dead, Nietzsche declaring, and a very rare species.

Death is the mother of—

No, that's not it.

Another dying friend. Another email. Another cancer. Another metastasis to the brain. Sorry not to have updated you sooner, but the fog is settling in so even this will have to be short. Not much news. I wish I could write something light and cheerful, at least something light and pomo-ish, but, fact is, cancer does suck. Or, rather, it's the treatment that sucks: makes me want to do nothing but sleep all day (and night). Not much pain—occasional headaches, joint aches. What's most scary is the felt deterioration of my mental abilities (such as they were)—each day, I get dumber and dumber, and know it. Memory loss, inability to follow conversations, inability to find words. B. finds it inevitably frustrating, seeing me standing in the middle of a room, clearly without a clue what I'm doing there; and never sure if I understand or will remember two minutes later something she asked me to do. Frustrating for me, too—feeling like a retard who needs to have notes pinned to his shirt, reminding him what he should be doing.

Every plot an education, ultimately, about how everything eventually ends.

Jerzy Kosinski swallows barbiturates and puts a bag over his head, as does Michael Dorris.

While I thought that I was learning how to live, Leonardo da Vinci wrote, I have been learning how to die.

Witkin's work performing an act of reminding.

Every narrative, ultimately, a study in death.

Freud overdoses on morphine.

How, as one gets older, deaths begin arriving closer and closer, like mortars zeroing in on their targets.

Death being the one idea you can't deconstruct, David Lodge pointing out.

How I was reading to my mother from Eliot's *Four Quartets* when she died. My wife Andi holding her hand. We were at her bedside, talking to her, trying to comfort her, love her out of this world, even though she was already unconscious, even though she had been for more than a day. After a while, I began reading to her, to us, a little from her favorite book, *The Bhagavad-Gita*, a little more from late Eliot. She suddenly flinched and stopped breathing.

She was herself and then she wasn't.

One thousand and one things change the meaning of any book on any given reading.

Alice Bradley Sheldon, aka James Tiptree, Jr., mercy-kills her terminally ill husband and then shoots herself.

Near death and incoherent, Nietzsche lay in his narrow bed in a small room on the top floor of the archives his sister Lisbeth had had built in Weimar. The people Lisbeth had brought in with the hope of establishing a lucrative cult around her brother were talking about literature. Nietzsche roused, opened his eyes briefly, and said: I too have written some good books. Then he faded back into nowhere.

Gregor Samsa starves himself, as does the Hunger Artist, as does Kurt Gödel.

And I have come to relinquish that most modern of stances: uncertainty, Carole Maso reflecting. I am certain now of what will happen.

How my mother changed tenses before my eyes.

They said the side effects of these last two chemo sessions would be the hardest, my dying friend emailing. The latest development is that I'll suddenly pass out for a few minutes. Yesterday I was teaching and woke up as they were loading me into an ambulance. They checked my vitals, did a quick EKG, I signed a waver stating that I didn't want to be taken to the hospital, and I went back to teach without incident.

Witkin's goal in line with Gaston Bachelard's: Art, then, is an increase of life, a sort of competition of surprises that stimulates our consciousness and keeps it from becoming somnolent.

Yes, and—

Edwin Armstrong, inventor of the FM radio, jumps out a window, as does Gilles Deleuze, as does F. O. Matthiessen.

In heaven all the interesting people are missing, Nietzsche declared.

Witkin asking his viewers to sympathize with the fragility of the human flesh, the human heart, the act of lessening that we call ourselves.

Birth was the—

The head. Not my head.

Everything else refusal.

Yes, I want to say, and—

It happened on a Sunday when my mother was escorting my twin brother and me down the steps of the tenement where we lived, Witkin told an interviewer, recounting the pivotal moment from his childhood. We were going to church. While walking down the hallway to the entrance of the building, we heard an incredible crash mixed with screaming and cries for help. The accident involved three cars, all with families in them. Somehow, in the confusion, I was no longer holding my mother's hand. At the place where I stood at the curb, I could see something rolling from one of the overturned cars. It stopped at the curb where I stood. It was the head of a little girl. I bent down to touch the face, to speak to it, but before I could touch it someone carried me away.

Remember that we are what we are.

How the angelic four-voice vocal texture of Guillaume Dufay's masses make the day on which you hear them feel thoroughly lived.

How your consciousness arranges the entire piece of theater called living into a series of remarkable paintings called recollection.

A polyptych.

How each morning, as you rise from your bed, the belief hums through your head that you are going to die, going to die, going to die, yes, surely, no doubt about it, but not today—an observation that will remain correct every morning of your life, except one.

2
AUTRE
BIOGRAPHIES

LITERARY AUTISM

Fever states, delirium, nightmares, daymares pervade the fictions of the father of postmodern fantasy, Franz Kafka, and two of his intertextual sons, Jorge Luis Borges and Alain Robbe-Grillet. Their readers sense that they are inhabiting a hypnagogic state more than a dream or hallucination—that in-between state of semiconsciousness and reverie we experience just as we are falling asleep, neither here nor there, floating away from the external as we are overwhelmed by the internal.

Like K. in *The Castle*, all Kafka's characters search for something through a world "hidden, veiled in mist and darkness"—the territory Faulkner loved so deeply in *As I Lay Dying* and *The Sound and the Fury*, twilight, that suspension between light and dark, comprehension and incomprehension, the natural manifestation of uncertainty itself. Borges's universe, packed with mirrors, with repetitions, mazes, and metalogical arguments resides in a state of "fundamental vagueness," like the compass from Tlön, "trembling faintly, just perceptibly, like a sleeping bird," always about to bleed into something else, even as Robbe-Grillet's shimmers with the "indefinite light of a rainy landscape" packed with a "labyrinth of streets," a "labyrinth of unlighted hallways," through which a psychotic Mathias or unbalanced husband shot through with pent-up rage wander, everything cast in a mathematical precision that unremittingly underscores its opposite.

These aren't the fantastic worlds of George Saunders or, in a very different register, Ursula K. Le Guin, designed to delight and liberate consciousness so that it may sport among a freeplay of imaginative and politico-philosophical possibilities. Rather, they are liminal worlds crowded with phobias, neuroses, feelings of entrapment and oppression whose topography, as Sartre notes in his essay, "'Aminadab,' or the Fantastic Considered as Language," is congested with "corridors, doors and stairs that lead to nothing ... signposts that lead to nothing ... innumerable signs that line the road and mean nothing. In the 'topsy-turvy' world, the means is isolated and posed for its own sake."

Such literary hypnagogia renders hermeticism nearly complete. At best it maintains only a fragile awareness of the outside world. At its most insistent it is fully self-absorbed, removed from the quotidian. It disintegrates communal plot (the public, the objective, the chronological, the mimetic) and substitutes a brooding, subjective plotlessness (the private, the atemporal, the indeterminate).

Bruno Bettelheim describes the enormous frustration, anxiety, and despair a child exhibits when he or she realizes she or he cannot completely control his or her cosmos. Utter defeat flocks in, manifesting, of course, through bursts of temper tantrums which usually abate when the child can begin again to imagine hope for the future. Equally possible, though, is that such feelings can be directed inward. "If a child is for some reason unable to imagine his future optimistically, arrest in development sets in," Bettelheim remarks. "The extreme example of this can be found in the behavior of the child suffering from infantile autism." Among its symptoms, according to *A Psychological Approach to Abnormal Behavior* are "seclusiveness, loss of interest in surroundings, disturbances in emotional responses to people, emotional blunting, reversion to 'primitive' types of behavior, negativism, mannerisms, sensitivity to criticism, physical inactivity, repetitive movement, and idiosyncratic speech and thinking."

By way of analogue, it isn't difficult to see how the fantasies of Kafka, Borges, and Robbe-Grillet are charged with frustration, anxiety, and despair before the recognition that the exterior is beyond their authors' control, that optimism is idle gossip. Closed structures, from small stuffy rooms whose doors are locked to cramped streets winding through illegible cities, serve as registers for isolation, that radical turn inward, the limits of the expectation. Even the long, gray paragraphs with which their fictions are built crowd with ambivalent facts. They are frequently unable to break open into dialogue, are jammed against the promise of white space, which is to say the promise of pause and breath.

In his parable of progressive contraction and withdrawal, Gregor Samsa lives in his shell, under a couch, behind a sheet, imprisoned in his room, confined within his apartment, lost among the twisting streets of an unnamed city about which the reader learns nothing save that a sign of disorder and affliction, a hospital, hovers foggily out the window. Borges voices a similar sense of disjunction between self and world when, in an interview at New York University in 1971, he comments: "I'm afraid there are no characters in my work. I'm afraid I'm the only character." And at the end of "Tlön, Uqbar, Orbis Tertius," the narrator loses all inquisitiveness about what transpires outside *his* window: "I go on revising, in the quiet days in the hotel Androgue, a tentative translation into Spanish, in the style of Quevedo, which I do not intend to see published, of Sir Thomas Browne's *Urn Burial*"—seclusive, incurious, inactive, spinning out a language no one else can understand (since English, French, and Spanish will disappear after the Tlönic takeover). Robbe-Grillet's Mathias in *The Voyeur* and the husband-lover in *Jealousy* regress, the former to the animalistic torture and murder of a thirteen-year-old girl, the latter to the car wreck and subsequent burning involving A . . . and Franck he imagines over and over again. Both Mathias and the husband find themselves stuck in a web of repetitive movements, Mathias's psyche continually returning to the room where he either witnesses or partakes in the strangulation of that young girl kneeling by her doll, the jealous husband-lover's psyche obsessed with the crushed centipede on the wall, objective correlative of his guilt, lust, and churning wrath.

Rather than taking place in our diurnal world, these fantasies take place in infinity, an imaginary duration, a fugue state, *la durée*, where claustrophobic interiors undo the ticking of the clock. It's the oddest thing, reading Kafka: that sense of time not keeping time—as in that Tlönic school that "has reached the point of denying time. It reasons that the present is undefined, that the future has no other reality than as present hope, that the past is no more than present memory." In *For a New Novel*, Robbe-Grillet asserts that time in his work "seems to be cut off from its temporality. It no longer passes. It no longer completes anything."

We discover ourselves in a perpetual oscillation between wanting and needing to participate in the authorial irrealities of these texts, on the one hand, and, on the other, wanting and needing to attain distance from their disorientation, their relentless troubling of stock responses about how reality functions and narrativity narrativizes. In what he called the Balzacian mode of the novel, Robbe-Grillet argues that "everything tended to impose the image of a stable, coherent, continuous, unequivocal, entirely decipherable universe. Since the intelligibility of the world was not even questioned, to tell a story did not raise a problem. The style of the novel could be innocent." Now, he goes on, the serious novel's deep-structure has lost its innocence, its forms becoming increasingly unstable and indecipherable.

Instead of "meaning," the reader confronts the literary equivalent of Freudian *Nachträglichkeit*, *afterwardness*, whereby the story almost makes sense, but not quite, and where the almost-having-meaning seems to promise that meaning has only been deferred temporarily. "Meaning" seems to exist, but only up the next flight of stairs, just through the next doorway, on the next page. Often, therefore, the operative genre of such fantasies becomes the detective story which won't resolve. The texts come into focus only through the characters' and reader's inability to achieve it.

Like sacred texts, those of Kafka, Borges, and Robbe-Grillet exist in order to be interpreted in polyvalent, contradictory ways. They are interpretation machines. Frank Kermode: "the reader will find none of the gratification to be had from sham temporality, sham causality, falsely certain description, clear story .... The reader is not offered easy satisfaction, but a challenge to creative cooperation." The reader becomes the ultimate protagonist, yet, as Maurice Blanchot offers in his seminal essay, "Reading Kafka," "the true reading remains impossible. Whoever reads Kafka is thus necessarily transformed into a liar, and not entirely into a liar." The reader may create his own "meaning," but only in a self-consciously bracketed sense.

Kafka criticism is a parody of such creative reading. The critics tell us that Kafka is both a religious thinker who strives toward an unattainable absolute, and a humanist who is only of this world which for him is devoid of significance. His work is imbued with Freudian substructures and is anti-psychological; firmly set in the author's Prague and outside political and geographical reality in the realm of myth. Susan Sontag: "it is always the case that interpretation of this type indicates a dissatisfaction (conscious or unconscious) with the work, a wish to replace it by something else." Close to the point, then, is Thomas M. Kavanagh's insight that Kafka's project uses the form of a parable, and "the parable itself becomes a set of semes from which an infinite number of possible subsets can be successively generated."

Another way of saying this: Borges could be read fruitfully as a commentary on Kafka commentary. In Tlön, all works "invariably include thesis and antithesis, the strict pro and con of a theory. A book which does not include its opposite, or 'counter-book,' is considered incomplete." In Babel's library, every conceivable book can be found, "everything which can be expressed, in all languages." The ramifications are frightening, for all possible meaning must therefore exist, "the faithful catalogue of the Library, thousands and thousands of false catalogues, a demonstration of the fallacy of these catalogues, a demonstration of the fallacy of the true catalogue," and so on.

The first paragraph of *In the Labyrinth* switches point-of-view twice, while asserting outside it is both rainy and sunny, cold and hot, windy and calm. Two pages further on, the narrator describes the outline of an object on a table. It could be, we are told, a cross, a knife, a flower, a human statuette, "or anything." The narrator of that text describes whole scenes only to end with: "No. It was something else." Robbe-Grillet launches that novel with a preface that claims the "reality in question is a strictly material one; that is subject to no allegorical interpretation." The reader, he says, should not give the text "either more or less meaning than in his own life, or his own death." And as he indicates in his essay "A Future for the Novel," the innovative text may suggest many interpretations, may, "according to the preoccupations of each reader, accommodate all kinds of comment—psychological, psychiatric, religious, or political," yet its "indifference to these 'potentialities' will soon become apparent." The discomfiture for the reader is that if all meanings are possible, then none are.

Another way of thinking about this is to suggest that readers of these texts become players in games whose goal seems to be meaning, but which in fact is the game itself. Playing becomes the *sine qua non*, since winning is no longer a viable option. One of the most fundamental notions in game-theory is that the game is essentially gratuitous, non-instrumental. Games, in other words, are ends in themselves. Play is a voluntary activity that creates order and hence "meaning" in a limited environment, fiction a game that proceeds within the mind's playground. Usually, there are three kinds of players: 1) those who play by the rules; 2) those who cheat; and 3) those spoilsports who refuse to play. In Kafka's, Borges's, and Robbe-Grillet's texts, there is also a fourth kind of player—the one who wants very much to play, but does not know, cannot know, how. He or she has chosen to play in a sport that goes on with or without her or him.

K. in *The Trial* relives the same scene in various forms: the trial itself, in which the expectation of finding the message-verdict is repeatedly short-circuited. From the beginning, he knows, it seems, that he can't win, yet he chooses (?) to play until realizing every assertion on his part is followed by its negation, at which time he succumbs to the other gamesters, named the Law, and admits defeat through murder/suicide. The librarian of Babel understands from the start that he will never find the book of answers, the book of ultimate codes, and yet he plays out his melancholy life among those unending shelves. And the jealous husband-lover will never be able to determine to what extent his paranoia concerning A … and Franck is justified, how much of a plot works against him: does A … lean over simply to give Franck a drink, or is there something whispered between them? Has there really been a breakdown that keeps the couple in the city over night, or is there an affair going on? Is the native on the bridge only that, or is he some sort of spy for the couple?

Giving up forms the nucleus of Kafka's, Borges's and Robbe-Grillet's operations. The narrator of "Investigations of a Dog" puts it this way: "People began to investigate after a fashion, to collect data … And though the truth will not be discovered by such means—never can that stage be reached—yet they throw light on some of the profounder ramifications of falsehood." One is left with knowledge of a system of lies. The greatest sense of sadness here is not that all hope is lost, for that at least would lend things certainty, but that Kafka and the others find hope never quite succeeds in being condemned. There is always one more dim winding staircase to mount. As the priest in *The Trial* tells K., the scriptures may be unalterable, but "the comments often enough merely express the commentators' despair." Borges's narrators are cursed with the disease of consciousness, yet "there is no intellectual exercise which is not ultimately useless." Robbe-Grillet's narratives are nothing if not a string of failed meetings, unattained goals. Wallas kills the man whose murder he is supposed to solve. A soldier wanders through a maze of streets trying to locate a man to whom to give a message, but that man is nowhere to be found.

Interesting to note in this context is that neither Borges nor Robbe-Grillet can produce long fictions, that the scant length of the latter is achieved only through frequent repetition. Kafka could only complete short stories. When he attempted length, he could never finish what he started. Their fantasies tend toward the fragmentary, the essence of which is mutilation. No wonder, then, that Georg Bendemann writes to no one, that the imperial message reaches no one, that the old manuscript is written to no one by the doomed survivor of a dying race. Communication fizzles, as Beckett would dub them, pervade Borges's work, where Funes labors to create his own system of noncommunication, a system of enumeration by which every number would have a separate name. The Borgesian subtext resonates with misery before the arbitrariness of language, its essential defectiveness for depicting the case. Robbe-Grillet's work reveals a similar sort of misery in the face of those "tentative noises that have no meaning." We read inward-turned monologues that have nowhere to go, nothing to say, no reason to say, no real belief that anyone is listening, no message but messagelessness to communicate, linguistic misfires rife with words that "are so faint that they disintegrate before [the speaker] has spoken them" so that "afterwards he even doubts whether he has actually pronounced them at all."

NOT-KNOWINGS

1. I want to consider an impossibility: Guy Debord's influence, especially through his theoretical meditation on the confluence of advanced capitalism and mass media, *The Society of the Spectacle*, published in France in 1967, on Vladimir Nabokov's first novel written in English, *The Real Life of Sebastian Knight*, published in the US two weeks after Pearl Harbor.

2. Debord was seven at the time *The Real Life* appeared. He didn't influence, couldn't have influenced, Nabokov's novel, which was composed in Paris between late 1938 and early 1939 in the bathroom of Nabokov's apartment, where the Russian émigré retreated to write (his desk improvised from his valise balanced over the bidet) while his son Dmitri slept and/or played in the one main room Nabokov and his wife Vera rented.

3. And yet such anachronous entanglement is not completely unimaginable, and not not completely unimaginable.

4. What I mean to say is that when talking about influence I am talking about a particular mode of it, the sort Jorge Luis Borges discusses in his essay "Kafka and His Precursors." Looking back on texts by six disparate authors (Zeno, Han Yu, Kierkegaard, Browning, Léon Bloy, and Lord Dunsany) written before the existentially helpless Praguian invented twentieth-century literature, Borges notes: "If I am not mistaken, the heterogeneous pieces I have enumerated resemble Kafka; if I am not mistaken, not all of them

resemble each other. The second fact is the more significant. In each of these texts we find Kafka's idiosyncrasy to a greater or lesser degree."

5. I am not talking about an historically based exploration of one writer's impact on another, but rather about a certain kind of reading, which is to say a certain kind of rereading and misreading.

6. A kind we cannot escape in our post-historical moment that isn't one where, as Roland Barthes argued from a Paris that had erupted into a series of general strikes and occupations of factories and universities the year after Debord—now 37—published *Society of the Spectacle* (theory always a deep and deeply disguised form of memoir): "A text is not a line of words releasing a single 'theological meaning' (the 'message' of the Author-God) but a multidimensional space in which a variety of writings, none of them original, blend and clash. The text is a tissue of quotations drawn from innumerable centers of culture."

7. Which is to say Barthes incorporated the ideological thrust of the student protests against political hegemony into his own undoing of textual hegemony, dismantling the authoritarian impulse and, as one of the slogans to appear in May 1968 had it: *Soyez réalistes, demandez l'impossible.* Be realistic. Ask the impossible.

8. I can only read, which is to say write, as myself. Each of us can only do so from the ahistorical (which is of course to say the historical) position which she or he discovers his or herself inhabiting, i.e., as if all texts existed simultaneously, as if all were in conversation with (or perhaps, to change metaphors mid-sentence, had already infected and been infected by) all others across space and time. This is exactly what we mean when we say the word *contemporary.*

9. Once, obviously, we already knew this. Yet somehow we seem to have forgotten the fact—forgotten to make visible what constitutes the seemingly invisible event of reading—regularly (as if willfully).

10. Let me begin again: Nabokov and Debord couldn't have had less in common. They couldn't have expressed more opposed imaginations.

11. Born in 1931, thirty-two years after Nabokov, Debord lost his father, a pharmacist, to tuberculosis the year following New Directions' publication of *The Real Life*. Debord's mother sent him to live with his grandmother in her family villa in Italy, which they were forced to flee during World War II. Debord became politically active in a Cannes high school and, shortly thereafter, joined demonstrations in Paris against the French war in Algeria. During the sixties, the self-proclaimed Doctor of Nothing led the Situationist International—that small but immensely influential group who had their finest hour with that near-revolution in Paris in 1968. While the mutiny may have in many respects failed (the Gaullist party came back stronger than before after the June elections), the Situationists' style and tactics have remained a blueprint for dissent against authority ever since, from punk rock to hacker culture and the anti-globalization movements.

12. On the evening of November 30, 1994, in Champot, near Bellevue-la-Montagne, Haute-Loire, Debord executed his final act of resistance, what we might term his closing anti-spectacle, by shooting himself through the heart. It was, as anarchist blogger Dorian Cope points out, "a fittingly provocative end; a suicide deliberately designed to stun the masses out of their collective ennui, conveying at once a scathing denunciation of the twentieth century's leftist hopes and a tactical political maneuver in the form

of the ultimate Situationist 'action' ... The master agitator who in life remained resolutely in the shadows in order to avoid being 'branded' by the consumer capitalism he so despised became in death a celebrity."

13. And so, let me begin again: Born in 1899—thirty-two years before Debord—to a wealthy, prominent St. Petersburg family that boasted fifty servants, Vladimir Nabokov was the eldest of five children of a liberal lawyer, statesman, and journalist. In the wake of the Bolshevik Revolution, his family was forced to flee the city, then the country. In March 1922—Nabokov now 21—a Russian monarchist assassinated his father in Berlin. Nabokov remained in that city fifteen more years, until a climate of growing antisemitism (his wife Vera was Jewish) forced him on the run again, this time to Paris. He settled among the 400,000 Russian émigrés living there from 1937 until May 1940, when he and his family narrowly escaped the advancing German troops and once again bolted, this time to the US where, after the publication of his literary hurricane a decade and a half later, Vladimir Nabokov became Vladimir Nabokov.

14. After his arrival in the 16th *arrondissement*, Nabokov—in addition to translating his novel *Despair* from Russian into English (feeling he possessed greater control over that language than French), finishing *The Gift*, and undertaking a number of other smaller projects—began *The Real Life*, through whose pages floats the vague double of Irina Guadanini, a divorced Russian poet who worked as poodle trimmer and with whom the real Nabokov entered a brief affair while living in what Humbert Humbert refers to in his *Lolita* screenplay as Gray Paree. *Gray* because, far from his childhood situation back in St. Petersburg, Nabokov found himself in difficult straits financially. When in 1939 his mother died in Prague, he was unable to attend her funeral due to lack of savings and regular income as much as

the political climate. For *The Real Life*, James Laughlin at New Directions—Harry Levin and Delmore Schwartz had recommended he consider the manuscript—paid Nabokov a $150 advance.

15. Two emblematic stories concerning Nabokov's conspicuous politics. One: while the Bolsheviks stormed the Winter Palace in October 1917, Nabokov, recently having inherited a 2000-acre estate and the equivalent of several million dollars, sat at home several blocks away, composing poetry and listening to the gunfire. Two: in 1965, when President Johnson underwent a gallbladder operation, Nabokov wired him, wishing him a speedy recovery and continued success in what Nabokov referred to as LBJ's "admirable work" in Vietnam.

16. Which is to say the man who once said he was raised "a perfectly normal trilingual child in a family with a large library" was the sort who vociferously disapproved of the student demonstrations in the sixties—except, he wrote, "in countries with real and grim dictatorships." The sort who claimed he ardently believed in democracy, yet never voted.

17. Despite his avowed apoliticism—the most political position one can strike—Nabokov couldn't help being part of that real, grim, and highly politicized decade and a half in Europe through the thirties and forties. And despite his protestations to the contrary, he engaged fully with those politics in his own quintessentially conflicted way. He wrote a biography critical of Nikolai Chernyshevsky in reaction to the Soviet Union's enforced implementation of socialist realism as the state anesthetic aesthetic, and launched several attacks on the Nazis, including one in the form of *The Waltz Invention*, a tragicomedy in three acts published during his Paris years about an infantile madman unleashed on history. Yet unlike Debord, Nabokov detested

being part of any group or endorsing abstractions like those espoused by Situationism. He rejected the very kind of spontaneous, aleatoric, openly political creation Debord championed because such work, Nabokov believed, flew in the face of the meticulous observation, care, and craftsmanship that were the hallmarks of serious—that is to say Nabokovian—art.

18. Nabokov's books worked behind his back, believed things he didn't—or didn't quite. Partly this is because texts by their nature accomplish more than their authors wish them to accomplish, remain by their very disposition over-determined, and partly this is because the act of reading is a variety of writing, as I say, and therefore a variety of rewriting, and therefore an endless exploration of texts' recursive character, a reminder that every author, when done with a work, is simply one more critic of it among a panoply of them.

19. In *Society of the Spectacle*, Debord traces the development of a mediascape where social life, a sense of felt community, human interaction, has been replaced the engines of advanced capitalism with representation (the core concept—speaking of influences—that enabled Baudrillard to become Baudrillard): with, that is, spectacles projected by the government and culture industry to distract us from the awareness that being has declined into having, "having to appearing." This condition, according to Debord, is the historical juncture at which we find "the world of the commodity ruling over all lived experience." Relationships among commodities, in short, have come to supplant relationships among human beings.

20. Passivity before the spectacle expresses itself as existential numbness, a condition consonant with Heidegger's notion of *Alltäglichkeit*, *everydayness*, in which the subject lives in a state of ceaseless overlooking, habitualness, boredom—in which existence has dimmed into indifference. For Debord, such existential numbness is expressed as political numbness, a ceaseless overlooking of the subject's position with respect to a web of power that has become so ubiquitous as to become unseen. This is the air we think through.

21. Debord's perceptual revolution: impede that passive relationship between human and spectacle, even if only for flashes; disorder the spectacular by devising instants that reorder life, give rise to sudden rushes of self-consciousness about one's being-in-the-world. Through the act of *détournement*—the creation of a new work inimical to the assumptions of an original (and usually commercial) one familiar to the target audience—Situationism appropriates and perverts the grammar of the distractive habitual in an attempt to interrupt it, making us aware both of the dynamics of spectacle and the possibility of alternative approaches to existence.

22. The Situationist project—Barbara Kruger's jamming of found consumer images with bitingly ironic text that reveals those images' connection to power, individual autonomy, and the body; Carlos Latuff's juxtaposition of Coke's logo with iconic imagery of weapons and murder that brings attention to The Coca-Cola Company's human rights abuses in Guatemala and contamination/over-exploitation of limited water resources in India—the Situationist project exists in order to remind us that we can imagine otherwise.

23. While clearly *The Real Life of Sebastian Knight* doesn't deploy blatant, politically charged derailment, Nabokov's novel does deploy (at least when read through the lens of a certain Debordian [non]influence) a more nuanced method of turnabout that in some measure accords with Debord's and his intellectual/aesthetic offspring's.

Nabokov's aesthetics suggest a politics other than the one promoted by the biological version of the author.

24. Plot I. In *The Real Life*, a narrator known only as V. (a vaguely metafictional stand-in for another, less sadly absurd Vladimir) has written the nominal biography we are reading (his first literary work) of his half-brother, the Russian-born English novelist Sebastian Knight, who died at 36 of the same heart ailments that took his mother—and will, years later, euthanize heartless Humbert Humbert on a different fictional planet. At the time of his death Knight, with whom V. has had at best a distant relationship, had already gained a great deal of literary notoriety for his five books.

25. Plot II. V.'s quasi-biography portrays his efforts to track down and interview various friends and acquaintances of Knight (as well as of V.'s readings of his half-brother's books) in an attempt, at least in part, to refute a previous biography produced by Knight's former secretary, one dubious Mr. Goodman, who "paints in a few ill-chosen sentences a ridiculously wrong picture of Sebastian Knight's childhood," among other alleged deliberate factual failures, in pursuit of a goal ("simple," V. avers, "as his philosophy") to prove Knight is "a product and victim of what [Goodman] calls 'our time.'" Goodman, in other words, according to V., conceptualizes writers as symptoms of history.

26. Thematics I. Yet by the second page of Nabokov's novel we find accuracy about earlier life-events interrogated. "Nor is it exact," V. writes, "as suggested in the British press after Sebastian's decease, that his father was killed in the duel he fought in 1913; as a matter of fact he was steadily recovering from the bullet-wound in his chest, when—a full month later—he contracted a cold with which his half-healed lung could not cope." If the British press's account is not exact, it is inaccurate, a thematic flag that yesterday's

events, rendered, go up for grabs. If the re-presentation of an event is troubled, then so it is with recollection. If one teller's reliability is questioned, so it is with the reliability of all.

27. Thematics II. The more V. tries to discover who his half-brother was, the less he learns—or, more precisely and importantly: what V. learns is precisely what he doesn't learn.

28. *The Real Life*, put another way, is an inverted detective novel where clues add up to less and less. By V.'s lights, Goodman's narrativization of pastness, like the British press's claims concerning Sebastian's father's death, is drastically deficient, if not purposefully—even, V. would like to argue, maliciously—flawed, his portrait of Knight (whose name suggests *night*, along with its connotations of darkness, obscurity, and ignorance) a series of slights and slips around an entity if not absent, exactly, then surely indecipherably present. Yet Goodman is far from alone in his be(k)nightedness. Sebastian's governess's memories of him as a boy were so "hopelessly distorted," "the past in her mind ... so blurred and displaced," that V. doubts their reality altogether, and even Sebastian's mother feels the real life of her son has "escaped" her, "that he will always remain an enigma."

29. Emblems I. V. visits the pension in the town of Roquebrune where he believed his mother died thirteen years before, only to discover after the fact that it was a different place with the same name. In the midst of V.'s interview with him, Knight's tutor at Cambridge confesses "my memory has shrunk in the washing." V's task of forming "a coherent picture" of his half-brother's life continually "eludes" him: "I could perhaps describe the way he walked," he admits, "or laughed, or sneezed, but all this would be no more than sundry bits of cinema-film cut away by scissors and having

nothing in common with the essential drama," a drama that for V. entails discovering a way to narrate coherence, even as his real life turns out to be something painfully more inconclusive.

30. Emblems II. As his quest for information about Knight's life lumbers on, V. comes to wonder: "Why was the past so rebellious?"—even as he comes to understand the best he will ever be able to write is "a book with a blind spot," "an unfinished picture" of his half-brother. As if to drive home the point, *The Real Life*, which the reader learns early on can never be real, never anything more than an approximation of truth, the imperfect puzzle that defines all interesting fiction, concludes with a scene—bookend to the one in which V. visits the town where he believes his mother died—in which V. is convinced he is visiting his dying half-brother in the hospital, only to realize that he has actually been sitting at the bedside of a stranger, that Knight died the day before.

31. His half-brother, V. learns, had planned to write a fictitious biography. Is that, I find myself inquiring, what we're reading when we read *The Real Life*—not V.'s biography of Sebastian at all, but Sebastian's mischievous biography of a version of himself whose narrator is a version of his estranged and absent brother?

32. Typing that last line leads me to think about the focal absences that impel so many of Nabokov's novels. Wondering once with my graduate seminar, Narrative Theory and Practice, if anyone gets out of *Pale Fire* unscathed, un-satirized, unironized, it occurred to several of us the answer might just be humble and bright Hazel, Shade's daughter, who, despite her homely suburban existence, is never lampooned in the key Kinbote and Shade are, never compared to anything but herself. She provides the gravitational force around which all the other characters circle, even though she only exists as a trace in Shade's poem, ends up leaving this realm, not because of any baroque shenanigans, but because it simply and achingly wasn't the one she had anticipated.

33. If so, Hazel becomes the distant fictional cousin of Dolores (another being wholly silenced in the text she inhabits; we only hear her speak as that speech is rendered through Humbert's gorgeously ghastly mouth), another sad ghost that drives a literary machine, the absence that makes a Nabokovian text present, the sole paper being in that novel with whom we are made to feel genuine, lasting empathy.

34. Or, with all the parallels to Nabokov's own past, from his almost-birthdate and exile from Russia to his affair with Guadanini, are we to imagine we are reading some Borgesian rendition of Nabokov's own autobiography in *The Real Life*? Is that perhaps what V. means, at least in a metafictional—if not a metaphysical—sense when he observes that "the only real number is one, the rest are mere repetition"? The only real number is the number that announces the self-enclosed subjectivity of what J. M. Coetzee refers to as *autrebiography*. If so, then, perhaps, we should take the last line of the novel literally: "I am Sebastian, or Sebastian is I, or perhaps we both are someone whom neither of us knows."

35. The noun/pronoun blur in that final sentence leads the reader in several fecund directions. First, it enacts a metaleptic blip—an unsettling violation of narrative levels that serves to remind the reader that the world of the told has been contaminated by the world of the telling, that the one is always in some sense the other. This tactic is used throughout *The Real Life*. V. learns it is out of the question to recount Knight's childhood "with anything like the methodical continuity which I would have normally achieved had Sebastian been a character of fiction"; he "yearns for the easy

swing of a well-oiled novel"; the reader navigates plot after plot of Knight's novels which don't, in reality, exist. That kind of metalepsis calls the reader's attention to her or his involvement in the event of reading, and hence to his or her involvement in the event of [re]writing in a manner analogous to those V. encounters during his own search for [the truth about] his half-brother. By its very nature, reading/rewriting will remain contrary to fact; [truth be told,] there are only bothered facts and fraudulent performances.

36. Second, the pronoun/noun blur has the effect of derailing—and here Debord reenters our conversation—conventional concepts of stable selfhood. This prompts the reader to recollect that identity happens only as worried construction and worrying construction-by-others; that identity remains contradictory, partial, and strategic; that we are forever being spoken through by the systems of which we are part and from which we wish to escape—which is to say, *The Real Life* (echoing Wittgenstein's news in *Tractatus*) performs a difficulty: our rules of grammar have been repeatedly misunderstood by Western culture as philosophy.

37. Third, that pronoun/noun blur has the effect of derailing, not a dominant politics, but rather two dominant and inherently naïve genres, which is to say ideologies: biography and memoir. Professed investigations into fixed pastness and selfhood, *The Real Life* contends through its very technē, are subsets of fiction that seek to uncomplicate yesterday. By perpetuating their illusions of causality, authenticity, and cohesion, they become insistent systems of fiasco.

38. *The Real Life* is ultimately a text, like so many by Nabokov, about epistemology—or, more exactly, about the limits of it.

39. *The Real Life* is ultimately a text about Not-Knowing, which is to submit that it presages Barthelme's observation in his

1987 essay on the subject: "Writing is a process of dealing with not-knowing, a forcing of the what and how."

40. Serious writing is a process, like serious reading, of learning how to linger in the unresolved.

41. *The Real Life* is ultimately a text about a particular kind of Not-Knowing: self-conscious narration aware of the myriad obstacles in talking about either personal or cultural history; about how events and confluent subjectivities are constantly being written, edited, rewritten, erased, reformatted, retold; about, to say it another way, the bafflement of knowledge itself. Or, as V. comes to understand about Goodman (and the reader comes to understand about V.): he "never quotes anything that may clash with the main idea of his fallacious work."

42. About the derailment of the very concept of temporality, and a special case of it: late-stage capitalism, where time is money and so is quantified, categorized, mechanized, stabilized, made to run in a beeline that disavows disorder and mystery … And, with that, a radical politics reenters the pages of *The Real Life* that Nabokov most certainly didn't believe.

43. Exemplary of Debord's clear influence on Nabokov is the carnivalesque line with which I should like to conclude, and perhaps my favorite in all of *The Real Life*—V. quoting from a work-in-progress sentence by his half-brother that disarranges the habitual at a syntactic layer, rouses us to our own reading practices, our own meaning-making ones, and thereby intimates by its presence that there are always other ways of constituting the reality of us, of our lives, instants that allow us to abandon (however fleetingly) the securities of our limitedness and enter new realms of examined consciousness:

44. *As he a heavy A heavy sleeper, Roger Rogerson, old Rogerson bought old Rogers bought, so afraid Being a heavy sleeper, old Rogers was so afraid of missing to-morrows. He was a heavy sleeper. He was mortally afraid of missing to-morrow's event glory early train glory so what he did was to buy and bring home in a to buy that evening and bring home not one but eight alarm clocks of different sizes and vigour of ticking nine eight eleven alarm clocks of different sizes ticking which alarm clocks nine alarm clocks as a cat has nine which he placed which made his bedroom look rather like a*

THE ART OF STUPEFYING MALFUNCTIONS

1. I want to say I was trying to be a writer.

2. I want to say it was 1971.

3. I'm probably making all this up.

4. Me fifteen, enfolded in an intensely white middle-class upbringing in a leafy Jersey crawling with pizza joints and surrounded by air-tight malls.

5. This the year I first noticed Donald Barthelme's fictions in *The New Yorker.*

6. When *The New Yorker* was still *The New Yorker* and not the thing it is not now.

7. That effervescent second of unearthing.

8. "Flying to America" (26 November). "The Catechist" (5 November). "Departures" (1 October). "Critique de la vie Quotidienne" (9 July). "Perpetua" (4 June). "Subpoena" (21 May). "The Story Thus Far" (23 April). "Engineer-Private Paul Klee Misplaces an Aircraft Between Milbertshofen and Cambrai, March 1916" (26 March). "The Genius" (12 February).

9. I was fifteen. I was sixteen. B. born four decades earlier, on April 7th, in Philadelphia, PA, a quarter century to the

month after Samuel Beckett, the man B. said made it possible for him to write.

10. Everything a manner of speaking.

11. B. Sr. an architect at the University of Houston, where B. Jr. would one day help found the prestigious creative writing program.

12. B. Sr. illuminatingly an advocate of the Bauhaus and utopian universalist belief that line, space, and form should be pared to their essentials, designing the house—an homage to Mies van der Rohe—in which B. Jr. grew up.

13. Reduction, simplification, concentration, B. Sr. used to say.

14. B. Jr. thereby spending his life unwriting the dead father who just wouldn't die.

15. I'm fated to deal in mixtures, slumgullions, which preclude tragedy, which requires a pure line, B. Jr. writing.

16. Famously.

17. All of us found ourselves at the same stoplights in different cities at the same time. When the lights changed, we all crossed the streets.

    Steve Katz once saying.

18. We may have crossed together, but we were heading in very different directions.

19. B. once declaring: How joyous the notion that, try as we may, we cannot do other than fail and fail absolutely and that the task will remain always before us like a meaning for our lives.

20. Like a *meaning*?

21. For me things sometimes flopping being more exhilarating than things sometimes succeeding.

22. An undergraduate at the University of Houston, B. founded a literary magazine: *Forum*.

23. Where he published Callois, Sartre, and Robbe-Grillet, among others.

24. Where he also fell in love with the visual opportunity called the page.

25. At thirty becoming the youngest director of the Contemporary Arts Museum in Houston.

26. His eye less a writer's than a painter's, an architect's.

27. Texts canvasses you move across, buildings you wander through.

28. Two prints hanging in the living room of his townhouse in the West Village: an Ingres, leader of the academic forces against the romantic barbarianism of Delacroix; and a Richard Lindner, whose bright erotic dreamworld of tightly corseted mannequins harmonized with the machine Cubism of Léger and the mechanistic wing of American Pop Art.

29. Yet Barthelme's imagination enjoyed greater affinities with the assemblages of Robert Rauschenberg: bricoleur art exploring its own geography, chance relationships, the topography of shapes and textures.

30. How, e. e. cummings wondering, can a typewriter redefine the part of writing called a sheet of paper?

31. B.'s fictions grew by accretion—like, he said, barnacles on a wreck or a rock: I'd rather have a wreck than a ship that sails; things attach themselves to wrecks.

32. Like Kafka, like Borges, Barthelme found it inconceivable to produce extended unified fictions, positing: Fragments are the only forms I trust.

33. His sole character being language.

34. The sidewalks were full of dogshit in brilliant colors: ocher, umber, Mars yellow, sienna, viridian, ivory black, rose madder, he writes in "The Glass Mountain."

35. Granular narratives about the futility of [[ ]].

36. Among other options.

37. I approached the symbol with its layers of meaning, but when I touched it, it changed into only a beautiful princess, ends "TGM."

38. Only?

39. Or almost. Then comes the line: I threw the beautiful princess headfirst down the mountain to my acquaintances.

40. And: Who could be relied upon to deal with her.

41. Then: Nor are eagles plausible, not at all, not for a moment.

42. Which I find funny as hell. Literally: as hell.

43. Like those few new leaves sprouting on the tree in the second act of *Waiting for Godot*.

44. Hole-in-your-heart sad, too, for its desperate recognition of all that emptiness.

45. How the word *dogshit* slips up the lyrical list of splendid colors from some artist's palette, its two hard syllables grating against that cluster of sweet smooth sounds.

46. Linguistic slapstick.

47. Discourse as a Three Stooges skit.

48. A sentence about sentences.

49. A lesson in how to break their backs.

50. Give me the odd linguistic trip, stutter, and fall, and I will be content, B. saying.

51. Yet he understood language about language's lack leaves one longing for more resonant slumgullions.

52. His fictions not only about the architecture of the page, the sentence as a buckled building by Frank Gehry, but also about the non-sequitured, buckled universe(s) we inhabit.

53. How his fictions make us feel as strange as we do living in this this-ness.

54. *On the other hand* announcing a philosophy.

55. How the giant mass hovering over a city in "The Balloon" becomes a metaphor for itself.

56. Let's call it the apotheosis of the postmodern allegory, which Charles Jencks (yet another architect in an essay full of them) says is enigmatic, because you don't know exactly

what the story being told is, nor do you know exactly what the myth it is being compared to.

57. "The Glass Mountain" rewrites a Norse tale in the notation of the contemporary. In the original, a poor young boy rides up a steep glass hill to win the hand of a beautiful princess on top.
    In B.'s version something else happens, but what?

58. How its last cryptic line lingers.

59. In my case, for a whole career.

60. *Nor are eagles plausible, not at all, not for a moment* not only an aesthetic gesture, but also a profoundly political one.

61. It says: Open your eyes.

62. And this is what I am sitting here in my writing studio thinking about as I write *And this is what I am sitting here in my writing studio thinking about*: Jessica Alexander, Ray Levy, George Saunders, Ben Marcus, Diane Williams, Laird Hunt, Lucy Corin, Norman Lock, Michael Martone, Kelly Link, Harold Jaffe, and all the others who wouldn't write as they do without B. having first been part of the solar system.

63. I am thinking about the teenage boy in that leafy suburb, I am thinking as I write *I am thinking about the teenage boy in that leafy suburb.*

64. About all the stupefying malfunctions awaiting him.

STAND BY TO CRASH

THE LETHALITY OF ART

At one blatantly metafictional moment in Robert Coover's *The Public Burning* (1977), we find ourselves at the Martin Beck Theater in Manhattan, not far from the Death Pageant in Times Square, early on the evening of Friday, June 19, 1953, watching a lonely and embittered Arthur Miller watch his play *The Crucible*, to which Richard Nixon that morning contemplated taking his wife, but then decided against the idea because he "couldn't risk giving it any kind of official sanction, and besides, Edgar [Hoover] was probably photographing the audience for his files."

Like Coover's novel, the play is a story about scapegoating, McCarthyism, and the brutal paranoia surrounding the Red Scare, and, like his novel, it involves witnesses bringing forth false accusations and misleading testimony, spectacular courtroom dramaturgy, the existence of a megalithic political force before which individuals feel powerless, and the eventual public sacrifices of several innocent people in a blackly ironic ritual cleansing and renewal of the tribe. Yet Miller, "an audience of one," sits in the near dark this evening, a few candles dimly illuminating his opus following a massive blackout, listening to the "mob of drunken lunatics outside," thinking to himself: "Ah, well: art ... not as lethal as one might hope."

Coover embeds three questions in Miller's rumination.

First, why is art not as lethal as one might hope? That is, how have the arts lost a good deal of their potential impact?

Second, what can artists in general and writers in particular do to remedy the situation?

Third, how can an artist create his or her way out of an art that has become exhausted?

If we were reading Coover's novel in the year it appeared, that word *exhausted* would no doubt trigger a line of associations within us that would conduct us to John Barth's piece on the subject, published a decade earlier, in which he argues that literature entered a state of "used-upness of certain forms or exhaustion of certain possibilities," and that "to be technically out of date is likely to be a serious defect" for the artist, since "art and its forms and techniques live in history," and so must change to reflect changing historical consciousness.

We aren't reading Coover's novel at the fag-ends of the seventies, however, but nearly half a century after its publication. Certain narratives and narrative strategies make sense only in retrospect, certain reading strategies only within specific diachronic contexts. While anyone concerned with experimental fiction in the seventies would have had a difficult time imagining *The Public Burning* without thinking of it through the Barthian triangulation of metafiction, literary exhaustion, and the nascent language of postmodernism, my sense is that anyone concerned with experimental fiction now will have a difficult time imagining Coover's novel without thinking of it through the triangulation of the Avant-Pop, hypertextuality, and the full-fledged language of a postmodern comic vision.

What interests me is how we might read *The Public Burning* today, from our current sociohistorical vantage point, when Coover's megatext has come to sit with ease in our minds alongside such encyclopedic American postwar achievements as Thomas Pynchon's *Gravity's Rainbow*, Samuel R. Delany's *Dhalgren*, Gilbert Sorrentino's *Mulligan Stew*, David Foster Wallace's *Infinite Jest*, and Don DeLillo's *Underworld*—those "big nasty books" that "pursue a holistic vision," as Frederick Karl dubs such poster-children of immoderation. If, as Thomas Pughe suggests, challenging novels like Coover's "are fashioned to provoke what Iser describes as a 'crisis response'—a crisis that is not confined to the text but is carried over into the reader's efforts at decoding and interpreting it," then what sort of crisis response does Coover's text elicit in us today?

How, in our own mediascape of public burnings—sensational impeachment trials, Nintendo wars, disinformation squalls, and the ever-more-frenetic commodification of desire—might we read it with fresh eyes?

AN AVANT-POPOLOGY

Larry McCaffery reformulates Arthur Miller's thought about the lethality of art in his 1995 manifesto-introduction to *After Yesterday's Crash: The Avant-Pop Anthology*:

> The biggest challenge facing contemporary American artists is no longer a matter of trying to figure out how to halt or deflect the progress of the [Yeatsian] beast [of apocalyptic change], but of learning how to coexist with it. For the beast is already here, having checked in a few years ahead of its originally scheduled arrival time, accompanied by its most recent live-in lover and caretaker, Hyperconsumer Capitalism.

Framing his discussion in terms of Jameson's argument in "Postmodernism, or the Cultural Logic of Late Capitalism," McCaffery theorizes that "pop culture has not only displaced nature and 'colonized' the physical space of nearly every country on the earth, but (just as important) it has also begun to colonize even those inner, subjective realms that nearly everyone once believed were inviolable, such as people's memories, sexual desires, their unconsciousness." We have entered the geography of "a multidimensional hyperreality of television lands, media 'jungles,' and information 'highways'" in which print-bound fiction of any sort—in particular that which aims to attack these very cultural centers—seems at best ill-equipped to persist. If this is the case, he asks, then what kind of lethal art can survive, respond to this set of historical circumstances in a positive, meaningful way, engage with and subvert the amorphous and ubiquitous forces whose will is to commodify aesthetic lethality and subversion themselves?

For McCaffery, at least one answer is the Avant-Pop, a term that conflates an obsession with pop culture with the avant-garde's mutinous mutant spirit. McCaffery appropriates the appellation from the eponymous 1986 Lester Bowie jazz album that itself features appropriations and reconfigurations of such classic rock songs as "Blueberry Hill" and "Oh, What a Night." These ideas of appropriation and reconfiguration form the essential aesthetic strategy for such Avant-Pop authors as William S. Burroughs, Philip K. Dick, J.G. Ballard, Raymond Federman, Kurt Vonnegut, Mark Leyner, Derek Pell, Gerald Vizenor, Stephen Wright, Don Webb, Paul Di Filippo, Doug Rice, Chuck Palahniuk, D. Harlan Wilson, and, needless to say, Robert Coover himself, who, among many others, "share[s] a fascination with mass culture and the determination to find a means of entering and exploring the belly of the beast without getting permanently swallowed or becoming mere extensions of its operations." They consciously absorb and commandeer pop-cultural artifacts from comix to science fiction novels, B-films to TV shows, which supply "citizens of postindustrial nations with the key images, character and narrative archetypes, metaphors, and points of reference and allusion that help us establish our sense of who we are" in order to turn the self-perpetuating mechanisms of these hyperconsumer capitalist products in upon themselves, dismantle and demythologize them, reveal their inner workings, and, perhaps, even make them ours while probing tentative means (if only briefly) to transcend them.

Art consequently regains its lethality, not by shunning the society of the spectacle in which it exists, nor by attempting to seal itself off from that society in some aesthetically antiseptic room, but rather by pirating and deconstructing the spectacle from within. As Harold Jaffe puts it succinctly in "Slash and Burn: A Narrative Model for the Millennium": "In the spirit of a guerrilla, find a seam, plant a mine, slip away." While McCaffery makes it clear in another central essay on the subject, "13 Introductory Ways of Looking at a Post-Post-Modernist Aesthetic Phenomenon Called 'Avant-Pop,'" that these authors don't by any means form a coherent movement, he underscores that their texts nonetheless do have in common "a set of related aesthetic and thematic tendencies specifically designed to counter the ideologies of consumption and hyperconsumption." They may go about their tasks in diverse ways, but those tasks are largely concordant.

If we commence focusing our attention on *The Public Burning* with this in our back pockets, we notice that the major players live within the pluriverse of hyperbolic commodification, information plagues, and an awesome surreality that the Avant-Popsters have made it their business to document, explore, and critique. Moreover, all the major players know that they live within such a realm, yet each understands this actuality in a singular way. Each, that is, approaches the late-stage capitalist mediascape in which he or she functions through a revealing perspective.

Uncle Sam, Eisenhower, and the Rosenbergs, multifarious as their ideologies appear to be, plainly bespeak premodern visions. By that, I mean they believe deeply in the binary logic of a politicized Judeo-Christian masterplot that pits good against evil, right against wrong, freedom against slavery, and, ultimately, the sons of light against the sons of darkness. They speak relatively the same language, though they often disagree at a fundamental level over its definitions. Furthermore, they frequently inhabit and are associated in the reader's mind with those alternating chapters told from the omniscient viewpoint of the Chronicler, that monologic, nigh deistic voice that knows all history, chronology, truth, people. His chapters (the voice is clearly patriarchal in tenor and tone) suggest a steroidal version of the newsreel sections from Dos Passos's trilogy. They embody the voice of postwar society itself, dwell within the integrated narratological and social space of an epic sensibility where, as

György Lukács remarks in *The Theory of the Novel*, "there is not yet any interiority, for there is not yet any exterior, any 'otherness' for the soul," and where a culture embraces "only answers but no questions, only solutions (even if enigmatic ones) but no riddles, only forms but no chaos."

Nixon, however, evinces a thoroughly modern one. His first-person, memoir-like, intensely subjective discourse harkens back to the introspective examination of consciousness reminiscent of the late-nineteenth- and early-twentieth-century novel. Ironically, while the biological Nixon of the fifties, sixties, and seventies seemed to be the cartoonish embodiment of a seedy politico, Coover's textual one is a richly resonant, sympathetic, thoughtful character who sees many similarities between himself and the Rosenbergs. In a conventional narrative move, Coover accomplishes this impression of character complexity by giving Nixon several strengths (contemplativeness, intelligence, even a strange kind of dignity in adversity), several weaknesses (connivery, social maladroitness, a buffoonish innocence), a fully-developed past (his severe parents, the premium placed on hard work and endurance during childhood, his inability to form mature relationships with women during adolescence), and a constellation of desires that grow out of those strengths, weaknesses, and past (a fixation on power, a need to be loved, a craving to be respected). Hence, while he often epitomizes the clown in Coover's novelistic three-ring circus, Nixon also often strikes the reader as more canny, sensitive, and at times even surprisingly warmer than his "unfortunate scowly sinister look" might initially indicate, and certainly more so than Uncle Sam, Eisenhower, the Rosenbergs, or the others we see externally rather than internally.

Nixon suffers as well from the modern disease of consciousness. He can't stop figuring, weighing, contemplating, working the angles. In a word, he's a reader, and he reads—many times misreads—his environment to discover connections where he is continually worried they don't exist. A would-be playwright, his approach to society is that of the paranoid: he seeks to script his private reality and the nation's public history into a meaningful whole, despite massive evidence to the contrary. Early in his debating career, he teaches himself "how to manipulate ambiguities when you don't have the facts and aren't even sure what the subject matter is." "The important thing," he learns back then, is "strategy, strategy and preparation: to marshal your facts, an army of facts, present them in pyramidal fashion to overwhelm your enemy." And this is precisely what he attempts to do as he sprawls on his office floor years later, surrounded by the messy piles of information that have accrued around the Rosenberg trial, though the more he thinks about it, the more he can read that information in several mutually contradictory ways. He pieces together shards of data into first one tentative pattern and then another, comprehending that he lives in "a random universe" where contingent patterns sometimes arise and begin to "turn and operate on the world" for no reason. He is intrigued by coincidence, accepting of uncertainty as a basic existential principle, "of reading sentences more than one way," always embarked on a quintessentially modern mission to shore up his factual and quasi-factual fragments against emotional and philosophical ruins, to locate relationships that will make disparate, often conflicting bits into a coherent (if static) system—yet constantly aware that his constructions are, at the end of the day, arbitrary, that they might well have been constituted other than they are.

We hear the Chronicler and Uncle Sam speak. We hear Eisenhower and the Rosenbergs speak, and on occasion read what they've written. We hear Nixon speak, read what he's written, and watch him think. The Phantom, on the other hand, the last of the novel's major players, exists less as a flesh-and-blood entity than as a shadow in the text, a rumor, the afterburn in a cloud chamber that tells us where subatomic particles once were, but never where or what they are. The Phantom embodies, then, that which Lyotard defines as the essence of the postmodern—as that which "puts forward the unpresentable in presentation itself." He is, we are told, the

"Creator of Ambiguities," the impetus that transforms universe into pluriverse. To a degree, he's the Native American Trickster writ large, but more to the point for this discussion, he's the "anti-everything," the "formless" incarnate that terrifies the Eisenhowers and Uncle Sams. Once loose in the world, the Phantom's presence, which is a kind of black-hole absence, "infects everything, our litterchur, art, religion, games." Before long he commingles in our minds with words we have come to associate with the heterological vision: disjunction, chance, dispersal, polymorphism, indeterminacy. For the purposes of the novel's metaphysics, then, the Phantom represents, not so much the personification of Communism and the Red Scare, as the reification of destructive energy in a culture, epistemological and ontological terrorism, the dark radical skepticism that throws everything about language and experience into question.

The Avant-Pop perceives itself as a positive response to these constricting and—in the cases of the modern and the postmodern—potentially despairing relativistic visions. It manifests in *The Public Burning*, not through the text's characters, but, as we shall see, through its thematics, structure, and overall *Weltanschauung*. A mode of perception that concerns itself, according to McCaffery, with "a renewal of precisely those qualities of optimism, confidence, and adventurousness ... missing from art in the aftermath of High Modernism," the Avant-Pop functions as a utopian liberation aesthetics that emphasizes the hopeful, the ludic, the emancipatingly transgressive—those transformative elements of the modern (e. e. cummings' verse, Duchamps' readymades, Charlie Chaplin's tramp in *Modern Times*) and the postmodern (Burroughs' cut-ups, Sonic Youth's *Daydream Nation*, Oliver Stone's *Natural Born Killers*)—especially those elements involved with the interrogation of hyperconsumer capitalism and its concomitant media industreality—and not (here McCaffery and I part company to some extent) a new practice of consciousness altogether.

MEDIA-TION: THEMATICS OF SPECTACLE & SIMULATION

By choosing to take Pat to the surreal Death Pageant on a stage in Times Square designed to simulate the execution chamber in Sing Sing instead of to the production of Arthur Miller's *The Crucible*, Nixon chooses spectacle over mere theater, suggesting that, while postwar art may run the risk of being less lethal than one might hope, outrageous entertainment never does. Rather, outrageous entertainment is all about fatality: of imagination, of private thought, of selfhood, of depth psychology, of fully lived life—and yet, as Coover has commented, "in America the search for meaning is tied up with the search for entertainment." We no longer experience unmediated natural landscapes (if we ever really did), yet, as McCaffery writes, mediascapes "so thoroughly interpenetrated by simulations, paranoia, and media archetypes that readers and characters alike are never quite sure where they are." This is the world of Debord, of Baudrillard, where Ronald Reagan, Esther Williams, Mickey Mouse, Betty Crocker, William Faulkner, Albert Einstein, Yogi Berra, "the whole dingbusted United State guvvamint," and more—various components of American culture, politics to sports, cooking to science, literature to journalism to comics, all of which have themselves simultaneously become entertainment and showed up this evening to behold death as entertainment's ultimate form—collect like Dr. Alfred Kinsey to study "the effects of electrocution upon the erogenous zones" in an orgy of sermons, lectures, dance numbers, singalongs, comic skits, freak shows, and even a flea circus in which the insects have been "renamed after characters in the Rosenberg drama," as Darryl Zanuck and Cecil B. De Mille project a documentary about the Rosenberg boys on the side of the Claridge Hotel.

And following the public burning? What happens then?

What else?

An instant replay.

The Death Pageant has much to do with the key ideas set forth in Debord's *The Society of the Spectacle*, published a decade prior to *The Public Burning*, and shortly after Coover originally conceived his scheme as "a little theater idea which grew into a series of rather raucous circus acts." Over the course of the last century, according to Debord, our species has metamorphosed from Homo Sapiens into Homo Spectator, as our society, dominated by hyperconsumer capitalism, has come to present itself "as an immense accumulation of spectacles ... where all attention, all consciousness, converges." Thus, "all that once was directly lived has become mere representation," "the effective dictatorship of illusion," "a social hallucination," an "inversion of life" into "non-life," and this "real unreality" has turned into a self-perpetuating "justification for the conditions and aims of the existing system." "Everything that appears is good," announces the spectacle; "whatever is good will appear." If former economies relied on possession, then the economy of the spectacle relies on impression, the depiction of depictions, so that "mere images are transformed into real beings—tangible figments which are the efficient motor of trancelike behavior." The consequence is an exploited population under the misconception that it is heterogeneous and free, a culture where communication is univocal, from media direct to the multitudes, and where the message is always "an uninterrupted monologue of self-praise" by those in power, whose totalitarianism to survive must "be attended by permanent violence."

The Rosenbergs, who garner increasingly impressive television ratings as their electrocutions near, don't move toward death, inasmuch as they are in many respects already dead in Debordian terms, but toward the core of the spectacle itself. As Cecil B. De Mille spells out to Warden Denno, "a practical-minded man, unaccustomed to the magical razzamatazz of showbizz": "Life and the real stuff of life aren't always the same thing, Warden—like, one don't always give you the other, you follow? So sometimes, to get your story across, you gotta work a different angle or two, use a few tricks, zap it up with a bit of spectacle—I mean, what's spectacle? it's a kind of vision, am I right?"

Spectacle *is* a kind of vision, both in the sense that it is the materialization of hyperconsumer capitalism, and in the sense that it is all about seeing, rather than, say, thinking, feeling, or being. Even Nixon—perhaps especially Nixon—knows, as he stands near the novel's conclusion with his pants bunched around his ankles on that stage in Times Square, "The American Showcase, Playland U.S.A., the Electrical Street of Dreams," Uncle Sam peashooting him in the testicles, that "this is a generation that wants to laugh, a generation that wants to be entertained." The only risk for the society of the spectacle is to let the pyrotechnics of entertainment plateau, fail to allow every image to surpass the one that preceded it in compass and delicious shock. It's imperative to keep the explosions coming, each bigger and better than the one before. Otherwise, even when those images happen to involve a public execution, audience members quickly begin to feel that "they've seen all there is to see the first time around—you just plug them in, they twitch and jerk awhile and shit their pants, then you unplug them and cart them off, ho hum." And so entertained they are by an escalating sequence of outlandish sights, sounds, and panoplies that don't culminate in Ethel's body flapping "like a sail in a high wind," "sizzling and popping like firecrackers," a kind of microcosm of "the final spectacle, the one and only atomic holocaust," but rather in Uncle Sam buggering the Vice President of the United States in a nightmarish display of power and a travesty of procreation.

The germ for the structure and the thematics of augmentational spectacle tracks back in Coover's work to "The Hat Act," a story that appears in *Pricksongs & Descants*. A metafictional metaphor masquerading as a dramaticule, "The Hat Act" lacks spoken language, yet is rich in vaudevillian slapstick; to this extent it is distantly reminiscent of such Beckettian playlets as *Act Without Words*. In it, a magician-artist creates something out of nothing again and again in a series of escalating hat tricks. First he pulls out a rabbit, then a dove, and soon rabbits are wildly pulling other rabbits from a multitude of hats, the magician is decapitated and re-comprised, and his beautiful assistant is brutally killed (or perhaps only apparently so; it's impossible to tell which, given the narrative's logic) when he jumps up and down on the hat into which she has seemingly disappeared. Only when he tries to repeat himself along the way does the audience fail to applaud and the boos begin. As long as he continues outdoing his previous performance, however, he keeps them enthralled. Magic, the subtextual argument seems to run, and by implication the magic of fiction, is in some fundamental way about the dictatorship of illusion, and, in this case, as in that of *The Public Burning* itself, the final entertainment is something approaching ritual slaughter.

Initially, it seems that to the extent the reader delights in Coover's story of magic and his novel of excess (themselves fictional spectacles narrating fantastic events through lavish language and unconventional structures), he or she is to some degree complicit in the larger society of the spectacle, somehow sanctioning the self-perpetuating mechanics of Debordian culture. If that were the case, it could then be argued that Coover's texts try to bugger the reader in the same way Uncle Sam does poor traumatized Nixon. But this interpretation seems too reductive and ungenerous by half; it gives Coover and the reader too little credit, converting the former into a malicious artificer intent on short-circuiting his audience's textual bliss, while converting the latter into a normative nineteenth-century reader unaware of the currents and concerns in contemporary innovative fiction. More on target is an interpretation that suggests in both "The Hat Act" and *The Public Burning* Coover invites the reader to collaborate (and collaboration, coevolution, are axial mechanisms in Avant-Pop) in the construction of a counter-spectacle, a literary extravaganza that itself interrogates the motives and means of the dominant culture's spectacle and attempts to predicament it through appropriation and reconfiguration.

If Debord focuses his attention on the society of the spectacle, Baudrillard focuses on the nature of that society's simulations.

In a postmodern retelling of Plato's parable of the cave, he recounts how, "under the pretext of saving the original,"

> the caves of Lascaux have been forbidden to visitors and an exact replica constructed 500 meters away, so that everyone can see them (you glance through a peephole at the real grotto and then visit the reconstituted whole). It is possible that the very memory of the original caves will fade in the mind of future generations, but from now on there is no longer any difference: the duplication is sufficient to render both artificial.

It is this aura of multiplication and artificiality that for Baudrillard defines hyperconsumer capitalist culture. There, the real disappears so completely into a succession of media images of the real that "it is no longer a question of imitation, nor of reduplication, nor even of parody. It is rather a question of substituting signs of the real for the real itself" until the simulation of the real no longer reflects or perverts reality, nor even masks an absence of reality, but instead "bears no relation to any reality whatever: it is its own pure simulacrum." Like Coover, Baudrillard soon fastens onto the powerful metaphor of Disneyland to underscore his point; in that synthetic fun zone, we find a space "presented as imaginary in order to make us believe that the rest is real, when in fact all of Los Angeles and the America surrounding it are no longer real, but of the order of the hyperreal and of simulation." We look up to discover "the dissolution of TV into life, the dissolution of life into TV," ourselves "doomed not to invasion, to pressure, to violence, and to blackmail by the media and the models, but to their induction, to their infiltration, to their illegible violence."

The thematics of simulacra, needless to say, pervade *The Public Burning* to such an extent that it is tempting to argue simulation constitutes its major trope. Politics becomes a sales campaign, religion a side show, and it doesn't take Nixon long to realize that, in the amusement park called today, reflective surface always takes precedence over substance: "form, form, that's what it always comes down to!"; indeed, it seems to him that "just about everyone in the nation, in and out of government, myself included [was] behaving like actors caught up in a play." Thus it's not for nothing that Eisenhower, Ethel, and he have all acted in plays as youths, that two of the Intermezzos take the shape of dramas, and that Nixon and Ethel can't stop acting even at this late date in their lives. After the Checkers speech, Zanuck phones the Vice President to tell him that Nixon has just put on "the most tremendous performance" Zanuck's ever seen. Nixon ludicrously acts like a dog, yapping at Pat and Tricia at the novel's close, and earlier disguises himself beneath a mustache and shades on his trip to see Ethel in prison, where he learns that both Rosenbergs tirelessly perform "like they're on stage."

Moreover, Nixon and Ethel continue performing during the course of their interview in the Death House: at first Nixon seems like the embodiment of governmental ideals, Ethel as political moral compass; soon they both begin acting like they're starring in some awful romantic B-film; and by the end Ethel acts like she might just love the V.P., or at least lust after him, though we know she has in truth humiliated him by lipsticking "I AM A SCAMP" across his buttocks. Richard Walsh points out, somewhat inaccurately, that "the Rosenbergs' presence in the novel is limited to the quotations from their Death House letters and from Ethel's clemency appeals," and goes on to propose that these are "for the most part given in support of Nixon's theory that the Rosenbergs are consumed by the roles in which they have cast themselves," but perhaps this doesn't quite go far enough. It often appears that the Rosenbergs, along with most of the other characters in the novel, are actors who don't have any bedrock personalities beneath their façades, any "essences"—that they are nothing but their acting, a regression of masks, like Harry Gold, the alleged courier among Fuchs, the Rosenbergs, and Greenglass, who invented a false life for himself but "had no sense of his own being"—and thus the incarnation of the Baudrillardian human, whose being marks "the end of interiority and intimacy," who exists as nothing but "pure screen."

Screen doubtless connotes *film*, a genre with which Coover has been intimately involved and which would lead him in 1987 to bring out a collection of stories focused on the topic: *A Night at the Movies, or, You Must Remember This*. If he had had the financial freedom to do what he wanted in life, Coover commented in a 1979 interview, he would quite possibly have preferred to work in film rather than fiction; he went on to recall the "religious experience" of watching ten-cent movies as a kid on Saturday mornings, and to affirm his delight in film's "mix of magic and documentary power"—this last phrase a fitting description, needless to say, of *The Public Burning* itself. The novel depends heavily on two filmic techniques, montage and jump-cut, while using film along with theater and television to emphasize the thematics of simulation, the slippage between the authentic and inauthentic, the public and the private, fact and fantasy, the real and the hyperreal in an age of information so dense, fast, and outwardly preposterous that it's increasingly difficult to tell what's true and what's hype, what's documentation and what's hyperbole, paranoia, or spectacular misrepresentation.

Eisenhower hardly reads because he finds books drab and lacking in splashy action; neither does he as a rule watch much TV or film, though when he does condescend, it is to pick up a western or watch *High Noon* in the White House basement because these help reinforce "his superpowers," his construction of self as comic-book superhero. Nixon is instinctively obsessed with all media, but particularly with television and film, always on the lookout for the good sound bite, always aware "that the fate of a great country can depend on camera angles." Unable to distinguish between fact and film, he leaps into a cab and yells "Step on it!" only to realize self-consciously that he's acting "just like in the old George Raft movies," and when traffic parts for the driver, an old Navy buddy of his, Nixon reports that it does so "like the crazy cars in the old Keystone Kops movies." When the lights come on after the blackout in Times Square, the clock having stood still like a long freeze frame, the crowd thinks that "it's just like coming out of a scary movie—nothing but camera tricks, the illusory marvels and disasters of Cinerama and 3-D, th-th-that's all, folks!"

Coover's novel itself dissipates reality by placing real subjects in reel terrain. Consequently, the reader often feels a little like that nameless Everyman who stumbles out of the Trans-Lux after watching Andre de Toth's *House of Wax*, 3-D glasses still on his face, viewing the world "through the eye-straining haze of alcohol and iodine." Disoriented, he moves from one phantasmagoric episode to another until the police cart him off as a madman, mark of the recognition that media-tion has turned reality into a horror flick, from which it is impossible to escape with one's sanity intact. Before long, simulation comes to feel like the real thing, and the real thing comes to feel like a very bad dream.

The largest imitation in *The Public Burning* is *The Public Burning* itself: a novel that mimics historical reality. By mixing magic and documentary power, it intermingles and confounds the two impulses—giving us, as it were, a lens of each to look through via our own readerly 3-D glasses, thereby engendering a metafiction whose job it is, as Linda Hutcheon notes, "to problematize the entire notion of external evidence, to question the objectivity of the reportorial, and to complicate the fragile and often unexamined concepts of the historical and the 'felt' within the humanist discourses of both history and literature." While the novel may be intrigued, as is Nixon, with discovering the connections, it also offers "a serious critique of the literally lethal results of such totalizing" structures, and thus, as Paul Maltby argues, "threatens the validity of any political reading of history proposed by its author," since such a reading "becomes just one more narrative construct." Yet, as Raymond A. Mazurek adds: "by emphasizing the limits of historical discourse in the America of the 1950's, it points to the limits of American ideology and the use of language as power." While

Coover's novel affirms history is fabrication, then, it also affirms that the historical discourse framing it—and the ideology such discourse articulates—is open to scrutiny.

So by investigating the Avant-Pop thematics of simulation in a society of the spectacle, *The Public Burning* attempts to unmake that society's narratives, reminding us of their fictionality and radical contingency, the fictionality and radical contingency of all narratives, and in the face of them the deep need to constantly (if also contingently) reinvent them.

SHATTERED BY THE EXPLOSIONS OF LAST WEEK

The thematic thrust against totalizing thought finds reflection at a structural stratum through the existence of hypertextual—or, better, hypertextoid—tactics. To be sure, I don't mean to suggest that *The Public Burning* is a hypertext fiction. Nor do I mean to suggest that Coover possessed an understanding of what hypertext was when he was writing it. He didn't—though that would change, and change profoundly, over the following decade. I do mean to propose, however, that the novel's structure is from certain vantage points analogous to that of a hypertext, and that it accordingly inhabits an historico-literary space alongside an assemblage of other proto-hypertextual novels from the fifties through the nineties, including Burroughs's *Naked Lunch*, Cortázar's *Hopscotch*, and Federman's *Double or Nothing*, all of which track back in numerous ways to an indispensable pair of proto-hypertextual novels, Joyce's *Ulysses* and *Finnegans Wake*, and a crucial proto-hypertextual poem, Eliot's *The Waste Land*, whose use of pla(y)giarism, mosaic, such filmic techniques as montage and jump-cuts, pop-cultural references, and an aesthetics of informational overload make it perhaps the Ur-Avant-Pop artifact.

Each of these works exhibits several of the following elements that we have come to associate with hypertextual fiction in the wake of Michael Joyce's extraordinary 1987 launch of the digital form, *Afternoon: A Story*, with its unpredictable quantum leaps between two or more storylines; typographical/configurative freeplay including but not limited to lists, footnotes, and visuals employed in order to rupture conventional linear reading strategies and foreground the technology of the page; an intermixture of prose and poetry, fiction and criticism, novel and drama, etc., used to question traditional genre distinctions in a postgenre age; digressive narrative structure where the overarching plotline frequently turns out to be less important than the individual page before the reader at a given instant, a technique that anticipates the power of a single hypertextual lexia; abrupt shifts in point of view; a query into polyphony, into doing the police in different voices; ongoing metafictional contemplation of aesthetic process and product; an appeal to greater readerly freedom and a participatory model of interpretation; an overall structural feel closer to music than to conventional narrative—one that often creates the impression that a reader can dip into the text at any point for a paginal snippet, since narrative forward force isn't what guides the reading experience any more than it does in lyric poetry or jazz improvisation; a kaleidoscopic neo-realism more in sync with the digital rhythms of the present than with what one might find in the narrative nostalgia accompanying, say, domestic suburban or regionalist fiction; and what Brooks Landon refers to as "the literature of information": texts, hypertextual and otherwise, in an electronic age that emphasize data glut.

As early as 1979, Coover, who would go on to launch Brown University's Hypertext Fiction Workshop a dozen years later, provocatively and premonitorily acknowledged that "one of the peculiarities of *The Public Burning* was that it was made up of thousands and thousands of tiny fragments that had to be painstakingly stitched together." In 1992, fewer than two years after establishing the Hypertext Fiction Workshop, he published an essay called "The End of Books" on the front page of *The New York Times Book Review* and accompanied it with a guide to hypertext composition software, key hypertext fictions, electronic and print journals dedicated to discussions of the subject, and several key scholarly monographs about it. In the essay itself, he traces the term back nearly twenty-five years to computer-scientist Ted Nelson's coinage "to describe the writing done in the nonlinear or nonsequential space made possible by the computer":

> Unlike print text, hypertext provides multiple paths between text segments, now often called "lexias" in a borrowing from the pre-hypertextual but prescient Roland Barthes. With its webs of linked lexias, its networks of alternate routes (as opposed to print's fixed unidirectional page-turning) hypertext presents a radically divergent technology, interactive and polyvocal, favoring a plurality of discourses over definitive utterance and freeing the reader from domination by the author. Hypertext reader and writer are said to become co-learners and co-writers, as it were, fellow travelers in the mapping and remapping of textual (and visual, kinetic and aural) components.

The precipitate, Coover observes, possesses "no fixed center, for starters—and no edges either, no ends or boundaries. The traditional narrative timeline vanishes into a geographical landscape or exitless maze, with beginnings, middles and ends being no longer part of the immediate display." What develops instead is—to exercise a familiar metaphor among hypertext writers and theorists—a Borgesian garden of forking paths without hierarchy. Quoting hypertext authors Carolyn Guyer and Martha Petry, Coover emphasizes that this sort of narrativity demands a special set of reading practices because "the form of the text is rhythmic, looping on itself in patterns and layers that gradually accrete meaning, just as the passage of time and events does in one's lifetime." He goes on to confess that he is not "an expert navigator in hyperspace," nor "likely to engage in any major hypertext fictions of [his] own," since he is at the verge of his "seventh decade and thus rather committed, for better or for worse, to the obsolescent print technology." Nonetheless, he is as "interested as ever in the subversion of the traditional bourgeois novel and in fictions that challenge linearity."

These interests have accompanied him from the outset of his career, and his fascination in antiforms that retrospectively strike us as hypertextoid appears as early as his most frequently anthologized story from *Pricksongs and Descants*: "The Baby Sitter," which begins as a work of the domestic fiction he seeks to implode, only quickly to elide into an investigation of multidimensional realities, offering up conflicting plot elements and chronologies that might refer to actualities, or the imaginings of the characters, or even of the metafictional author himself, or that, most likely, constitute an attempt on Coover's part to mimic the televisual ecology of the sixties in a (proto-Avant-Pop) form which augurs hypertextual structure. By the time we reach *The Public Burning*, we discover that obsession with the mediascape at full throttle, the hypertextoid quality of the novel approximating and evaluating the continual bombardment of the individual by data, electronic and otherwise. Coover submits through the novel's structure of immoderation that a deluge of such information doesn't set you free, but rather functions as a generative engine of confusion and imprisonment, that the "magical" thing about TV, as the Chronicler comments in passing, is that "everything seems to happen at once on it, the near and the far, the funny and the sad, the real and the unreal."

Too much information makes it impossible for her or him to know where facts conclude and fantasy, conspiracy, chicanery, or schizophrenia commences. This is the hypertextoid zone with no fixed center, a maze of "raw data" without beginnings, middles, or ends that "is paralyzing, a nightmare" because "there's too much of it and man's mind is quickly engulfed by it"—a place, as Nixon comes to understand, where there are "no necessary patterns, no final scenes," "just action, and then more action." Disconcertingly, "all men contain all views" here. Purposes, causes, and so on convert from epistemological givens into mere reading strategies among other reading strategies, "stuff we make up to hold the goddamn world together," one language game apparently as good (or as bad) as another.

Coover accordingly presents the reader with "the abundant overflow of events, 'an effective mosaic' assembled from 'the fragmentary documents' of life": epic catalogs, newspaper reports, headlines, the trappings of parajournalistic documentary in the lineage of Truman Capote's *In Cold Blood* and Tom Wolfe's *The Electric Kool-Aid Acid Test* ("There's nothing of mine in any of those three Intermezzos," Coover told one interviewer. "Every word spoken comes from some document or other."), plays, songs, poems, diatribes, letters, first-person memoirs, third-person biographies and annals, trial transcripts, the language of marquees and billboards, librettos, experiments in paginal layout, and, within these, slivers from classic American film lore, the history of New York City in general and Times Square in particular, baseball talk, comedy shticks, Horacio Alger and old west narratives, all in a grand display that announces "Design as a game. Randomness as design. Design ironically revealing randomness," conveyed acutely in the following excerpt from Chapter 10, in which the Chronicler chants a Burroughsian omnium gatherum garnered from the pages of *The New York Times*:

> Prince Karl Rudolf Marries. SOME HOPES FOR U.N. / TOO HIGH. Trouble on First Hole. HERE IS WHAT YOU CAN DO ABOUT IT (if you really care ...): The Goddess Strapless in fine white Push-Button Loading. DULLES' REMARKS SHARP: Don't Neglect Slipping FALSE liquid will help you to handle expanding demands as well as to weather adjustments Fair and a little warmer today highest temperature near 23980 entries in McCalls' dress-your-best Candidate for the worst-dressed woman scattered with black polka dots RED PLOT! "What's happening? Where am I?" they scream, tearing frantically through the shrine, plowing into other pilgrims, slapping up against the slabs: "Let me out!"

The public smears into the private and we locate, not serious psychological stream-of-consciousness, but parodic electronic stream-of-information, an insane surge that adds up, not to resonant subjective enlightenment, but to the impression of superficial commotion by "an opportunistic thief, a pastepot-poet who steals from everybody," as the Chronicler christens America's poet laureate, thereby placing him (like, of course, proto-Avant-Popster Coover) among the "great eclectics, gatherers and enhancers of the detritus from the passing flux," or what Derrida, himself parasitically shadowing Lévi-Strauss, would eleven years earlier label the bricoleur: a do-it-yourselfer; someone who uses "the instruments he finds around him, those which are already there, which had not been especially conceived with an eye to the operation for which they are to be used and to which one tries by trial and error to adapt them, not hesitating to change them whenever it appears necessary, or to try several of them at once, even if their form and their origin are heterogeneous."

I mention Derrida in this discussion of hypertext, as Coover does Barthes in his, in order to italicize a point made by George P. Landow in his book on the subject: that hypertextual (and, I would argue, hypertextoid) strategies mark the convergence of poststructuralism and the digital technosphere in that both accent the notion that "we must abandon conceptual systems founded upon ideas of center, margin, hierarchy, and linearity and replace them with ones of multilinearity, nodes, links, and networks"—that both, as McCaffery implies in his introduction to *After Yesterday's Crash*, must address and shape an art "which has been visibly shattered by the explosions of last week": by, in other words, the filmic, the televisual, the digital, the hypercommercial, the hyperreal, in which speed is no longer manifested by the individual's movement through a single environment, but by countless environments whipping by the individual on countless screens.

Unlike such moderns as Eliot and Joyce, and unlike such characters in *The Public Burning* as Nixon, Coover doesn't shore up his textual and cultural fragments against the ruins. Rather, in an Avant-Pop corrective, he hollows out the dominant cultural myths he appropriates, reconfigures them to highlight and confute their fictionality, and leaves the fragments (at least in a certain sense) as fragments, delighting in their fragmentariness, loving the amplification of lexia as a state of mind. This is not to offer up *The Public Burning* as a fragmentary text; it's obviously far from that, closer in constitution to a beautifully designed supremely artificial whole. Nonetheless, that very design, made up as it is of "thousands and thousands of tiny fragments that had to be painstakingly stitched together," bespeaks something other than a suggestion of ultimate order, the presence of a grand narrative beyond this massive one. It bespeaks, instead, the keenly provisional status of any design, the presence of randomness just beyond the book's covers.

Coover's structure seems to indicate that the contemporary human does not shape texts in order to create meaningful product out of chaos (it's never quite clear how guilty or innocent the Rosenbergs actually are within the novel's universe of discourse, simply that the government is trying to scapegoat them) so much as to enjoy the process of shaping itself, the playful activity of networking disparate data in absorbing ways.

PANTS DOWN FOR GOD & COUNTRY!

At the nexus of the Avant-Pop thematics of the spectacle and simulation, on the one hand, and the Avant-Pop structure of hypertextuality, on the other, resides the topography of Coover's comic vision. As I have already proposed, this vision takes the form of a utopian liberation aesthetics that emphasizes the ludic, the emancipatingly transgressive, and hence the affirmatively transformative elements involved with the interrogation of hyperconsumer capitalism and its concomitant media industreality. It takes the form, that is, of an arrangement of many of the most positive traits we have come to associate with postmodern consciousness over the last century: a sense of robust skepticism rather than despairing paralysis, openness rather than constriction of conformations and attitudes, satiric sport rather than severe sobriety, active coevolution between reader and writer rather than the traditional textual paradigm of a unidirectional broadcasting channel, appropriative intertextuality rather than "original" monotextuality, paratactical organizations rather than hypotactical ones, and literary mutation rather than chromosomal regularity—traits, to return to Arthur Miller in that dimly lit Martin Beck Theater once more, that can reenergize art, allow it to reengage with the culture around it in rewarding and illuminating ways, recharge it with a healthy dose of vigorous lethality.

Coover's use of counter-spectacle and perceptual variegation presumed in the creation of a hypertextoid novel accords nicely with the concept of carnivalization Bakhtin sets forth in *Rabelais and His World.* In a carnival, itself a collective and popular event like Coover's Death Pageant, or in a carnivalized text like *The Public Burning*, hierarchies are inverted (the Marx Brothers pirate the roles of the Rosenbergs and the executioner and turn them into Avant-Pop skits in Coover's novel, the Vice President finds himself with his pants down before the American people, the somber mood traditionally paired in the reader's mind with the electrocutions collapses into hyperbolic political cartoon); opposites are mingled (Uncle Sam's sadism joins with Nixon's masochism, the literal darkness of the blackout joins with literal light of the incandescent public burnings, "objective" documentary joins with "subjective" hallucination); and the sacred is made profane (the mob responds to the monumental face of death with a screwball orgy, the dignified Supreme Court judges slip and skid in the elephant dung, the mythic discourse of ritual rebirth elides with Ethel's carcass ludicrously "flapping out at the people like one of those trick images in a 3-D movie") to such an extent that a joyous relativity is released—the rigid, the authoritarian, the univocal are relaxed, subverted, fractured. "Truth" is not a monologic absolute and finds existence as perpetual polyphonic interchange, as what Jack Halberstam talks about as transitivity (a mode which "holds off the certainty of diagnosis"), and realism gives way to postmodern fantasy, mimetic uncertainty, the feel, as Coover well knew, of a hippodrome world.

Even Uncle Sam (a hypertextoid pastiche of conflicting discourses, including those of the preacher, stand-up comic, frontier man, supernatural demigod, con artist, politico, carny barker, cheerleader for the USA, southern tall-tale teller, snake-oil doctor, patriarch incarnate, and thespian cousin of the King and Duke in *Huck Finn*) sees the social benefit of "an occasional peak of disorder and danger to keep things from just peterin' out," though he'd just as soon make such social disjunctions short, sweet, and government-sponsored; otherwise, he soon comes to feel "swarmed about with fears and absences"—that is, as Nixon understands, he soon comes to sense the embodiment of the comic vision, the Phantom, himself "the dissolution of the natural limits of language, the conscious invention of a space, a spooky artificial no-man's land, between logical alternatives." The Chronicler may desperately wish to impose inelastic order atop these motley happenings through his omniscient patriotic viewpoint, but the juxtaposition of his chapters with a host of others (in a host of other forms, other voices) ultimately devalues the regulation he attempts to exert. As Richard Walsh notes, Coover even goes so far as to subvert the traditional reader's monologic "reflex response" to his materials: "An unequivocal sympathy with the victims against the establishment is resisted by a sustained distance from the Rosenbergs; the portrayal of Nixon, while acutely satiric, is also unexpectedly empathetic; Uncle Sam too has an appeal that conflicts with the monstrosity of his character."

In his often-overlooked discussion of the novelistic genre, Leonard Lutwack distinguishes between two methods of presentation in fiction: uniform and mixed style. Texts employing the former—Lutwack cites *Pamela* and *The Ambassadors* as examples—signal the presence of a writer's conviction about a single, unambiguous, coherent view of reality. "A uniform style is assimilative in that it helps to create under a single aspect of language a single vision of the multiplicity of reality," he writes. "It is a bond between author and reader, ensuring that no different adjustment to language and viewpoint will be demanded from the reader than that established at the outset." Conversely, texts that employ a mixed style—*Moby-Dick*, say, or *The Sound and the Fury*—signal a writer's lack of conviction about a single, unambiguous, coherent view of reality. "A mixture of styles has the effect of making the reader pass through a succession of contradictory and ambiguous attitudes," Lutwack contends. "It offers no sure stylistic norm by which the reader may orient him permanently to the fiction and to the point of view of the author." To put it slightly differently, not only the vocabularies but the values and visions they reflect are shown to be both tenable and arbitrary. Such carnivalized ambitextrous fictions spotlight decenterment, demystification, and detotalization: simultaneous acts of destruction and construction.

What we are left with in the case of Coover's megatext isn't earnest political critique (which we might find in Miller's morally stable drama), or *simply* earnest political critique. It's a subtle investigation into the limits of such a critique, into the complexities and complications necessitated by undertaking such a univocal enterprise within the multivocal reality of today. In place of such a critique—or, perhaps closer to the point, concomitant with it—we discover a forcefully disarming charge of slapstick, black humor, sexual winks and innuendoes and double entendres, scatological wit, exaggerated boasts, flat-out absurdity, tall tales, massive irony, folk humor based on the use and abuse of power relations, and the enactment of comic theories based on the release from restraint and surprise—all culminating from chapter twenty-seven forward in a Menippean *Walpurgisnacht* that makes Ulysses in Nighttown seem a little understated and listless in comparison, and all with the purpose of confounding any purely no-nonsense approach to the text.

Nor does such an immense cathexis of polyphonic funniness serve solely to vex popular earnest political readings; it also helps vex popular earnest mythological ones. Frisking with numerology, Coover repeatedly calls attention to the fact that the executions occur on June 19th. Given his novel's hypertextoid structure, focus on an extremely limited time-frame for its central action, and appropriation and reconfiguration of myth, it doesn't take the reader long to realize the fortuitous connection to Bloomsday, June 16th—nor, given such literary mythic resonance, the fact that the Jewish sabbath begins at sundown on the day of the killings, and that day's proximity both to patriarchal Father's Day and to the richly symbolic first day of spring. If one adds the numbered chapters together with the Prologue, Epilogue, and Intermezzos, one attains the sum thirty-three, Christ's age at the crucifixion, and hence a nod (further accented by the structural and thematic nods to *The Waste Land*, itself an ambitextrous work that appropriates and reconfigures both Jessie L. Weston's and James Frazer's studies of fertility rites, scapegoating, and tribal sacrifices) toward the fact that the Rosenbergs are indeed perceived to be, by Le Monde and others, "expiatory victims of the cold war." Yet Coover's play is self-conscious and, as John Ramage and others have registered, strongly parodic. There is no final communal enlightenment here, no transcendence. Demons, sins, and diseases aren't driven out; after all, Uncle Sam, Nixon, and the Phantom are all left standing at the end of Coover's drama. Instead of rebirth and renewal followed by a symbolic journey to the sacred marriage chamber, we witness the incorporation of our country's gruesome insemination of the Vice President. We don't, that is, experience an entry into mythic time, cyclical temporality, but the simulation of myth, pseudo-cyclical time—in a phrase, spectacular time—and we thereby come to understand, as does Debord, that "our epoch, which presents its time to itself as essentially made up of many frequently recurring festivities, is actually an epoch without festivals ... Mass pseudo-festivals, with their travesty of dialogue and their parody of the gift, may incite people to excessive spending, but they produce only a disillusion—which is invariably in turn offset by further false promises."

We are left with a deeply conflicted crisis response both within Coover's novel and within ourselves in the face of decoding and interpreting it, sensing as we do that his seeks to disrupt all centers of authority (political, mythical, analytical, etc.)—including our own, his own—while through its radical incongruity of form attempting to investigate, reveal, and short-circuit hyperconsumer capitalism's repressive impulses (said attempt, it goes without saying, a kind of ironic will toward authority). Before such wickedly shocking, contradictory, and hypertextoid Avant-Pop laughter, the only thing we can do in the face of our spectacular society is stand by to crash.

QUEEN OF THE PIRATES

EPISTEMOLOGICAL STUTTERS

Kathy Acker, arguably the most significant postwar pirate queen of avant-fiction, returned to her home planet at 1:30 a.m. on Sunday, November 30, 1997. She departed from the American Biologics clinic in Tijuana, surrounded by her closest friends, her exit papers listing the cause of death as cardiopulmonary failure from complications due to metastasized cancer.

She was born Karen Lehman to wealthy assimilated German-Jewish parents in New York City in the Roswellian year 1947—maybe. The Library of Congress gives 1948 instead, *The New York Times* 1944. Somehow that epistemological stutter strikes me as perfect. She studied Classics at Brandeis, fell for writing and moved to the University of California-San Diego, where she worked with David Antin and Jerome Rothenberg, graduated in 1968, and went on to attend two years of graduate school at the City College of New York, where she specialized in Greek. Along the way, she married several times (*Acker* was her first husband's last name), was disowned by her family, and ended up working in everything from vegan bakeries to sex shows on 42nd Street to make ends meet.

Diagnosed with breast cancer in April 1996, she had a full mastectomy in San Francisco and moved to London to recuperate. A year later she began suffering from digestive disorders and pneumonia. When she returned to San Francisco, she visited the Davies Medical Center and learned the cancer had spread to her liver, pancreas, spleen, and lungs. She decided to cross the border with a handful of friends on 1 November and take her chances at a holistic clinic near the seedy main drag of the aptly named Avenue de la Revolution.

She was barely 50 and virtually broke.

A BOOK OF TRANSFORMATIONS

Kathy Acker left us early because she had already collected enough data about our species to file her report back home.

We don't come off looking very good in it.

"I don't know," she once told an interviewer. "I don't think humans have done well figuring out what it is to be human."

For me her most influential and crucial work will always remain her punk novel, *Blood and Guts in High School*, written in the seventies. Acker mimeographed pages from the growing manuscript, DIY, and passed them out on street corners in the East Village. The whole was copyrighted in 1978, but it wasn't officially published until 1984. The narrative chronicles the life of Janey Smith, a name that translates to "Kathy Acker" in her native planet's tongue, and here reads as the feminine equivalent of John Doe. Janey's mother dies when Janey is one year old. Her abusive father abandons her at ten. She travels from the Yucatan to New York where she's kidnapped and sold into white slavery, then gets cancer. Disgusted, her white master forsakes her. She journeys to the Middle East, has a tempestuous relationship with Jean Genet, wanders into the desert, and dies. The novel doesn't stop there, but rather maps Janey's afterlife, where she searches for a book of human transformations, longing to leave behind her alligator form and become a bird.

That book of transformations, of course, is a metaphorized version of *Blood and Guts* itself, of all Acker's work—more than ten volumes, including *Empire of the Senseless* and *Pussy: King of the Pirates*—which takes the shape of polyformal proto-hypertextual collages comprised of dramaticules, sexually explicit drawings, maps, poems, rants, translations from the Persian, and Acker's signature pla(y)giarism: rewriting and re-righting key patriarchal texts like Hawthorne's *Scarlet Letter*—all shot through with an awareness of two theorists in particular, she told me (Kathy and I were friends for several years before her death) she was reading while she composed: Georges Bataille and Julia Kristeva.

Acker wrote in what Barthelme called back-broke sentences—sentences that rupture conventional syntax and grammar, the assumptions behind such ordering, smoothness, and intellectual ease, while embracing an Aesthetics of the Ugly that tracks back through her anarchistic sensibility of the seventies, the Black Mountain School anti-formalist verse of the sixties, Burroughs's viral language and vision of the fifties, and arrives at last somewhere in the poems that are Baudelaire's *Les Fleurs du mal*, the first to embrace the dislocated, dark, marginalized, transgressive, polluted, multidimensional underworld of urbanization.

LITERARY TERRORISM

In other words, Acker's work functions as an act of literary terrorism. Janey articulates this clearly when she tells Genet "terrorism is letting happen what has to happen ... Tremendous anger and desire." More important, Janey learns, in an echo of European Romantic thought, that "terrorism is a way to health," and that "health is the lusting for infinity."

"I like books that are primitive," she told an interviewer. "I trust them ... I prize animal thoughts rather than cerebral thoughts." Hers was an imagination that set itself against rigidity, systematization, and sleepiness in all forms, yet, perhaps paradoxically, every one of her protagonists is on a spiritual quest, obsessed with literary patricide, the complicated slur of gender and identity, stowage aboard a mothership of pirates, aliens, witches, outlaws, and others whose lives telegraph fluidity and exile.

"We may not always have agreed with her," critifictionist Raymond Federman emailed me as Acker lay on her deathbed and, scattered across the country, we all waited for the inevitable, "but we always admired her guts." Through her work and presence, she taught an extraordinary generation of innovative writers—among them Eurudice, whose *f/32* tells the story of an escaped vagina; Doug Rice, whose *Blood of Mugwump* Jesse Helms cited as a reason for terminating the NEA; and Shelley Jackson, whose hypertext *Patchwork Girl* pla(y)giarizes *Frankenstein*—to be more extreme.

And she taught a generation of readers that we can only really alter things if we alter how we perceive things from the ground up.

A BEAUTIFUL DEATH

Though we'd been in touch intermittently since 1988, I first met Kathy in the fall of 1994 when she visited the University of Idaho, where I was teaching and directing the creative writing program, to lead a fiction workshop for a week and give a reading. We were to meet at The Garden Lounge, an outdoor bar in Moscow, after she'd had a chance to settle into her hotel.

Right on time, a small, muscular, blue-jeaned, middle-aged woman with close-cropped orange hair ambled up the block sucking a cherry lollipop. We exchanged pleasantries, ordered beers, and sat back to watch life roll by on Main Street. Everything was autumnally sunny and warm. Within five minutes Kathy was telling me about her embarrassment at accidentally leaving her gnarly vibrator behind on the bed at the B&B in Oregon she'd stayed at the night before. She was too mortified to phone the owner. "What do you think the lady who runs the place is thinking about me right now?" she asked. Then she leaned back and laughed the most wonderfully textured laugh from deep down where joy is sometimes rented.

Over the course of the week, she turned out to be one of the most generous, nurturing, and emotionally volatile people I've ever met. Students fell profoundly in love with her. When she got up to read in the standing-room-only auditorium, people whooped and whistled as if she were a rock star. I'd never seen a reaction like that to an author. Just for a moment, it made me feel like what we did counted for something in some alternate dimension, like we weren't just the literary equivalent of the last pterodactyls—forlorn, hopelessly out of step with the times, dead in some absolute sense years before the reaper actually planned to drop by to say hello.

Almost three years to the day later, Matias Viegener, Acker's close comrade (who would become her executor and head of the Kathy Acker Literary Trust) provided us with the final paragraph: "Kathy was very clear, looked us both [Matias and Connie Samaras, her friends at her clinic bedside] in the eyes—we were caressing her and telling her she was all right, that she was safe—and just stopped breathing. She gasped a few times and then just stopped. If there is any thing as a beautiful death, this was one. She knew exactly what was happening and all her fear seemed gone; she had a beaming, open look on her face. Connie and I just held her gaze, as though elevated with her. Then her whole body relaxed, her palms turned upward."

READING MILORAD PAVIĆ READING

"I thought how houses are like books," writes one of the bibliophilistic narrators of Milorad Pavic's *Dictionary of the Khazars*. "So many of them around you, yet you only look at a few and visit or reside in fewer still." This in good part continues to be the case with Pavić's work in the US. Visit much of the rest of the world, however, and you'll discover Milorad Pavić the famous and respected poet, dramatist, short story writer, and novelist whose work has been translated into more than sixty-seven languages and who has been nominated on several occasions for the Nobel Prize. You'll discover a stunning innovator with a fierce, always startling, deeply metaphoric, and richly puckish intelligence whose complex linguistic and formal playfulness represents some of the most original and accomplished in the last century.

You'll discover a secondary Pavić as well: the university professor who has translated Pushkin and Byron and is an expert on Baroque and Symbolist poetry; a theorist; a scholar of seventeenth-, eighteenth-, and nineteenth-century Serbian literature. It's this shadow-self you will see if you study the photographs on the back of his books: a dead-ringer for Lech Wałesa with that jowly face, toothbrush mustache, thick eyebrows, and dark hair parted neatly on the left. His eyes are congenitally kind, his smile as unassuming as the plaid sports jackets, white shirts, and ties he always seems to be wearing. This is the Pavić who talks to himself while puttering around his Belgrade apartment, drives against traffic on one-way streets through the capital, and takes pride in the fact that his family has produced at least one writer each generation since 1766.

Born October 15, 1929, the son of a philosophy professor and a sculptor who built houses for a living, Pavić is quick to underscore that "I have been a writer for two hundred years now." Yet he didn't publish his first modest collection of poetry until he was nearly forty. Instead, he studied literature and the violin and soon showed a knack for rapid language acquisition. He tried his hand at writing fiction in high school, but stopped almost immediately, discouraged by the realization that his instinct was to invent against social realism. Such mimetic work, attempting as it does to mirror external reality in a beeline fashion, didn't concern in the least the eccentric man with an arabesque mind who became obsessed years later with generating new unrealities that mirrored the intricacy of our pluriverse. He thus slid into the apolitical life of literary critic and translator in the fifties, married another literary critic, Jasmina Mihajlovic (who would eventually take on the role of his biographer, bibliographer, and one of his most astute readers), and with her had a son, Ivan (who would grow up to become a painter in Paris and illustrator of one of his father's novels).

Pavić continued to publish poetry and, increasingly, short fiction through the seventies and early eighties, virtually unknown in his country. Then, in 1984, at 55, everything changed. *Dictionary of the Khazars* exploded. A radical innovation, it poses as a lexicon that combines a furious storytelling impulse with a Byzantine sense of surface decoration, intellectual abstraction, and exquisite formality of design. Four years later Knopf brought out Christina Pribicevic-Zoric's translation in the US and, over the course of the following decade his next novel, *Landscape Painted with Tea*, which takes the form of a crossword puzzle, and his novella, *The Inner Side of the Wind*, which takes the form of a clepsydra, or water clock. In 1998, Dufour Editions, a small press in Pennsylvania dedicated to publishing noteworthy European writers, brought out *Last Love in Constantinople*, which structures itself around a Tarot deck. The son of a builder, indeed.

What we don't have here, even now, except for bits and pieces in the odd journal, are his four volumes of short stories, his play, his several books of poetry, or his academic monographs. And the novels we do possess are often notoriously difficult to get hold of since most have slipped out of print and off the bookstore shelves. Nor do we have much by way of criticism to help in our appreciation, the one notable exception an issue of *Review of Contemporary Fiction* (edited by Radmila Jovanovic Gorup), which carries a key interview with and essay by Pavić in addition to seven illuminating critical forays into his work and a bibliography.

Why this seeming lack of interest in our country for a writer who commands such impressive attention on the international stage of letters? One reason might be that Pavić's novels tend to reveal a remarkably European sensibility. Art, Pavić once asserted, "must move continuously in order not to sink. If art stops moving, even for a moment, it will drown." His is the craft of continual formal and definitional investigation that finds easy company among a constellation of European and European-influenced Latin American innovators, among them Calvino's *If on a Winter's Night a Traveler*, and faux-American Nabokov's *Pale Fire*, with its ornate narrative hall of pseudo-scholarly mirrors invented by a genuinely scholarly awareness. Borges's dense, resonant, acutely philosophical metafictions that sometimes read as five- or six-page notes for the novels Pavić actually composes almost go without saying, as does Cortázar's proto-hypertextual novel, *Hopscotch*, which is electrified by a surrealist impulse. In another register there's Gabriel García Márquez's *One Hundred Years of Solitude*, which instances both a stupendous unhinged ingenuity and a profound passion for a rich oral tradition daedal with deep mythological undercurrents. Behind them all, naturally, stands the textual generating machine of *One Thousand and One Nights*.

All those authors would agree, along with Pavić himself, that "there are no definite borders between the real and the imaginary world." Assume such an anti-pragmatic (which is often to say anti-American) position, and one's writing transforms into a perpetual act of liberation, life itself into a chronic metalogical startle aswarm with passing strange coincidence, indirection, and tease after thoughtful tease, which lead to larger and larger questions about the nature of literature and the plexus of existence. For Pavić, this means a fiction whose basic state of being is amazement. Consequently, its basic modus operandi is a peculiar textual haunting that leads to readerly wonderment—not only at the level of plot, where, say, a woman can begin to write letters to a younger version of herself at her old address halfway across the globe to feel a little less lonely in her new home, but also at the level of abrupt parenthetical deadpan detail: the girl whose shadow, we learn in a passing clause, carries the scent of cinnamon; the old man whose bones are made of gold; the fellow whom people won't stop slapping (for no apparent reason) as he attempts to make his way down the street one day toward some more central narrative action.

Such hauntings enter the architecture of Pavic's sentences. One character asks another in *Landscape Painted with Tea* if children have souls before they are born, and another answers:

> If you do not christen [their souls before they are born], they'll turn into tiny winged children, unalive and unchristened, who fly, whistle, and piss from the air into the ears of passersby. They will roam forever ... elongated like wrung-out fish, with beards on top of their heads, they will shriek with the spring down the streams, in cemeteries, they will scream in underwater voices in the night air and attach themselves to the bellies of nursing mothers, playing their breasts as though they were bagpipes. Screeching, they will call on your house, too, they will sob under overturned bowls and bite your progeny and their brothers with wise dreams.

Several planets away from statutory sentences—those kind that embrace a lucid anonymity and predictability by furthering the illusion they are panes of transparent semantic glass through which we view what we once thought of as communal reality—Pavić's self-reflexive ones strive by means of narrative hair-pin turns, hyperbolic formulations, and outlandish landminings of expectation to foreground themselves as sentences: highly artificial constructs designed to call attention to the magical narration in which the reader takes part and to the very act of begetting such narration. Reading a sentence by Pavić (not unlike reading one by Nabokov, by the way) is like playing a diminutive game of chess with a master—or, maybe, to remain within the bounds of our overarching metaphor, wandering through a small-scale mosque. It's a short step to conclude that reading Pavić's poem-prose language becomes an act of reading about the act of reading.

This assuredly is what all his work is about sooner or later. When a critic commented that *Dictionary* isn't so much novel as "parable about the novel," she could have been referring to any corner of Pavić's self-conscious project, which, like Borges's, is peopled with a pantheon of literate heroes: scribes, publishers, scholars, translators, librarians—those whose reason for existing is the composition and interpretation of words and thus systems of meaning. We are often tempted to say that Pavić is a writer's writer, but closer to the mark might be to submit that he is a reader's reader. Central to his poetics is his distinction between reversible and nonreversible art. In championing the idea of a literature that is "reversible"—that can be wandered in or around without a sense of specific aim, like a building, like a bust—he announces his mission: driving the wrong way on narratological one-way streets.

He fabricates texts that thwart conventional reading and interpretational blueprints while nudging the reader into making a series of self-conscious choices about how to navigate them. "In my opinion," he contends, "the book is going through a period of decadence and crisis, but the novel is not. If there is something in crisis it is the way of reading." Hence those four elaborate narratives in the respective forms of lexicon, crossword puzzle, clepsydra, and Tarot deck—sophisticated texts that call attention to themselves as three-dimensional structures in our hands while concomitantly inviting us to become co-participants in the fabrication of their meaning which, we are invited to keep in mind, is and always will be a personal engineering enterprise.

Pavić's novels quite literally invade the world outside their narration while the world outside their narration quite literally invades his novels—not, it should be italicized, simply to perform one more act of self-indulgent textual brinkmanship, but rather, according to the intrusive narrator of *Landscape*, "because any new way of reading that goes against the matrix of time, which pulls us toward death, is a futile but honest effort to resist this inexorability of one's fate, in literature at least, if not in reality." To disrupt the story that itself mimics life, with its unstoppable slide from start to stop, amounts to nothing short of an assertion, however short-lived and in the long run inadequate it may be, of human freedom.

Dictionary, as a case in point, masquerades as the modern reconstruction of an original 1691 edition, itself unreliable, based on three sets of texts (one written in Greek by Christians, one in Arabic by Muslims, and one in Hebrew by Jews) about events which may have taken place in the eighth century (though maybe it was the ninth; there is much debate) concerning the warlike nomadic tribe called the Khazars which came to settle and establish an empire between the Caspian and Black Seas. Where they came from and where they went and why remains a mystery. As a matter of fact, almost everything about them remains a mystery, including the key event in their history referred to by specialists as The Polemic. Here wise men from each of the great monotheistic religions traveled to the Khazar empire, interpreted a knotty dream by its ruler, the Kaghan, and, doing so, won the Khazars over to Christianity, Islam, or Judaism (it's unclear which, each religion after the fact asserting the Khazars converted to it).

Dictionary takes the shape of not one but three lexicons, one for each religion. All three lexicons contain encyclopedic entries (usually discordant with their sibling entries in the other lexicons) on the life, customs, stories, major (and minor) figures, and the beliefs of the Khazars, along with a multitude of references to the Bible, miscellaneous myths, sermons, the Cabala, Russian novels, the German Romantics, and so on, many of which are historically accurate and some of which are not, drafted by scholars over the course of more than eight centuries. In the original 1984 edition of *Dictionary*, each lexicon was printed on different-colored paper, red for the Christian, green for the Muslim, and yellow for the Judaic, and the 1988 American variant arrived in either a "male" or a "female" version (each reader chooses which to buy), identical except for a single paragraph—though the author never specifies exactly which paragraph that is; such business is for the meticulous adventurer to ferret out by carefully comparing the two versions. (The answer is located on pages 293 and 294, when an Arab man's thumb accidentally brushes against a Jewish woman's hand during breakfast in a hotel garden: the female version slides briefly into sentimentality in the face of that act, the male into murderous hatred).

A trinity of lexicons, *Dictionary* can be opened anywhere, read in any order. Many of the key figures and events are cross-referenced through a series of conspicuous icons on the page, meaning that no matter where one starts one is soon carried into a narrative web that exists among the different lexicons and often-discordant versions of the same stories. It is therefore effectively unthinkable for the reader to become anything other than an active party in significance manufacture. But she or he is aware all the while that he or she is cooperating with a book whose essence subscribes to a hermeneutics of indeterminacy with a mercurial view of words, texts, and "truth." Just as many characters in the novel teeter on the edge of becoming someone, something, or somewhere other than they are, sliding between beings and dimensions (like the inhabitants in Itil, the Khazar capital, "where, when two people—who may be quite unknown to each other—cross paths, they assume each other's name and fate, and each lives out the rest of his or her life in the role of the other, as though they had swapped caps"), so too the text itself is a translation of translations, a compulsive study of textual and existential metamorphosis. This isn't so much a classically proportioned edifice designed by Leon Battista Alberti, then, as it is the Hagia Sophia designed by Escher in one of Dali's dreams.

Which is to say the enigmatic Khazars become emblematic of the text as a whole. They possess no clear origins, no clear endings, and at their story's center churns nothing other than a nexus of conflicting interpretations. Accordingly, *Dictionary* is not an easy book to parse if one is looking for a plot and coherence, but it is always a strictly amazing one, one whose individual sentences and paragraphs are rare pleasures, a poem in drag:

- The Khazars believe that deep in the inky blackness of the Caspian Sea there is an eyeless fish that, like a clock, marks the only correct time in the universe.

- On Monday evenings, he could take a different day from his future and use it the following morning, in place of Tuesday. When he came to the day he had taken, he would use the skipped Tuesday in its place, thereby adjusting the total. Under these conditions, of course, the connecting seams of the days could not fit together properly, and cracks appeared in time, but this matter only gladdened Petkutin.

- In 867 AD, the brothers set out with their followers on one of those journeys where every step is a letter, every path a sentence, and every stop a number in a large book.

- In Constantinople one morning in 1699, he [Yabir Ibn Akshany, a lute player who may also have been Satan for a while] tossed a laurel leaf into a pail of water and

> dipped in his head to wash his pigtail. It wasn't for more than a few seconds, but when he lifted his head from the water and took a deep breath, Constantinople and the empire in which he had washed were no longer there. He was now in the Kingston, a luxury Istanbul hotel, the year was 1982 after Isa, he had a wife, a child, and a Belgian passport, he spoke French, and all that was left floating at the bottom of the sink made by F. Primavesi & Son, Corella, Cardiff, was the laurel leaf.

Pavić as postmodern Scherazade foregrounds idea, inventiveness, wild narrative non sequitur, intelligence, voice, playfulness, appropriation, and readerly freedom even as he undoes chronology, attention to the senses, homogeneous points of view, Aristotelian plans, dialogue, rounded character, and fleshed-out scene. Such pyrotechnic disturbances serve to highlight a certain thematic unity, sometimes one way and sometimes another: if not today, then tomorrow, we shall all become Khazars, an undone and lost people unreadable by our children's children's children, and existence will thereby remain at best a series of tentative trips lacking arrivals.

Still, Pavić's first and perhaps most successful novel (certainly his most well-known) is not so much about the Khazars as it is about reading about the Khazars, which is to say an epistemological venture. One of its key parables is that which appears in the "Preliminary Notes": "Imagine two men holding a captured puma on a rope. If they want to approach each other, the puma will attack, because the rope will slacken: only if they both pull simultaneously on the rope is the puma equidistant from the two of them." One of those men is the author of the untamed text, the other the reader. They are involved in an intricate interpretive dance. And the "punishment for shirking this responsibility," Rachel Kilbourn Davis asserts in her essay on the topic, "is death—not just the literal death of the text but the intellectual and spiritual deaths of both the writer and the reader."

"If you do not forget the books you've already written," Pavić told an interviewer, "you cannot write new ones, because every new book is like returning to the beginning." While there may be something cerebral and remote about his first novel, his second, *Landscape*, carries with it the full range of human emotions in addition to a strong narrative drive and a sure-footed pacing. That notwithstanding, there's no doubt who brought it into being. *Landscape* employs the fundamental metaphor of art-as-building to relate the odyssey of a Serbian architect manqué named Atanas Svilar, who gives up his creative endeavors to become the tremendously wealthy executive of an environmentally dangerous chemical corporation in California. The novel's fairly familiar narrative overture quickly fissures into a mosaic of testimonials to Svilar involving confessions, family chronicles, letters, newspaper articles, memoirs, and authorial interruptions that divide the world into two kinds of people: cenobites or solidaries, on the one hand, who affirm communal life, and idorrhythmics or solitaries, on the other, who affirm a "shallow but impenetrable solitude." Alienated from his past, his self, and the natural world, Svilar is of the latter sort. In looking for his father, who disappeared near the end of World War II, he looks for a real home, a source of selfhood and ecological harmony, but is doomed to defeat. The reader, meanwhile, sets out on her or his own search for a home in the text, which takes its shape from a crossword puzzle that said reader, following the author's instructions and diagrams, must choose to experience either "down" or "across," only to learn that he or she is the ultimate solution to the novel's fulfillment, especially since one of the central characters in it has gradually fallen in love with her or him.

Pavic's novella, *The Inner Side of the Wind*, also asks the reader to make a decision, though here that ask comes before he or she even opens to the first page. On the inside flap (the front and back covers are indistinguishable, except that one is right-side up, the other upside down, just as the first part of the book is printed right-side up, the second part upside down) is the following note: "This book can be read from either the front cover or, by flipping it upside down, the back cover. The choice is yours." Start one way, you meet a retelling of mythological Hero's story set in the twentieth century. Start the other, and you meet a retelling of mythological Leander's set at the turn of the eighteenth. Only here Hero is short for Heronea Bukur, a chemistry student and amateur fiction writer who teaches French on the side. Leander is Leander Chihorich, a mason, merchant, and one-time musician who commences another Pavićian journey—this one as much temporal as spatial. Leander swims like his mythic namesake, but is borne in this version through the darkness of time rather than the sea by various fires. While Hero and Leander never actually come together in this recapitulation of their story, images, phrases, and scenes from their narratives echo back and forth, and their tales do kiss in the androgynous center of the novella, which has taken the form of a device for measuring time by marking its flow through a small opening.

Last Love in Constantinople is accompanied by a set of twenty-two Tarot cards from the Major Arcana, along with an explanation of their meaning and use and three diagrams of possible ways to lay them out to obtain different sequences of reading the text at hand, each of whose chapters is named after and controlled by one of the cards. However one chooses to proceed, one soon enters the story of a conflict between two Serbian families during the Napoleonic Wars, the French-aligned Opujices and the Austrian-aligned Teneckis. Sofronije Opujic, whose father killed the patriarch of the Teneckis years ago, returns home from military duty to learn one of his sisters wants to marry into the hated family. What follows is a series of resourceful reprisals that spiral through the years toward a final showdown in Constantinople involving various fated deaths. Pavić's use of those deaths and that Tarot deck draws our attention to the idea of prophecies which fill the pages of this book, sometimes coming to fruition and sometimes not, recalling for us that the future is the one place we will never reach.

Pavić's attraction to unpredictable leaps among proliferating storylines, typographical and configurative freeplay, and what have you, suggests an abiding kinship between his work and hypertext. While his early novels might best be thought of as unconsciously proto-hypertextual, his later work is fully cognizant of its hypertextuality. Pavić's wife, in one of her two contributions to the Pavić issue of *Review of Contemporary Fiction*, makes the link succinctly while chronicling the efforts in Serbia and the US to convert *Dictionary* into a CD-ROM version, and in Malta to do the same with *Landscape*. Pavić himself concludes "The Beginning and the End of Reading—The Beginning and the End of the Novel" with an affirmation of the digital form that can "break free of the conditions and laws of Gutenberg's galaxy and emerge into a new galaxy … that has no more connection with a printed book." His 1997 play, *For Ever and a Day*, is a love story that comes with a menu from which the audience, actors, or director can choose one of three beginnings and one of three endings (a tragedy, a comedy, an ecological tract), while his 1998 Web-based hypertext, *Damascene*, is rich with electronically forking paths that invite us to choose the chamber we'd like to visit to deliberate upon that magic act of human choice in narrativity's tomorrow, which has apparently happened some time ago now.

TERMITE ART

"If you know that here is one hand, we'll grant you all the rest." —LUDWIG WITTGENSTEIN (LW)

"It's a myth that truth is stranger than fiction. Actually they're about equally strange." —DAVID FOSTER WALLACE (DFW)

REALITY TERMITES VS. WHITE ELEPHANTS

LW: "Might I not believe that once, without knowing it, perhaps in a state of unconsciousness, I was taken away from the earth—that other people even know this, but do not mention it to me?"

DFW: "It seems important to find ways of reminding ourselves that most familiarity is meditated and delusive."

The fifth time you read Milorad Pavić's *Dictionary of the Khazars* isn't the first, which is to propose the more one inhabits a difficult text, the less difficult it becomes. In part that's because humans are constructed to adjust and accommodate, in part because we are arranged to make sense of things, even if the things in question resist our understanding. After all, how long can any of us actually live in a state of Pynchonesque anti-paranoia? How long can any of us retain the bracing uncertainty we felt on our initial encounter with Theresa Hak Kyung Cha's *Dictee* before we set about trying to finalize it, develop a discourse to contain it, a context through which to colonize it? That impulse is embedded in our genes.

And yet difficult texts (perhaps all texts to one degree or another) are built to refuse us. They leave some remainder of unknowability in their wake, some sensed enigma, a rejection of our will to resolve and categorize. That's why reading isn't a math problem or video game. The hyper-metalogical writing in Mark Leyner's *My Cousin, My Gastroenterologist* or Ben Marcus's *Age of Wire and String*; the temporal static of Robbe-Grillet's *Jealousy*; the smashed narrativity in Burrough's *Ticket that Exploded*, Leslie Scalapino's *Dahlia's Iris*, Renee Gladman's *Event Factory*—these are both disabled texts (in the most vibrant sense of the word) and disabling texts (i.e., texts made to teach us how to re-think and re-feel).

Many years ago, William Gibson introduced me to a term that has helped me contemplate these sorts of texts: Termite Art. It comes from a 1962 essay by the iconoclastic film critic Manny Farber. Farber distinguishes between two kinds of creation. The first, for which he holds contempt, he names White Elephant Art. This is the kind that embraces the idea of a well-regulated, logical arena. It's embodied in the films of François Truffaut. Proponents of this quasi-neoclassical school produce pieces that are "weight-density-structure-polish amalgam[s] associated with self-aggrandizing masterworks." Termite Art, on the other hand, stands opposed to high culture, welcomes freedom and multiplicity, is embodied in the films of Laurel and Hardy. Proponents of this school produce pieces that go "always forward eating [their] own boundaries, and, likely as not, leave nothing in [their] path other than the signs of eager, industrious, unkempt activity." Termite Art is a stubbornly self-involved mode of creation concerned with process over progress, question over solution, messy ambiguity over crystalline explanation.

THE SCAVENGER BELLY

LW: "Philosophy is not a theory but an activity."

DFW: "What?"

Ludwig Wittgenstein and David Foster Wallace, in spite of their countless differences, share a Termite Consciousness. Derrida would consider them thinkers rather than philosophers, that variety of human beings that rejects conventional writing practices in order to better work through the scrambled world. "What is the use of studying philosophy," Wittgenstein asked a student, "if all that it does for you is to enable you to talk with some plausibility about some abstruse questions of logic, etc., and if it does not improve your thinking about the important questions of everyday life?"

This said by the Viennese savant who, as Wallace writes, "by all evidence lived in personal torment over the questions too many of his academic followers have made into elaborate empty exercise." Who was gay, a congenital outsider, an indifferent student, an ascetic, a soldier, an aviator who would whistle along to a repertoire of forty Schubert songs that his boyfriend and collaborator David Pinsent (to whom the musically structured *Tractatus* is dedicated) performed on the piano. Who in 1913 submitted to hypnosis hoping the resulting trance would allow him to arrive at clear answers to questions of logic, and lived for more than a year in a secluded hut on a mountain in Norway; debated entering monastic life; donated large sums of inherited money to needy Austrian poets and artists (Rilke and Trakl among them); was a grade-school teacher until he began to worry his intellectual influence on children was probably harmful; disliked universities and academia; was, like Kafka, relieved to hear he was dying; and published exactly one book in the course of his life, leaving behind 20,000 unpublished pages.

Wittgenstein's and Wallace's imaginations take nothing for granted. Doubt is their cardinal virtue. The former may have begun as a modernist searching through his picture-theory for what can be said honestly and accurately about experience. He ended up, though, drifting in a post-*Tractatus* twilight wondering if he could be even relatively sure he possessed a hand.

The movement from the *Tractatus* to *On Certainty* is the movement from cubism to cloud chamber, Joyce to Beckett.

Wallace, one of the Viennese savant's intellectual great grandchildren, is, after a fashion, Wittgenstein in Avant-Pop clothing, one of the first generation to be raised inside the television screen. "Popular culture," says the narrator of "Westward the Course of Empire Takes Its Way," "is the symbolic representation of what people already believe." Like many authors who shop in the global K-Mart, he's made of the stuff, imbued with Andy Warhol's aesthetics of trash, Laurie Anderson's ironic media-infiltrated being, Pynchon's hip convoluted language, cartoonishly named comic characters, maximalism, Don DeLillo's thematization of television and William Vollman's interleaving of real and fictional characters in order to puzzle out the historicity of both, not to mention Barth's metafiction ("Westward" is, Wallace tells us on the title page of *Girl with Curious Hair*, "written in the margins" of "Lost in the Funhouse").

17.3.92

LW: "Does my telephone call to New York strengthen my conviction that the earth exists?"

DFW: "Bees have to move very fast to stay still."

In a 17 March 1992 letter to me, Wallace remarked that his father (a philosophy professor at the University of Illinois-Urbana for 49 years) studied with Norman Malcolm, one of Wittgenstein's students, at Cornell. Wallace, an English-philosophy major at Amherst who graduated *summa cum laude* (his senior thesis in philosophy and modal logic was awarded the Gail Kennedy Memorial Prize and posthumously published as *Fate, Time, and Language: An Essay on Free Will*), took a seminar on Wittgenstein taught by William Kennick, another student of the philosopher. Wallace was "deeply taken" with the *Tractatus*, but felt "the *Investigations* were silly because they retracted the cold formal beauty of the former (the *Tractatus*'s first proposition is 'The world is everything that is the case,' which along with Crane's 'The Open Boat''s 'None of the men knew the color of the sky' is the most beautiful opening line in western lit)." This led to him in the summer of 1990 publishing a 22-page essay in *Review of Contemporary Fiction* about David Markson's *Wittgenstein's Mistress* that, besides giving Markson's book a sharp, thorough, and sometimes critical reading (Markson, among other things, doesn't get women right, says Wallace), serves as a lucid introduction to many of Wittgenstein's central concepts and clearly establishes Wallace as an understanding and self-proclaimed "fan" of the philosopher.

LENORE SR.'S MEASUREMENTS

> LW: "Whereof one cannot speak thereof one must be silent."
>
> DFW: "Suppose Gramma tells me really convincingly that all that really exists of my life is what can be said about it?"

In the same letter, Wallace explained that Lenore Sr., Lenore Beadsman's great-grandmother in *The Broom of the System*, "is based loosely, physically, on Alice Ambrose, a very old former Smith professor who lived near me and had been one of the students whose notes were comprised by Witt's Blue and Brown books." Lenore Sr. is a "small, birdish, sharp-featured thing," "a hard woman, a cold woman, a querulous and thoroughly selfish woman, one with vast intellectual pretensions and … probably commensurate gifts," who lacks a body-thermometer and hence has to dwell in excruciatingly hot rooms, thermostats locked at 98.6—a rich metaphor both for her cold-blooded, hermetic life and, quite possibly, for the cold-blooded, hermetic methods of logical positivists everywhere. In the 1920s she studied at Cambridge "under a mad crackpot genius named Wittgenstein, who believed that everything was words," as Rick Vigorous puts it.

Lenore Sr. consequently serves as a skewed, gently ironic introduction to Wittgenstein's philosophy in Wallace. For her, whose prize possession is an autographed copy of *Philosophical Investigations*, language is a system of symbols that filters our experience of reality. We only know our lives through what we can say about them. Our understanding of the world arises from our ability to talk about it. Put another way: language shapes what we perceive and how we perceive. Moreover, both the post-*Tractatus* philosopher and Lenore Sr. believe language possesses no meaning except in how it's used at specific times in specific places in specific linguistic contexts. The use of a word or a sentence is the language game in which it plays a part. "Meaning," as Lenore Jr. says, "is nothing more or less than its function."

Hence the central metaphor of Wallace's first novel: the broom. Lenore Jr. relates how when she was a child Lenore Sr. showed her one and asked which was more fundamental to it, the bristles or the handle. Lenore Jr. answered the former. "'Aha,'" Lenore Sr. says, "'that's because you want to sweep with the broom, isn't it? It's because of what you want the broom for, isn't it?' ... And that if what we wanted a broom for was to break windows, then the handle was clearly the fundamental essence of the broom ... Meaning as use." What happens, though, if one's life has no use? Then it has no meaning. And that's the problem Lenore Sr. finds herself in. She's been tucked away in the Shaker Heights Nursing Home in Ohio. Twenty-four-year-old Lenore Jr. (who, like Wallace, was a philosophy major in college) and a few other patients are her sole visitors. She's stuck, in other words, in stasis. Which explains the main plot of *Broom*: Lenore Sr. attempts to invigorate her life with use and therefore meaning by proposing to Stonecipher Beadsman III, Lenore Jr.'s dad and chief of the Stonecipheco baby food company, some research into a drug that speeds development of (what else?) language skills and comprehension in children.

In a madcap plot that brings to mind *The Crying of Lot 49*, Gretchen Yingst, one of Lenore Sr.'s cronies at the home, had a husband who used to work for Consolidated Gland Derivatives in Akron. He came up with a cattle-endocrine derivative on his own, writing the results down on Batman tablets before his death. Stonecipher goes for the idea, but Lenore Sr. reconsiders and steals back the tablets and test-samples, which she feeds to Lenore Jr.'s pet cockatiel, Vlad the Impaler, giving the bird the gift of gab, or at least gabble. She then absconds to the phone tunnels beneath the Bombardini Building, aided and abetted, apparently, by Dr. Jay, Lenore Jr.'s and Rick Vigorous's psychologist, where there is at least fleeting evidence that she eventually dies.

There is more to that titular broom, though. The word is related to the Anglo-Saxon word *brom*, the Low German word *bram*, the Dutch word *brem*—the last two of which are closely allied to *bramble*, a word deriving from the Sanskrit *bhram*, meaning *to be confused*. In a roundabout way, then, the actual title of the novel might translate into something like *The Confusion of the System*. Language is the primary system of this text, and confusion of language and other corollary systems (much to Lenore Sr.'s and Wittgenstein's chagrin) forms the spanner in the works.

Wittgenstein understood his life-project to be explaining the nature of sentences which, early in his career, he believed model or picture reality. Each element in one corresponds to the state of affairs it represents, though not everything that can be understood can be said: certain religious states, or love, among others. Wittgenstein thereby saw one function of philosophy as demarcating what cannot be said by pristinely presenting what can be said via his picture-theory of language, along the way uncovering errors that had given rise to various philosophical doctrines.

His basic concern, then, was the relationship of language to world, and his world started out, as Wallace comments in his essay on the philosopher, "a logical heaven," but ended up "a metaphysical hell." The more post-*Tractatus* Wittgenstein probed the relationship between language and world, the more he intuited language didn't contain the clear-cut structure he'd been hoping for. In fact, he started to believe the philosophical ideal he'd put forward in the *Tractatus* was an increasingly dubious one. As his life went on, the impression grew that there wasn't so much a universe of meaning out there as a multiverse of bemusement. By granting that the meaning of a word or sentence is in its use, rather than in its reference to a stable and knowable out-there, the hope of a mythically pure inspection of reality began to gunk up, and the idea of totality began to break down. It's a short step from believing context determines meaning to arriving at the doorstep of philosophical relativism.

Question: Where then do all those important moral and ethical values Wittgenstein sought in his daily life find a place?

Answer: Nowhere.

Result: A broom in the system.

Wallace from time to time parrots the methodical, clean, subject-verb-predicate sentences of the *Tractatus*, as in these lines from the opening of "Little Expressionless Animals":

> It's 1976. The sky is low and full of clouds. The gray clouds are bulbous and wrinkled and shiny. The sky looks cerebral. Under the sky is a field, in the wind. A pale highway runs beside the field. Lots of cars go by. One of the cars stops by the side of the highway. Two small children are brought out of the car by the young woman with a loose face. A man at the wheel of the car stares straight ahead.

This sort of "realist" language functions as analogue for Wittgenstein, tracks back through Carver's, Ann Beattie's, and Hemingway's, perhaps all the way to Flaubert's doorstep in *Madame Bovary*, certainly before him to the language of Stendhal, who set forth in *The Red and the Black* the scientistic belief that language is a mirror held up to experience. These traces find voice through characters like Faye, who, in "Little Expressionless Animals," doesn't like the complexity of lyrical language because "it beats around bushes. Even when I like it, it's nothing more than a really oblique way of saying the obvious, it seems like"; or Bruce, who, in "Here and There," wants to be a Poet of Technology and assumes "literature will get progressively more mathematical and technical as time goes by ... Meaning will be clean":

> No more ... warm clover breath, heaving bosoms, histories as symbol, colossi; no more man, fist to brow or palm to décolletage, understood in terms of thumping, thudding, heated Nature, itself conceived as colored, shaped, invested with odor, lending meaning in virtue of qualities. No more qualities. No more metaphors.

Ezra Pound's Imagist obsessions stalk this passage, a desire for the clear and concentrated, as does, of course, the early Wittgenstein. But Bruce's story ultimately turns out to be Wallace's critique of that way of expressing, which is to say thinking (Wallace in his syllabus at Illinois State University: "I draw no distinction between the quality of one's ideas and the quality of those ideas' verbal expression"). Bruce is more in love with a picture of his girlfriend than with his girlfriend herself, with the representation rather than with the thing. When he moves from ideal picture-theory to grubby praxis, trying to fix a broken stove, he soon realizes the stove is like the world: "a crude piece of equipment."

Even if Wallace's mind tells him the first sentence of the *Tractatus* is the most beautiful opening line in Western lit, his gut tells him otherwise: that the world is enigma, a nexus of perplexity. Consequently, his sentences usually sound more like this one from forty-two-year-old Rick Vigorous visiting his alma mater:

> As I joined the serpentine line of students walking up the ungentle hill to the Art and Science Buildings, all of us falling into the vaguely floppy, seal-like gait of the hurried hill-climber, most of us seals apparently late for class, one

> of us late for an appointment with a tiny ocean of his own past, stretching away and down beside the carved dock of his childhood, an ocean into which this particular seal was going to pour a strong (hopefully unitary) stream of his own presence, to prove that he still is, and so was—that is, provided of course the bathroom and toilet and stall were still there—as I joined the line of seals in short pants and loose short-sleeved shirts and boat shoes and backpacks, and as I felt the fear that accompanied and was in a way caused by the intensity of the wash of feelings and desires and so on that accompanied even the thought of a silly men's room in a silly building at a silly college where a sad silly boy had spent four years twenty years ago, as I felt all these things, there occurred to me a fact which I think now as I sit up in bed in our motel room, writing, the television softly on, the sharp-haired object of my adoration, and absolute center of my entire existence asleep and snoring softly in the bed beside me, a fact which I think now is undeniably true, the truth being that Amherst College in the 1960's was for me a devourer of the emotional middle, a maker of psychic canyons, a whacker of the pendulum of Mood with the paddle of Immoderation.

Those 283 words forge labyrinthian clauses, parenthetical phrases within parenthetical phrases, chaotic cataloging, syntactic indirection, and confusing syntactical frameworks. Nor is its information density, as somebody might be inclined to argue, simply a revelation of Rick's mixed-up neurotic mind, though it is, certainly, in part, that. It's just how Wallace writes most of the time. Remark the following 122-word knot, an excerpt from a book review he wrote for *The Los Angeles Times*, and which *The New Yorker*, perhaps predictably amused, reprinted under the title "Sentences We Hated to Come to the End Of":

> If pop is the argument between sub-culture (as conceived by the cultural outsider when that outsider happens to

> be a genius) and the redemptive, relentlessly consuming appetite of the community, then the arc of Elvis' career, from starving white trash to musical insurgent to heart-throb to B-movie mainstay to corpulent Vegas schmaltz-king "performing a kind of enormous victory rather than winning it" ("Mystery Train"), limns also the living and fatal paradox of all popular US art: that this art, which is produced via raw difference, the special fecund anguish of non-inclusion, attacks, seduces and is devoured by a mass-art market that redeems and even deifies the artist while it drains his productions of the denial and pain that is its voice.

Wallace's sentences are effusions that correspond, not to some mathematically pure realm of being, but rather to some multi-dimensional space of becoming intricate as the involved surface of a brain. Like all Termite Art, they move ceaselessly forward, gnawing away at their own perimeters, revealing themselves as ardent and disheveled processes rather than cool, prudish productions, reflecting nothing if not their author's and characters' bedragglement before living.

"Good Old Neon": "What goes on inside is just too fast and huge and all interconnected for words to do more than barely sketch the outlines of at most one tiny little part of it at any given instant."

STRATEGIC MISREPRESENTATION

> LW: "I don't know why we are here, but I'm pretty sure that it is not in order to enjoy ourselves."

> DFW: "The truth will set you free. But not until it is finished with you."

They're funny as well, Wallace's sentences, in a self-reflexive register akin to those in Beckett's trilogy or Jeffrey Deshell's

S&M. If early on Wittgenstein's consciousness is the harvest of Rilkean earnestness, his later inquiries ("A serious and good philosophical work could be written consisting entirely of jokes.") are something altogether different. Wallace's consciousness is the harvest of both impulses: earnest, tender, deeply empathetic, but concomitantly ironic, mischievous, and eccentric—and both impulses are ever engaged in larger philosophical issues that are consonant with Wittgenstein's.

Many characters in *Broom* misunderstand each other and misrepresent themselves. Lenore Jr., raised in a family that made "just a huge deal out of what got said," and Mr. Bloemker, administrator of the Shaker Heights Nursing Home, go at it for over two pages trying to define what *missing* means with respect to Lenore Sr., while Lenore Jr. and Rick go at it a lot longer than that trying to determine whether Lenore Jr. actually loves him. That cockatiel, Vlad the Impaler, mouths pronouncements the Reverend Hart Lee Sykes believes profound but which are as a matter of fact just this side of gibberish. LaVache, Lenore Jr.'s one-legged cynic of a brother at Amherst, deliberately misnames his phone *lymph node* so he can honestly tell his father he doesn't own a phone, while he rechristens his friends with aliases like Heat and Breather because, he says, their real names don't matter much anymore. An important part of the college experience, he adds, "is learning how to lie. 'Strategic misrepresentation,' we call it." He wants people to refer to him as the Antichrist instead of Stoney because Stoney, his family handle, makes him part of a system he'd just as soon not be associated with.

Meaning may be use, but what happens if use becomes unclear, either accidentally or on purpose? If someone hands you a broom, yet doesn't tell you what you're supposed to do with it, and it dawns on you that sweeping is only one option among many? If use (and thereby meaning) edges toward some borderline state, toward the nebulous and puzzling?

Confusion of the system—or, in this case, systems: of language, meaning, narration, actuality itself. Near the end of his life, Wittgenstein wrote: "All testing, all confirmation and disconfirmation of a hypothesis takes place already within a system. And this system is not a more or less arbitrary and doubtful point of departure for all our arguments: no, it belongs to the essence of what we call an argument. The system is not so much the point of departure, as the element in which arguments have their life." It may be the case, as the narrator of *The Unnamable* asserts in his paean to aporia, that "the thing to avoid, I don't know why, is the spirit of system," yet systems are impervious to avoidance. We're part of them, they of us. We'd like to hope they somehow bring the world into clearer focus. Instead, they limit our ability to speak, which is to say our ability to see, which is to say our ability to be.

Wallace, harkening back to post-*Tractatus* Wittgenstein, thematically challenges persistent identity in *Broom*. Lenore Jr. is briefly bewildered, as a case in point, when the new nurse at Shaker Heights thinks Lenore Jr.'s making a bad joke when she announces she's Lenore Beadsman, there to see Lenore Beadsman. A more pronounced illustration is the ritual the Spaniard family acts out before the laser disk playing on their television set: they don masks and tell a tale about how, when they talk of themselves as part of a family, they both feel part of a larger whole (a whimsical nod in the direction of Wittgenstein's "family resemblances") and like they've lost parts of themselves (what's under those masks, anyway, and how many layers of masks, figuratively and otherwise, do they possess?). Lenore Jr.'s other brother, John, who is admitted to Lake Lady Medical Center in Chicago because he's convinced he's not himself anymore, but a perpetual gameshow contestant, serves as a figure for all of us because, in a very real sense, none of us is us. Rather, we're all, in the world according to Wittgenstein and Wallace, contestants in a multifaceted system of language games.

Except, in Wallace's universe, it's not always clear who's winning.

Or who's playing what.

GRAMMA SAYS

> LW: "Suppose some adult had told a child that he had been on the moon. The child tells me the story, and I say it was only a joke, the man hadn't been on the moon; no one has ever been on the moon; the moon is a long way off and it is impossible to climb up there or fly there. If now the child insists, saying perhaps there is a way of getting there which I don't know, etc., what reply would I make to him?"

> DFW: "Gramma says any telling automatically becomes a kind of system, that controls everybody involved ... Every telling creates and limits and defines."

No wonder Wallace foregrounds the very act of narrativity itself. Telling is, as writers and therapists know, one of the great pattern-making gestures, a method of testing, labeling, dominating. We seem configured to locate the stories we can live in. "The truth," Dr. Jay claims, "is that there's no difference between a life and a story." LaVache reminds Lenore Jr. that Lenore Sr. believes "that you're only real insofar as you're told about, so that to the extent that you're real you're controlled, and thus not in control, so that you're more like a sort of character than a person, really—and of course Lenore would say the two are the same, now, wouldn't she?"

Many players in *Broom* are obsessed with getting the scripts that are their lives right, but maybe none are so obsessed as Rick, a kind of Scheherazade who works, suitably enough, for a publishing firm and as the fiction editor of a small literary review. He tells Lenore Jr. stories, often not his own, often in bed, often with the point that things can always get worse: babies can die without warning, cars crash through ceilings and kill the innocent, malicious psychologists cheat with wives while mute blind paraplegic husbands lie helplessly by. He also tries creating some tales of his own, as with "Love," which involves the discovery that a neighbor has been taking photos of and collecting artifacts belonging to the little boy next door (unbeknownst both to the little boy and his parents) as part of some dark infatuation—a story, by the way, like several by Rick, that distantly replicates his own infatuation with Lenore Jr.

The stories Lenore Jr. tells frequently attempt to figure out the plot she seems to have been unwillingly written into, some (again that word) Pynchonesque conspiracy Lenore Jr. feels herself, existential sister of Oedipa Maas, to have entered the moment Lenore Sr. vanished, but which may be nothing more than a series of coincidences or product of an overactive imagination. It's all a little like the game of Telephone, where, by the time the message (from Lenore Sr.? Lenore Jr.'s father? someone else?) reaches Lenore Jr., it's traversed so much white noise that it's become nearly indecipherable, in which case those malfunctioning phones at Frequent & Vigorous, symbols of communications gone awry, are fitting images indeed for the novel itself which is one grand system of communication sizzling with white noise in its master network, as it leaps around atemporally, shifts from third-person to first-, whole chapters wrought out of Barthelmesque swatches of untagged dialogue only to introduce the characters speaking later, morphing from fiction to transcript to monologue to journal entry to magazine article to legal contract to duty log, flustering traditional narrative boundaries along the way, hybridizing genres, and thereby producing the novelistic equivalent of philosophical relativism. It's appropriate that it ends mid-sentence, some skier caught just as he lifts from the jump, unsure how he'll land, a final broom of the system, though we surely know (we think) the word that finishes the sentence that finishes the novel: the only real Wittgensteinian choice: *word*.

One of the most significant narrative systems that informs Wallace's project is television, NBC to MTV, Ronald McDonald to David Letterman, Merv Griffin to Jack Lord. A character in the short story "My Appearance" reminisces about those parodies of commercials that *Saturday Night Live* used to broadcast after the show's opening:

> Such great parodies that it always took you a while to even realize they were parodies and not commercials? And how the anti-commercials were a hit? So then what happened? ... [T]he sponsors started putting commercials on "SNL" that were almost like the parodies of the commercials, so that it took you a while to realize that these were even real commercials in the first place. So the sponsors were suddenly guaranteed huge audiences that watched their commercials very, very closely—hoping, of course, that they'd be parodies.

A system of commerce co-opts a system of art, which was mimicking a system of commerce, in order to mimic a system of art mimicking a system of commerce in order to make the viewer think she or he is watching a system of art mimicking a system of commerce and not a system of commerce mimicking a system of art mimicking a system of commerce, all in order to push product. Baudrillard, be still.

In Wallace's work, media become pervasive as background radiation. Televisions seem like they're always on. (This was the case, incidentally, when I visited Wallace on several occasions.) Which turns out to be not so much a critique of the media on Wallace's part as it is just a video recording the way things really are for those generations raised on airwaves. The extreme case is the character in "Little Expressionless Animals" who begins wondering which side of the tube she's really on. That is, she begins wondering, like all actors who sense they're part of some bigger, sometimes pretty intricate, screenplay: Where did self-hood go? Human interaction? And where, finally, that ultimate language game: "reality"?

Broom was published in 1987, but is set for the most part in the very near future-world of 1990, now our past. This future-world, no longer our future-world, isn't our present world, either. Nor is it exactly not our present world. Stonecipher Beadsman II has shaped East Corinth to resemble Jayne Mansfield's profile, and grotesque Norman Bombardini, right out of the *Meaning of Life*, wants to eat everything in sight and grow to infinite size. There are those magical realist frogs growing in the pit of the Thermos woman's neck in one of Rick's early stories, and Vlad the Impaler's newfound speech in the real-world (which isn't the real world) of the novel. Alternate geography crops up in the form of the Great Ohio Desert, surreality in Rick's goofy sexual dreams of Queen Victoria, absurdity in Dr. Jay's (read: Dr. Hilarious from *The Crying of Lot 49*) hygiene-anxiety therapy. Reality termites are everywhere.

A GREAT LUMP OF OPAQUE PIG IRON

> LW: "But what about such a proposition as "I know I have a brain"? Can I doubt it? Grounds for doubt are lacking! Everything speaks in its favour, nothing against it. Nevertheless it is imaginable that my skull should turn out empty when it was operated on."

> DFW: "Rarely is our uncritical inheritance of early Wittgensteinian & Logical Positivist models so obvious as in our academic & aesthetic prejudice that successful fiction encloses rather than opens up, organizes facts rather than undermines them."

Guy Davenport, late modernist nephew of Wittgenstein, subscribed to the notion that the philosopher who thought his way through the *Tractatus*, *Investigations*, and *On Certainty* was the sort who made honesty look dishonest, he was so honest:

> Nothing—nothing at all—was to be allowed to escape analysis. He had nothing up his sleeve; he had nothing to teach. The world was to him an absolute puzzle, a great lump of opaque pig iron. Can we think about the lump?

> What is thought? What is the meaning of *can*, of *can we*, of *can we think*? What is the meaning of *we*? What does it mean to ask *what is the meaning of* we? If we answer these questions on Monday, are the answers valid on Tuesday? If I answer them at all, do I think the answer, believe the answer, know the answer, or imagine the answer?

Or, perhaps better yet: the world to Wittgenstein was a welter of impaired language games. Wallace, needless to say, is right behind him. To question the efficacy of language is to question the validity of systems of meaning, which is to question the efficacy of systems of narrative, which is to question the validity of systems of identity, which is to question the veracity of systems of reality.

Et cetera.

Lenore Sr.'s antinomy in *Broom* is the guiding metaphor for this: "the barber who shaves all and only those who do not shave themselves." Does he shave himself? He can't. And yet he can't *can't*. Puzzles, paradoxes, mysteries. Lenore Jr. is an enigma to Rick. She's someone who "soundlessly invites one to play a game consisting of involved attempts to find out the game's own rules." Rick is a riddle to Lenore Jr. Lenore Sr. is a riddle to everyone. If we don't fully understand—let alone know—the rules, we don't fully know or understand the games. Most of the characters inhabiting Wallace's pluriverse are as baffled before life as those poor patients in the Shaker Heights Nursing Home. They live in a persistent state of philosophical extremis, instability their only norm. "How might one even begin to orient oneself with respect to such a series of changes in the fundamental features of the world?" Mr. Bloemker asks, thinking of those patients and what they've seen of the twentieth century. "How to begin to come to some understanding of one's place in a system, when one is part of an area that exists in such a troubling relation to the rest of the world, a world that is itself stripped of any static, understandable character by the fact that it changes, radically, all the time?"

Lenore Sr. adores antinomies. She wants less to interpret the world as she does to contemplate its fraughtness. Philosophy is a less stabilizing doctrine than an activity of mind. Just because you know one state of affairs, Wittgenstein asserts, doesn't mean you can necessarily infer another from them—and yet this is what one does when trying to speak about the future. To this extent Wittgenstein and Wallace are kindred spirits with Kafka, who in many ways is the ambassador of our Age of Uncertainty. Like Gregor Samsa, we continually wake in our beds with the funny feeling that that uneasy dream we just had wasn't one.

ONTOLOGICAL METALEPSES & THE POLITICS OF THE PAGE

The first book by Steve Tomasula I came across was the manuscript for *VAS: An Opera in Flatland*, which I read when I was chair of FC2's Board of Directors. This was, I want to say, sometime in 2002. Only the first 20 or 30 pages had been laid out as they currently appear in order to give the Board a flavor of the imagined aggregate so that we could discuss and vote on it. The rest, as I recall, looked like a more or less conventionally typed novel. I wrote up a reader's report that was energetically positive. It talked about how impressed and excited I was by Tomasula's bracketing of the page, his unnatural narrative gestures and production of an art book that wasn't actually an art book because it had been designed to be (relatively) mass-produced. How *VAS* was a novel about the problematic text of the body that was also a text about the problematic body of the text.

In the end the other readers on the Board disagreed with me and decided to pass on *VAS*. I still count that among FC2's real editorial missteps, although I'm happy to say the press has been fortunate enough subsequently to bring out Tomasula's *The Book of Portraiture*, *TOC*, *Once Human*, and *Ascension*.

Yet when I speak of Steve Tomasula as the author of a hardcopy novel like *VAS*, the narrative (printed in a trade paperback whose cover approximates flesh traced with blood vessels) concerning a [[man]] named Square's decision about whether or not to undergo a vasectomy, or a hypermedia project like *TOC*, a digital compilation of steampunk aesthetics, creation myths, an audio recitation about a model's husband kept alive on a respirator after a terrible accident, and a continuous meditation on the unimaginable nature of time—I am misspeaking.

I don't mean what I say, or, closer to the point, I mean it in a modified sense, because the author-function in *VAS* apparently possesses two names: Steve Tomasula, the writer at Notre Dame who initially conceived the project, produced and compiled the text, mailed it to FC2, and Stephen Farrell, the associate professor of visual communication at the School of the Art Institute of Chicago, who created the art and designed the layout. As with most other books, that is, the author-function in *VAS* also possesses myriad invisible collaborators—editor, publisher, printer, distributor, reviewer, reader, teacher, blogger, tweeter, and so on.

With *TOC*, which itself exists within a bifurcated physicality—it is available both as a DVD one may upload onto one's computer and as an app one may download onto one's iPad—and which Tomasula initially imagined as a unique genre inhabiting the aesthetic space "somewhere between reading and [watching a] film—a Frankenstein of a book," as well as a chamber opera, "a story told to an audience of one, on a tiny stage, as if a 12-inch monitor were puppet theater"—with *TOC*, as I say, the author-function possesses yet more collaborators, and yet more nebulously. In addition to the usual suspects, there was programmer Christian Jara, and a number of artists, animators, musicians, and actors—fifteen in all scattered across three countries, most of whom never met or interacted with each other during the ten-year-long undertaking to bring that project into being.

My point is obvious and yet invisible to most of us: when any writer touches pencil to paper or fingers to keyboard, when she or he commences to commence even imagining to imagine a new work, she or he can't help launching into collaborative exercise, embarking on an intricate conversation across history, geography, and technology with other creators, with the inventors of his or her means of production and distribution, with the genre with or against which she or he is working, with specific texts (in *VAS*, for instance, Edwin A. Abbott's 1884 satire about Victorian culture's myopia, *Flatland*, scientific graphs and flow charts, *et cetera*)—not to mention with several thousand years of language development.

The reason I bring up this evident fact that isn't one is to point to how in both *VAS* and *TOC* Tomasula sets about revealing what has become concealed in our culture by virtue of its ubiquity. Tomasula is not simply author of a novel, but rather director of a film or digital program, conductor of a soundtrack, producer of a *Gesamtkunstwerk*, or perhaps a grant application to fund it. Being so, he seeks to make strange bookish ecology, call attention to its dynamics and definitions, flag his undoing of the Romantic myth concerning the solitary artist-genius by announcing through his texts' overt materiality and intertextuality that creation is invariably a Barthesian collaboration all the way down, every text always textured.

To approach a Tomasulian text is thereby more times than not to enter into a larger problematics concerning [[identity]], both with regard to that of the text itself—i.e., the nature of its technological delivery system: if this isn't a book that behaves quite like a book, then what is it, and how do we begin to find a language to discuss it?—and to that of the status of the actants moving through its narratives.

I (and I use the pronoun loosely) hesitate to use the word *characters* because many if not most of Tomasula's actants don't evince deep psychology, full roundedness—"the old myths of 'depth,'" as Robbe-Grillet used to call it. Many if not most tend to exist externally rather than internally, Skinnerian black-box beings reflecting the issues surrounding the posthuman subject position. They function as placeholders for something closer to theses than modernist Freudian selfhood or conventional plot-drivers, as abstract ideas rather than plump paper people, thereby calling into question the philosophico-cultural assumptions behind various modes of characterization itself.

And so let me begin again, this time in someone else's voice: *Lulled into somnolence by five hundred years of print, literary analysis should awaken to the importance of media-specific analysis, a mode of critical attention which recognizes that all texts are instantiated and that the nature of the medium in which they are instantiated matters.*

With that, N. Katherine Hayles urges literary analysis to become more attuned to the materiality of the medium under investigation—a point that underscores the fact a story is never merely a story. Each is mediated not only through the systems of narrative discourse by which events in it are rendered, but also remediated through its tangible means of being-in-the-world.

How a text matters to us should matter to us.

By contending that texts are comprised of quotations drawn from innumerable centers of culture, Barthes advocates an intersectional approach to reading. Intersectionality posits a continuous process of writing and rewriting. By encouraging such an analytic strategy, Hayles argues, Barthes becomes both textual liberator and blind man—the former because he sets free a mode of engagement with texts that in many ways initiate[s] semiotic and poststructuralist approaches to discourse, arguably among the most important developments in literary studies in the last hundred years; the latter because suddenly every medium becomes every other medium: all texts come to evince a textual existence that fails to register the textural.

In treating everything from fashion to fascism as a semiotic system, Barthes's method has the effect of eliding distinctions, never a fruitful enterprise.

Children, we should remember, are taught differently: think of pop-up and other sorts of text/image books. As a teen, an undergraduate, a graduate—no matter our field of interest—we are habituated to conceptualize pages as meticulously Windexed® windows through which we tumble into story worlds. If we come to think about the page at all, it is typically as we sit composing at our computer screens within the context of what Bill Gates has guided us into believing a page should be and look like by means of Microsoft Word (its margins, its movements, its fonts, its flatness) which, of course, Gates unthinkingly absorbed from those five hundred years of print history.

Tomasula's texts short circuit the non-ergodic reading process by making reading a non-trivial, even visceral event, the foreignness of the reading/writing instant (and hence of meaning-making itself) foreign once more.

Hayles redux: *The crucial move is to reconceptualize materiality as the interplay between a text's physical characteristics and its signifying strategies ... In this view of materiality, it is not merely an inert collection of physical properties but a dynamic quality that emerges from the interplay between the text as a physical artifact, its conceptual content, and the interpretive activities of readers and writers. Materiality thus cannot be specified in advance; rather, it occupies a borderland—or better, performs as connective tissue [there's that word again]—joining the physical and mental, the artifact and the user.*

Once upon a time we talked about politics and metalepsis at the level of thematics, but Tomasula, along with many others over the course of the last few decades, if not the last few centuries—Max Ernst, Tom Phillips, Anne Carson, Chris Ware, *et al.*—are invested in the politics of structuration as well: in how, that is, every narrative procedure, every material choice in composition, be it in the replacement of commas with em dashes or insertion of a black page in *Tristram Shandy*, the creation of a book that shows up as a sheaf of loose pages in a box that invites the reader to choose the order and amount s/he reads in Marc Saporta's *Composition No. 1*, or the archeological layering of different colors of paper comprising *The Book of Portraiture*, implies a cluster of political and metaphysical resonances.

Deciding to render a narrative one way rather than another, out of one substance rather than another, *means* profoundly, and so the question for the innovative writer always takes some form of the following, either consciously or unconsciously: do I retell received stories, thereby perpetuating their deep-structure lesson that the world should remain as it is, or do I wrench those stories, invent counternarratives? Because, once upon a time, *travel* and *travail* were the same words. The *OED*'s first definition of the former: to torment, distress; to suffer affliction; to labor, toil; to suffer the pains of childbirth. Serious travel—whether through a radically alien country or a radically alien text—is accompanied by an element of calamity that can run the gamut from mild discomfort to affliction, depending on who you are, when you are, where, with whom.

Why, I wonder, hasn't more been written about reading as a mode of productive pain—a theory of writing/reading as a mode of S&M?

The travail, one could argue, of traversing *TOC*, is how it arrives—as do many hypermedial texts—foremost as a reading dilemma, a series of questions minus familiar solutions. How, the reader/viewer/listener is asked to ask, do I travel such a complication, not in a figurative sense (with regard to establishing the impression of a coherent plot, sense of character, architectural thematics), as she or he might in most novels, but physically? How, the participant is asked to ask, do I pilot this prosthesis for my brain with mouse or finger? To a greater degree than with most novels, nearly every manifestation of the hypermedial becomes a fresh (dis)embodied exploration of not-knowing, an irruption of the material in the immaterial.

And so let me begin again, this time in Barthes's voice: *No literature in the world has ever answered the question it asked, and it is this very suspension which has always constituted it as literature: it is that very fragile language which men set between the violence of the question and the silence of the answer.*

Darko Suvin speaks of science fiction as the literature of cognitive estrangement. So it is with most formidable writing practices. By the medium's nature—that is, by means of the medium's continuous cognitive estrangement of meaning making, its disquietings of normalizing practices—*TOC* brings forth the constant somatic code-breaking calculus by which we make a work to a greater or lesser extent intelligible. We could say *TOC—VAS*, too, but more on that soon—operates as performance of disclosure.

Das Heimlich (*the homey* as well as *the secret*) is also *Das Unheimliche* (*the un-homey* as well as *the uncanny*), but *Das Unheimliche* has been displaced from plot or character into shape itself.

Late in *VAS*, the narrator recounts how strange the family's move to Flatland has made Square feel. It used to be the case that his wife Circle would follow him as he followed this or that job prospect. Now their roles are reversed: Square finds himself following her as she follows her own options. And hence he spends all his time being-at-home not being at home, solo and adrift (daughter Oval is off in school much of the day): "So, he did what spouses of the-one-with-the-job have always done: Gone boating. But since there weren't any oceans in Flatland, his sail was a blank whiteness and his oar a pen and he began to write, *First pain, then knowledge* ..."

With that, Square starts composing a version of the book we are reading, whose opening words are exactly those: *First pain, then knowledge*. They take us back to the novel's inaugural language, where Square accidentally receives a paper cut and kisses his finger, part Judas, part lover, examining "the world he'd been writing into existence" on the page lying in his lap. The weird winks and withdraws. Partially this is because there is a good chance the reader has forgotten through an operation of underreading that the third-person narrative mash-up she or he is wandering originated from Square's pen, that Square is the narrator of Square's story, that we are reading something like his autrebiography, since it isn't quite his memoir (he thinks of himself throughout as someone else; he seems to be writing, impossibly, both as we are reading and after the fact), and partially because he or she has just been further mislocated in a text built on mislocation, where textuality itself has been made uncanny in Ernst Jentsch's sense of a situation producing "intellectual uncertainty" as well as in Freud's of an encounter with "something that was long familiar to the psyche and was estranged from it only through being repressed," then encountered again in a different form.

In this case ("his sail was a blank whiteness and his oar a pen and he began to write ..."), the uncanny arises through Tomasula's adoption of a particular narrative technique: *metalepsis*—that frame-rupturing procedure, that unsettling violation of narrative levels common to metafiction wherein the world of the told becomes contaminated by the world of the telling. Such moments call the participant's attention to her or his own engagement within the unfolding event of reading, and hence to his or her own engagement within the constantly unfolding reminder that reading is nothing if not re-writing.

Yet it isn't merely that the words *first pain* initially appear at the beginning of *VAS*. It is also how they appear: in a comic-book font inside a drawn box below which floats a comic-book sign for the tiny explosion of hurt Square experiences as the hospital form he is filling out (and not, as we are led to believe when this compressed scene is reiterated-cum-variation later in the novel, a page from the autrebiography he seems to be composing) slices his finger (proleptic intimation of Square's vasectomy encountered down the narrative highway—and hence those references to lover and Judas, both, when he kisses his finger). The materiality of the page physically changes Square's relationship to it even as in another sense it changes the reader's.

Besides that tiny explosion, the page on which the words *first pain* first appear is blank, the word-duet unsituated in time (which is to say unsituated in narrative), but fully situated in space (which is to say situated in design), untethered to the right and slightly below the page's center. The reader must turn the leaf to find the thought completed and hence signification established: *then knowledge*—although, oddly, that *Then* is capitalized, suggesting paradoxically (more on paradox in a bit) that it is the beginning of a new thought rather than the completion of a previous one. If the reader has read *VAS* before, she or he also knows that, given the novel's last scene—the doctor preparing his surgical instruments for Square's surgery—the novel's first words are a continuation of its last scene, its climax, which completes, not with a period, but an ellipsis, thereby forming an infinite hermeneutic loop.

That sort of narratological stutter-step permeates *VAS*, where paratext (here unfixed comic-book design) adulterates an already visually impure text constituted precisely from other paratexts (those forms, graphics, marginalia, and so forth) that are integral to the primary text, which means paratext collapses into text even as text collapses into paratext.

Or to rephrase using the language of artist books: *sign* becomes *gesture* even as *gesture* becomes *sign*. "That is," *VAS*'s narrator—who both is and isn't Square—tells us, "the message is the material. People and their stories being as inseparable as they are. Material also being the message, logically." Materiality also being the missive: the body of the text about the text of the body and a body called language calls attention to itself as a (de)formed, (dis)abled anatomy, a change in the nucleotide sequence of the literary genome we refer to as the novel—and, as we all know, genetic mutations are integral to evolution, which is to say bodily/textual/aesthetic innovation: a constantly fluctuating form based on constantly fluctuating forms. One could thus call Tomasula's a recombinant narrative—i.e., a narrative mutative as the DNA that is referenced throughout its physical and conceptual being(s)—and a narrative that recalls for us a possible definition of The Novel: an omniphagic literary undertaking always in the process of figuring out what it will be next.

Turning a page in *VAS* is similar to clicking a link in *TOC*: a surge of turbulence followed almost immediately by a surge of acclimatization, a Heideggerian concealment followed almost immediately by a Heideggerian unconcealment, as our eyes and hands decipher where to settle, how to proceed.

H. Porter Abbott speaks about narrative jamming as that technical maneuver which "arouses and then refuses to satisfy our narrative perceptions," and he cites by way of illustration how a painting like Francis Bacon's "Three Studies for Figures at the Base of a Crucifixion" discomposes a straightforward response by means of its ambiguities of subject matter, form, context, and lack of indications about what code-breaking strategies the viewer should enlist to provide interpretive coherence.

Tomasula jams narrativity in both *VAS* and *TOC* by two kinds of metalepsis: rhetorical and ontological. For Marie-Laure Ryan, the former (an instance of which we see enacted in that pair of *first-pain-then-knowledge* passages) "opens a small window that allows a quick glance across levels, but the window closes after a few sentences, and the operation ends up reasserting the existence of the boundaries," whereas the latter "opens a passage between levels that result[s] in their interpenetration, or mutual contamination." Alice Bell and Jan Alber take the distinction between rhetorical and ontological metalepsis further, pointing out only the latter involves "disorienting transgressions of boundaries that are physically or logically impossible, and hence properly unnatural"—in other words, properly anti-mimetic in the sense that they violate logic by re-presenting situations that are contrary to fact in the actual world.

Metalepsis is the primary mode of narrative jamming in both VAS and TOC because, no matter which others are brought to bear in the texts, the reader is aware (as part of an ergodic operation of which she or he isn't aware when moving through normative narratives) that he or she is part of a corporeal event.

That event evinces itself both *in* the text (*VAS*'s posthumanist de-emphasis on deep character that asks us to contemplate in what other ways character might be conceived as a marker for our social sense of diffused, plural, messy identity) and *of* the text (which is committed, as Tomasula has pointed out, to "making art that mirrors biological processes"—literal literary genetic and generic permutation).

To pick up *VAS* is to be asked to ask what the relationship is between its epidermal cover and the organs within; whether or not that cover (unlike most codices, which are designed and controlled by publishers rather than authors) is where we are meant to begin making semiotic sense of the text; how we should treat and physically navigate the various sorts of charts, photographs, drawings, tests, scribbles, epigrammatic narraticules, and other formal elements in *VAS* that are part of the signifying system we term this text; what sort of work our eyes should do with the DNA sequence that confronts us with twenty-five pages of genetic code (the words *THE FACTS*—indicating we are nothing if not our biological [and cultural and aesthetic] codes—are easy to miss, buried as they are deep within the twenty-fourth); what sort of work our hands should do when they encounter a fold-out page on one side of which is printed an elaborate family tree echoing the satiric impulse on the reverse where the participant comes upon the fusion and confusion of DNA data with a lyrical meditation about the generative potential of genetic/generic/linguistic impurity.

To pick up *TOC* is in certain ways an even more complicated affair because to pick up *TOC* is exactly not to pick up *TOC*, while it is at the same time to pick up a plurality of *TOC*s. The participant must first choose between the DVD iteration (which no longer functions on the current Apple OS) and the iPad app (which doesn't function on other tablets). Choose, and one is no closer to holding the thing itself. At best, the participant can hold a device that holds *TOC*—and yet she or he is more conscious of the holding than ever when holding the normative codex exactly because the holding is concurrently a not-holding.

In order to begin interacting with it, the participant is made aware of physically manipulating her or his cursor or his or her finger-as-cursor; made conscious he or she has entered an ontologically metaleptic field of play (and pain?) where she or he is both prosthetically inside and corporeally outside the text, *here* having infiltrated *[t]here.*

Click on the faux-button that opens the app (accompanied with the sound of a bell, sonic indicator of passing minutes), and meet a polymodal prelude in the form of an epigraph from St. Augustine's *Confessions* about the unknowability of time hovering across the image of a star-misted galaxy accompanied by a warped (one could almost say out-of-time) waltz soundtrack: *What then is time? If no one asks me, I know; if I want to explain it to a questioner, I know not.*

In addition to announcing *TOC*'s principle thematics—or, better, its essayistic thesis—those sentences reveal one of the project's fundamental structuring devices: paradox, that self-contradictory concept expressing possible veracity, the word descended from the Greek *paradoxon*: a statement which is contrary to expectation, unexpected, strange (one could almost say uncanny). St. Augustine's observation fades out even as a narrator's voice begins to speak: "A distant world shines from another's past that is simultaneously our future. Is this a ripple in time, or in life?" An instant, and then text scrolls across the screen: "How is it possible for a day to start at dawn and also midnight? Is it time, language, or us that has such fuzzy boundaries?"

With that, the participant drops like Alice down a digital rabbit hole into an investigation of duration that, structurally, is to a great degree—again paradoxically—actively spatial.

The human mind organizes time (*chronos*) by narrativizing events, which is to say by means of rational discourse (*logos*), but *TOC* problematizes temporality even as it problematizes narrativity by making the borders between the two permeable, the ideas on either side of the binary both commensurate and incommensurate.

Such tensions are literalized through the myth of Chronos and Logos to which the text turns next. Chronos, we learn, believes he should ascend to the throne because he is first born. Logos believes he should ascend to the throne because he is first born. Both are—yet again paradoxically—correct and incorrect: the ship on which their mother, Ephemera, birthed them as she fled her troubled homeland crossed into an earlier time zone during its journey. While Chronos was therefore born first early Friday morning, Logos was also born first late Thursday night. A never-ending struggle ensues between the brothers (and the seeming binarism they represent); and the participant, like the inhabitants of the island on which Ephemera and her sons finally settle, is directed to wager who will win by plunking a digital stone into one of two digital boxes.

The answer, given the hypermedia's narrative logic, is neither and both, the point being that the two boxes are really one box (and not precisely one box) seen from dissimilar angles: narrative is time organized even as time is narrative organized. Each term (dis)arranges the other. Drop the stone one finds on the right side of the screen into Chronos's box (even if at first glance the eye is unclear where to go, what to do, whether the object represents stone or something else, whether it is a significant locus of attention or whether one's reconnaissance should take one in another direction altogether), and the top slides off to expose a player-piano roll interface and half-hour-long audio narrative (which, like that ellipsis at the end of *VAS*, forms an infinite hermeneutic loop). This postmodern reconfiguration of the oral tradition concerns an unnamed Vogue model whose husband hovers in a timeless coma following a terrible car accident. An embodiment of the posthuman as an "organic machine," he is attached to a respirator and pump circulating his blood. The model—pregnant by her brother, a "man of scientific bent" with whom she has had an affair (another bio-cultural binary made impure)—sits beside her husband's hospital bed in another kind of timelessness, torn from her hectic, glitzy routine, waiting for something to happen even as it already has, contemplating both an abortion (a clinamentic beginning) and unplugging her partner from life support (a clinamentic conclusion).

But the narrative begins re-looping before she makes her decision: that non-moment of choice remains pregnant, both a prebirth and afterbirth, the fairytale assumptions connoted by the once-upon-a-time pivot undone by time moving forward relentlessly, while also going in circles, while also forever fetched up at the cusp of resolution.

Drop the stone one finds on the right side of the screen (even if at first glance the eye is *et cetera*) into Logos's box and the top slides off to expose a player-piano roll interface which the participant must physically probe before understanding how it works. Touch that interface and crosshairs appear. Every time it zeroes in on one of the highlighted slots, a bell (like the one at the entrance to *TOC*) sounds: the red slots link to short videos; the blue slots link to a series of mythological narratives written on what appear to be sepia-colored text scrolls within a bell-jar frame; the green slots link into Ephemera's past, which also illogically seems to be her future.

Everybody's body is in essence a kind of time machine—a Difference Engine, of which Ephemera is inventor and with which, impossibly (or, perhaps better, metaphorically), she is pregnant (thereby echoing the Vogue model's situation of a vital gravidity that is simultaneously a kind of death)—a time machine that experiences the second law of thermodynamics from the inside out. And so it is, we learn, with civilizations. Ephemera's comes apart, but before it does she escapes onto a ship where she will birth, one imagines, the belligerent brothers Chronos and Logos.

Another way of saying this: we are confronted with another metaleptic leap that corrupts one narrative frame with another: *TOC* ends where it begins, and the participant finds him or herself reading myths created by the cultures apparently founded by Ephemera on her newfound island. Yet those micro-narratives—like the ones housed in the bell jars, containers built to protect precious relics as well as mere bric-a-brac—are what Barthes calls artificial myths, the kind reconstituted and turned back upon themselves in order to rupture the ideological coherence and naturalness implied by controlling mythologies.

In a Debordian gesture, *TOC* derails Myth even as it perpetuates "myths."

Both *VAS* and *TOC* lead to forced dislocation wed to an invitation to contemplate the idea of locality, and they question the concept pregnant within itself: Where am I when I am reading/rereading, writing/re-writing?

I recall Oliver Schneller's soundscape *Polis. Istanbul—Cairo—Jerusalem—Beirut*, an eight-channel aural montage commissioned in 2009 by the Berliner Festspiele as part of an exhibition entitled "Taswir: Pictorial Mappings of Islam and Modernity." Schneller's sonic installation generates the illusion on the listener's part of being in four places at once by producing ambient noise from a quartet of geographically disparate locations through an octet of speakers: 11:00 a.m. in Cairo, 11:00 a.m. in Beirut, 11:00 a.m. in Jerusalem, 11:00 a.m. in Istanbul. What, the listener is asked to ask, does auditory identity sound like, if it sounds like anything at all?

VAS and *TOC*, through their deployment of onotological metalepsis, raise a similar question with respect to the happening labeled reading, re-reading, writing, re-rewriting: the participant reads as she or he listens, listens as he or she views, touches as she or he forgets (and doesn't forget) about touching, is ceaselessly reminded of being both fully *here* and *there* even as he or she is neither fully anywhere, yet many places at once.

What's extraordinary for me about these texts is the kind of static they introduce into the various mechanics of meaning construction. The consequence of such unnatural structurations allows what our culture has made inconspicuous through its mobilization of the chronic to become discernable again, not simply for aesthetic reasons, but as a means to re-open a space of radical politics. Through the creation of an aesthetics of contamination inimical to the ones familiar to target audiences (here let us call those familiar ones myths, in Barthes's sense, as well as expressions of the corporate novel), Tomasula appropriates and perverts the grammar of the distractive habitual, while making the participant re-conscious both of the procedures of the spectacular—which is to say the dynamics of power, which is to say the dynamics of reading and writing—and the opportunity for non-normative narrativity in the world, which is to say non-normative modes of individual and social existence.

LOST IN AMERICA

Painting Daniel Boone's portrait, Chester Harding asked the frontiersman if he had ever been lost. "No, I can't say I was ever lost," Boone replied, "but I was bewildered once for three days." I was bewildered once for seventeen years, the whole of my childhood near the interminable climate-controlled stretch of shopping malls and parking lots called Paramus, because for some reason I always had the sense that New Jersey and New York and for all I knew the whole of the Northeast had been mysteriously grafted onto the real America. So I ended up going to the midwest for college and to the southeast for graduate school, and afterwards I took a job at the University of Kentucky because I intuited that I would get a better education teaching there than at one of the bigger schools in one of the bigger urban areas. During the autumn of our second year in Lexington, my wife, Andi, an artist who taught art history part-time at the University, was reading the real estate ads in a local greensheet in her office before class one evening for a kick when her eye caught this: "FOR SALE: Remote cabin on 15 acres, Red River Gorge. Cliffs, caves, waterfalls. 1000 sq. ft., 2 BR, electricity. Great for relaxing, hiking, writing. Under $12,000." When she showed it to me I couldn't believe what I was seeing. We phoned the owner immediately and drove out the next weekend to have a look.

Remote was seventy miles east of Lexington, in Meniffee county, first on a highway and then on a series of winding and increasingly hilly and wooded backroads through towns with names like Camargo (pop. 450) and Bagdad (pop. 250) and Grants Lick (pop. 50); past fields of yellow-green tobacco and the Primitive Baptist Church which was no larger than a small sagging garage; past the Lucky Stop Pentecostal Barn which doubled as a used-car lot; past block letters in white paint on the side of another gray barn that spelled SECULAR HUMANISM IS THE DEVIL'S WORK; and into and out of the last town, Frenchburg (pop. 296), which consisted of a Methodist church, a Piggily Wiggily Food Mart, a post office and Mom's Kuntry Kitchen. Remote was first running out of paved road and then running out of graveled road and then finding your white Dodge Colt spattering through seven-inch-deep mud puddles and lurching through hip-high wild grass and bobbing over dried red dirt to the point you weren't sure if you were on a road anymore or not. Remote was no running water and no indoor plumbing and no heating and no insulation and holes in the roof and the glass in the front door shattered last winter by a hunter searching for some warmth who left a thank-you note tacked on the wall near the fireplace. Remote was heaven in my head and the real America pounding through me crazily. We bought the place the next day.

Initially we drove up once or twice a month. We brought tools and secondhand furniture and we worked. We had the roof fixed, a phone put in, a new front door put on, sunk a well whose water we discovered was undrinkable because of the coliform count. We decided we couldn't afford insulation and that a hot water heater was pretty much an extravagance that would probably crack come a cold winter anyway. We labored through the fall, spent a frigid Thanksgiving and New Year's there, and set our noses to the grindstone again the next spring. By early summer we had begun to think of our house in Lexington as a place to do our business and our cabin ten miles outside of Frenchburg as our place of grace.

"If I seek the sense and skill of children, the information of a thousand books, the innocence of puppies, even the insights of my own city past, I do so only, solely, and entirely that I might look well at a creek," Annie Dillard writes in *Pilgrim at Tinker Creek*, one of my first favorite nonfiction books. My goals were neither so high nor so noble. All I wanted to be able to do was look well at our outhouse. It was a gorgeous thing, redwood and tidy, with the remains of an indoor-outdoor carpet on the floor and a bucket of lime and a plastic dove-colored cup in the corner. You sit with the door open in summer for the breeze and with the door open in winter for the view of naked pines and cedars sloping down gently in front of you and then abruptly falling away off a limestone cliff into thousands of acres of uninhabited forest. It is futile reading in there, futile thinking of any political system save democracy, perched as you are above the most egalitarian one in creation. My mother on her first slightly recalcitrant visit could not bring herself to say the word outhouse. "Let's call it The Cathedral," I suggested, and she did, and my wife and I soon picked up the same habit.

All I wanted to be able to do was look well at the five-inch-long acorn-brown lizard that waited every morning on our top step, head raised with dignity and alertness, reptilian grin frozen on his face. Or at the thousands of large astonishing jelly-bubble sacks of frog eggs in the puddles sprinkled through the woods; the blueblack rat snake that forms a black scrawl like a discarded bicycle innertube among the wild blueberry bushes and sassafras shrubs near the ledge at Whippoorwill Point on the eastern end of the property that rises 200 feet above the forest floor; the undulating bands of chestnuts and hourglasses which are the copperhead that coils in the leafy shadows of a rotten log, arrogant and only apparently lethargic.

John Chapman, better known as Johnny Appleseed, could see snakes better than I. Once he was bitten by a poisonous one and lived to tell about it and someone later asked him what had become of his assailant. "The poor thing!" Johnny Appleseed responded. "Hardly had it touched me that I, overcome by godless passion, cut off its head with my sickle." I shot mine. The spring after we bought the cabin, I bought a 38-gauge shotgun. All my northeastern discomfort about the evil of firearms vanished in a flash the first time I saw a short stubby ochre squiggle looking up at me with its black glassbead eyes. There are few things as powerful and as concentrated as the joy of killing a symbol of darkness, except perhaps running a chainsaw at full throttle in the afternoon sun, that megalithic roar in the head, that spray of magically scented woodchips collecting around you. Opal Smallwood, my farmer-neighbor a mile up the road, knew this better than I. One spring he shot no fewer than twenty-three rattlers in one of his fields alone.

Now I better understand all those shotguns you see in the back windows of those shiny black pickups with over-sized wheels speeding along the backroads at twilight. I better understand the bangs you hear at midnight down in the forest somewhere behind the screech of cicadas. People are coon hunting. As you lie in bed you can hear the dogs barking. My neighbors did it for fun, but more importantly they did it to survive. No one within a five-mile radius of my cabin had a steady job. Or to put it more plainly, their steady job was subsistence. They farmed two or three acres. They made squirrel burgoo. They made that sour smell that comes drifting into the cabin with birdsong on hot foggy summer mornings—the stills down in the nearby hollow. My neighbors ran them for a little extra cash.

I don't, however, understand all those rebel flags you see in the same back windows of those same shiny black pickups with the same over-sized wheels speeding along the same backroads at twilight. "Remember the Civil War!" the flags seem to be saying. "Remember the South!" But Kentucky was on the north's side. It had wanted to stay neutral, only in 1861 Confederate troops invaded from the west and so the legislature created a military force to drive them out, and Grant helped. So did most of the Kentuckians. Seventy-five thousand of them fought for the Union. Only 35,000 fought for the Confederacy. That seems to me a lovely signature of the state, a place that can never quite parse what it is, what it was; can never quite decide whether it should side with Abraham Lincoln or Jefferson Davis, both of whom were born in this part of country less than a hundred miles apart. Those rebel flags ask, "Should we be northern or should we be southern, eastern of midwestern, rich or poor, Democrats, Republicans, or what?"

Such regional schizophrenia was registered by my students at the University as well. They found book learning useless because books, they believed, didn't help you bag a coon or cook up lamb fries, but they also sensed that book learning was associated with success, whatever they thought that meant. So my coeds diligently took notes in my American survey course but, like students everywhere, had utterly no sense of the past. History was thin as air at 39,000 feet. Come exam time, they informed me with sure seriousness and the best of intentions that Freud published *The Interruption of Dreams* in 1900 and the Civil War took place between 1964 and 1968 at Columbia University. On weekends they packed up and traveled for hours—the state is 350 miles from the eastern border to the western, 175 miles from the northern to the southern—back to their all-white counties (during the sixties only one building burned on campus and that was because of an accidental electrical short), in which the ten commandments are pegged to the wall of every schoolroom, and where their parents referred to Lexington as Sodom and Gomorrah and where everything made perfect sense to them. They have an iron-strong and near medieval sense of community, so it's not for nothing that my colleague and friend there, Guy Davenport, in an essay called "Hobbitry," tells how interested J. R. R. Tolkien used to be in Kentucky. And it's not for nothing that one of my students, a woman in her forties, dropped a class of mine after first telling me she would pray for me because she learned that I had been raised Unitarian. And it's not for nothing that at the end of their formal education students leave the state for twelve months, maybe twenty-four, even forty-eight, but give them enough time and pretty soon you'll see them strolling the streets of their hometown again, tugged back to Kentucky by some irrefutable gravity of common roots and common thought.

There is another side to such a strong feeling of place and people, and that is an almost unbelievable sense of kindness. Opal Smallwood was over one morning for coffee and noticed out the window that a large dead pine was threatening our cabin. I told him I would have cut it down but I didn't have the knack yet of aiming felled trees and was worried it might hit the electrical lines or, worse, the roof. We went on talking about other things and soon I forgot all about the pine. The next day Opal showed up with his brother Virgil and Virgil's chainsaw and without asking they cut down that tree and two others which looked as though they might give me problems if a storm came up. Afterward, I asked if I could pay them for their work. "Ain't there such a thing as bein' neighborly?" Opal asked, befuddled.

Gurney Norman, another colleague and Appalachian writer-friend, tells the story of how he visited an eighty-year-old woman who had spent more than a month sewing an exquisite crazy-quilt for him. When Gurney asked how much he owed her for her effort she said forty dollars. He offered her 200, arguing that her time alone was worth more than that, not to mention the dazzling beauty of the thing itself, but she wouldn't hear of it. So he paid her the forty dollars and then sought out her son, who was working in a nearby gas station. Gurney asked him to change the oil and while the son worked Gurney explained what had just happened with the quilt. "Christ," the son said after a while, "the old folks ain't got no sense of the price of things these days. You go right back there and tell her I said she got to take your money." "I'll do that," Gurney said, relieved. "By the way, how much do I owe you for the oil change?" "That'll be a dollar twenty-five," the son replied.

Walter Abish came to the University to give a fiction reading one spring (I had put together a series of innovative writers featuring Ronald Sukenick and William Gass), and Andi and I took him out to the cabin to show him what sort of America we had found. We met Homer Ingram, another neighbor, whom we had hired to build us a porch. Homer was measuring and sawing wood in back of the cabin when we arrived. Walter was obviously a little flustered to meet a native Kentuckian but he recovered almost immediately and, eager to make pleasant conversation, put on his lovely European charm, picked up a board that was lying close by, and asked in his faint Germanic accent: "Is this what they call a two-by-four?" Homer gently took the board from Walter and asked: "You work at the University, too?"

Every Friday evening was visiting night around Frenchburg. Often, and always without warning, Homer stopped by with his wife and daughter around eight o'clock. Andi and I offered them coffee. Invariably they turned it down. An academic, I can't stand space that isn't busy with language, so I invented small talk, asked Homer what to do in case a copperhead bites you. "Dip your arm in kerosene," he said. "Kerosene?" I repeated, always just a little on guard in case I was missing some irony. "Yep," he said. Then he settled back and smiled, and his wife smiled, and his daughter smiled, and Andi and I smiled, and we went on like that for perhaps five minutes. It took me a number of these visits to realize Homer wasn't shy and he wasn't tongue-tied and he certainly wasn't being ironic. He just didn't have anything to say and he didn't see the use of wasting words.

My mother came to visit for a week and was terrified at the prospect of accidently stepping on a snake, so took our snake-bite kit with her wherever she went. Walking down the gravel road late one afternoon, we ran into Ferrell Bailey. Ferrell was a retired school teacher and blind in one eye. He had a house maybe a mile down the road from us. My mother explained the worst thing about Kentucky was the prevalence of reptiles. "They aren't so bad,' Ferrell said. "You just shoot 'em." I thought my mother would hoot and run back to her car and drive away and I would never see her again. I thought she would be so afraid of bullets that I hid my shotgun before she came and never even mentioned I had one. But she didn't even flinch. "How?" she asked. "How what?" I asked. "How do you shoot them?" she asked Ferrell. Ferrell came by the next day and showed her with his rifle filled with birdshot. He took her into the woods and for an hour I heard snap after snap. When they returned again she was holding the gun. Ferrell said he would lend it to her for as long as she needed it. He also showed her how to pick raspberries and brought out a jug of moonshine for her once because she had wondered aloud what it might taste like.

One autumn after a rain Andi and I picked up our walking sticks and went out for a hike. The sky was a solid heavy gray and the leaves were all down and a keen chill was in the air. We followed a new trail to the forest floor and then deeper and deeper into the woods. The wet birches were the color of cinders. We could see our breaths and our fingers grew stiff and pink. We walked and talked for several hours, listened to wild turkeys in the distance, then decided to head back. But when we turned around we saw the trail had disappeared. It must have been growing smaller and less well marked the last mile or so. All we made out were trees and we were far enough down in the valley that we had no way of seeing any landmarks. "We're lost," Andi said. My heart clattered, then stilled, and with her words I suddenly realized we'd finally gotten to where we had been heading all along.

3

SPEECH ACTS

WITH FLORE CHEVAILLIER

In your essay, "Fourteen Notes Toward the Musicality of Creative Disjunction, or Fiction by Collage," you observe the increasing production of "critifictions," or texts that break down the distinctions between criticism and fiction. Could you explain why you find this mode of writing particularly valuable in the context of fiction's present?

I'm not sure I'm interested in the question of "value" with respect to fiction's present. I'm not even sure I quite understand the use of such a word when discussing aesthetic issues, since it houses within it connotations of commerce, of monetary or material worth, of quantity—connotations inimical to serious writing practices.

Perhaps it would therefore be useful to replace the world "valuable" with "significant." If we ask why the increasing production of critifictions is particularly *significant* in the context of fiction's present, my answer would take some form of the following: the kind of fiction I've been responding to most over the last few decades, the kind that has been referred to as "innovative," "experimental," "alternative," "avant-garde," "postmodern" (all overdetermined, troubled and troubling terms), has been inextricably linked with a certain critical, or, better, theoretical consciousness. From one perspective, naturally, all narrativity save the most acutely cookie-cutter varieties (Harlequin romance, pulp science fiction, potboiler porn, and so forth) is "experimental" in that it involves countless acts of exploration and discovery on the part of the author and the reader. From another, however, such a statement is devoid of nuance, a sense of the larger conversation across time and space called literary history, and an understanding of the (ir)realities concerning the pragmatics of the contemporary American publishing industry.

Maybe closer to the point might be some provisional statement suggesting "experimental" narrativity is that which asks such questions as: *what is narrative? what are its assumptions? what are its politics and social dynamics? its limits? how does such narrative engage with the problematics of representation? identity? race? gender? temporality? spatiality? empathy? psychology? genre? ideas of "literature" and "the literary"? authorship? readership and the act of reading?* Another way to approach a tentative definition of "experimental" narrativity, in other words, might be to suggest it is the sort that includes a self-reflective awareness of and engagement with theoretical/narratological inquiry, concerns, obsessions.

What's significant to me about the proliferation of such postgenre, postcritical prose—this collapse of criticism into its object, this ongoing rich complication of the accepted difference between privileged and subordinate discourses—is the varieties of extraordinary forms, aesthetic and social critiques, and play to which it gives rise: The Difficult Imagination, I've called it, the sort that challenges what we suppose about texts (the world, it goes without saying, being one text among others).

How does the collapse of "theory and fiction" affect your writing?

My work is contaminated by a theoretical awareness, my criticism by a fictive one. And once you've left the Edenic garden of narrative innocence behind, well, there's no return ticket. I've been fascinated for decades by what Raymond Federman dubbed *critifiction*, but, in many ways because of my own training in the academy, I tried to keep my criticism and fiction categorically separate for a very long time, like two misbehaving children—until the turn of the century, when I began my novel *Girl Imagined by Chance*, a story concerning a childfree couple who invent a little one to appease the culture committed to being fretful and multiplying. Everything changed after that.

One of the principles that governs *Girl* is "hovering"—a refusal to nail down that occurs at different strata in the text. Obviously there's that hovering between a certain theoretical imagination and a certain creative one (Baudrillard is a strong presence in the book), between nonfiction and fiction, between fiction and poetry, even between words and image (in many ways, *Girl* is ultimately a text about the difficulties inherent in the idea of representation that employs photography as its dominant metaphor). There is also the hovering at the stratum of plot concerning the invented girl's physicality. Given the narrator's slightly unhinged mind, it's not surprising that his prose also exhibits a kind of hovering, a jitteriness, a failure to stick with any idea or feeling for more than a few arrhythmic heartbeats, thereby giving rise to what I hope is a kind of aesthetics of doubt.

Behind that aesthetics floats Wittgenstein's ghost. What I've always loved about him is how, toward the end of his life, he became increasingly possessed with trying to say what we might be able to know about the world with anything like conviction. The more possessed he became, though, the less he could be sure about. Something analogous seems true to me about any photograph: the more you study and contemplate one, the less you know about it. What can you say with anything like conviction about what's going on in it? When it was taken? What its relationship is to "reality"? How much has been "staged"? How much is "authentic"?

And one form of hovering that engaged me a great deal in *Girl* was between autrebiography and fiction. *Girl* is particularly intrigued by how much our memories of ourselves, our pasts, those events we think of when we set out to construct who we are, carry a deeply fictive charge, how we compensate for our lives being a series of distinct photographic instants in a sea of forgetfulness by generating narrative links, turning discrete shots into filmic (and forever disputable) narrative.

That critifictional frame of mind has followed me through my last several books, and is especially ascendant in *Anxious*

Pleasures, a retelling of Kafka's *Metamorphosis* that fractures the original (which, it turns out, wasn't strictly original to begin with) into a number of different points of view, some of which masquerade as (and some of which in fact quote) scholarly engagements with Kafka's text.

History is also central to your work. Can you say more about the relationship between fiction and history in your novels?

I'm drawn to artists and thinkers out of step with their times, those who tend to proceed through paralogy rather than homology toward creation, who believe, as Lyotard once pointed out, that "invention is always born of dissension." Now I'm not sure how much, if anything, my Kafka, or my Nietzsche, or my van Gogh have to do with the flesh-and-blood people who once shared those names. The relationship of fiction to yesterday in writing is nothing if not tricky. Those characters remain, despite the research I've done on them, constructs for contemplating the role of the artist or philosopher in our culture, as well as nuisances incarnate of what we think about when we think about selfhood and how it's manufactured for us and by us. That is, my characters ask in what sense all history, biography, and memoir are subsets of storytelling, what the connection might be between subjects acting in "the world" and "subjects" translated into syllables and sibilants.

My novel *Calendar of Regrets* is arguably more obsessed with these questions than most of my work. The text takes the shape of twelve interconnected narratives, one for each month of the year, all having to do with notions of travel—through space, through narrative, through death itself, and, of most consequence to our conversation, through history. For the first half, each of the first eleven narratives breaks off midway through, at which point the next narrative commences. For the second half of the text, each of the first eleven narratives concludes inconclusively, but in reverse order. Hieronymus Bosch inhabits one storyline, Dan Rather another, Iphigenia another, a journalist in Burma in 1976 another, and so on. Each of *Calendar*'s narratives is connected to the others, not through plot events or character, but rather through a musical structure of recurring metaphors and images, transpositions of the same scenes and/or phrases, and temporally transmuted subjectivities. The result, I like to wish, is a multiple narrative about narrativity itself, the human passion for trying to make sense through storytelling, how we tell ourselves and our cosmoses again and again in an attempt to stabilize them.

Writing that imagines itself to be history creates the illusion of endeavoring to get every bloodless fact right, whereas writing that imagines itself to be fiction can do something shockingly different: it can allow a reader to experience an experience from inside out, from within a character's consciousness, from motley subjective perspectives, release the scent of diesel into the air, the background sounds of trams clanking on the streets bordering Oosterpark in Amsterdam, the way the light falls on a field of wheat at twilight after a hot day in Auvers-sur-Oise, the cadences of a fanatic's voice. That's what really engages me: the complexities of a moment felt.

You mention the "(ir)realities concerning the pragmatics of the contemporary American publishing industry." Could you say more about such pragmatics, both as a writer and as the Chair of the Board of Directors at Fiction Collective Two?

If we checked in on American publishing in New York in the early sixties, we would discover more than a hundred thriving houses bringing out a plethora of innovative writers: Coover, Pynchon, Gass, Ishmael Reed, John Barth, Donald Barthelme. All of that began to change with the recession brought on by the 1973 oil crisis. Attention in the publishing industry shifted increasingly and inextricably from daring artistic investigations to the bottom line. Great editors were laid off. Publishers went under or were absorbed by larger conglomerates. What we've seen over fifty years or so, then, is what one might call the McDonaldization of US publishing: culture as fast-food franchise.

We could say the worst has already happened in the world of books. By and large they have come to seem an increasingly conservative, market-driven form of communication. In addition to the publishing situation in Manhattan, even bestsellers now exist in a secondary position in our society to the spectacles of film, television, the web, video games, the iPod, the iPad, the surveillance-capitalist devices we call our cellphones. Currently not a hundred thriving houses, but three behemoth media corporations dominate commercial publishing while employing the print arms of their swollen multinationals as tax write-offs. They consider low sales figures and small audiences tantamount to failure. More disheartening still, many independent presses have decided to mimic in miniature this preposterous paradigm rather than trying to subvert, re-imagine, or otherwise stand in opposition to it.

That isn't to suggest, of course, that Manhattan isn't bringing out some vibrant and surprising work (one need think no farther than José Saramago, David Mitchell, Don DeLillo, and Lydia Davis), but it is to suggest that Manhattan is bringing out less of it—far less of it—than it once did. Nor would I want to suggest that alternative presses don't bring out some embarrassingly bland, simple, sloppy work. Still, those alternative presses by and large remain sites of energized aesthetic, political, and philosophical resistance. They exist as aesthetic opportunities and where the work of such corporate authors as Dan Brown, John Grisham, or Danielle Steele simply aren't seen as enlightening.

It's as though, next to the universe of commercial publishing, there has come to exist an alternate one, as if we were living in one of Borges's stories, made up of authors who live completely different existences with completely different aims and ethics than those who are drawn to Manhattan. They bring out each other's work, read and review it, teach it at colleges and universities across the country, study it in essays, urge others to start up journals and presses to help get the word out about the fiction they love, fiction that takes the act of exploratory, frequently demanding writing in earnest—all that, and those people write their own fiction, too. I think of them, with the greatest respect and admiration, as literary activists.

If it's the case that the early twenty-first century is the worst of times for American fiction because of those market pressures that favor novels and short story collections that want to be films when they grow up, it's also the best of times because of these sorts of people. Competition in their universe has been replaced with collaboration. Corporate paradigms have been replaced with collective ones.

FC2's story in particular points to one future of American publishing by offering a successful model based on alliance and partnership, a production paradigm run by and for authors, the idea that it is less important to make a profit than it is to disseminate important heterodox projects. There are ways of caring about such fiction that Manhattan, to put it bluntly, can't begin to fathom. If executives there exhibit The McDonaldization Effect on publishing, the small, independent presses that have been proliferating across the States over the last three or four decades offer the equivalent of a mom-and-pop Vietnamese bistro down the block.

The one constant for Fiction Collective, and now Fiction Collective Two, is that there have been no constants except a commitment to its mission statement: "to publish books of high quality and exceptional ambition whose style, subject matter, or form push the limits of American publishing and reshape our literary culture." The Collective has always stood against, as one of its founders, Peter Spielberg (others, by the way, included Jonathan Baumbach, Steve Katz, and Ronald Sukenick), pointed out in 1974, its first year in existence, "books designed by cereal packagers, marketed by used-car salesmen ... and ruled or overruled by accountants."

That's more the case now than ever before. The Collective fashioned itself as an adaptable, flexible entity, and here we are nearly fifty years later (originally the idea was to put together a literary experiment that might last two or three, tops), with the help of such leaders as Curt White and R. M. Berry, having brought out some of the most diverse innovative writers of the second half of the twentieth and first half of the twenty-first centuries: Brian Evenson, Toby Olson, Leslie Scalapino, Raymond Federman, Lidia Yuknavitch, Harold Jaffe, Stephen Graham Jones, Noy Holland, Doug Rice, Samuel R. Delany, Michael Martone, Clarence Major, Vanessa Place, Aimee Parkison, Elisabeth Sheffield, Michael Mejia, Joanna Ruocco, and on and on. In addition, we established two contests to help identify and celebrate innovative writers not yet published by the Collective: the Sukenick, which comes with $1000 and publication by FC2, and the Doctorow, which comes with $15,000 and publication by FC2.

You also teach at the University of Utah. How does your understanding of formally innovative writing's current state and goals affect your teaching and translate into the institutional setting of the university?

It's pretty easy, unfortunately, to write merely competent fiction—the kind cranked out in most of the 350-or-so creative writing programs across the US: so-called well-crafted domestic realism where character is fleshy and Freudian, style transparent, plot pleasantly arced, and adversity always giving way to luminous moments of human connection and insight. My own approach to teaching writing is to dilemma that approach, become self-conscious about it, invite my students to conceive of fiction writing as an opportunity to explore, question, and rethink narrativity and its assumptions (which is to say explore, question, and rethink living and its assumptions)—all in workshops that are the opposite of therapy sessions. I call those spaces (the word *workshop* fraught down to the bone) Askings, where students conduct interviews with the authors whose writing is up for conversation. I urge my students to remain inquisitive and realize it's only at the brink of failure that liberating, illuminating breakthroughs occur.

At their best, I think, creative writing programs can be special, energizing zones of mutual support, mutual challenge, and personal-aesthetic growth by means of exposure to a profusion of defiant voices and approaches, both "creative" and "theoretical," both contemporary and historical. (In my creative writing zones, we're as likely to spend time discussing an essay by Bataille or Barthes, a novel by Ourednik or Pavić, a story collection by Garielle Lutz or Lucy Corin, a poetry collection by Susan Howe or Stephanie Strickland, a hypermedial project by Steve Tomasula or Young-Hae Chang, as student work.) At their worst, creative writing programs can be stultifying assembly lines that spit out flat, faded, predictable, well-made products in order to fill classrooms and make money for the institution, because making money is what education has devolved into, bringing us once more to the doorstep of McDonald's. But in either case—and perhaps this is their greatest contribution to our culture in the end—creative writing programs generate careful readers, thoughtful readers, close readers, self-reflective readers at a time when many literature courses teach how to think in sweeping ideological terms while employing texts in quite general terms as symptoms.

When talking about them, it's useful to keep in mind that creative writing programs usually exist within English departments that usually exist within some form of humanities divisions that exist within the larger institution of the college or university that is in ongoing crisis due to recent budget cuts, but, more importantly, due to the corporatization of higher education. Just yesterday I came across a story emblematic of this trend in, of all places, *USA Today*. A biology professor at LSU, Dominique G. Homberger, was removed from her teaching position mid-semester for refusing to artificially inflate her grades. Her transgressions, according to those in power, included giving quizzes at the beginning of each class, both to check on attendance and encourage students to keep up with reading, and failing to grade her tests on a curve (believing "students must achieve mastery of the subject matter, not just achieve more mastery than the worst students in the course"). Not only was she yanked from the classroom, but the administration also raised her students' grades after Homberger left—a gesture that brings up all sorts of sad questions about grade ballooning and professor autonomy, but also one that suggests just how much our institutions of higher learning are becoming places that value customer satisfaction over something like real critical thought and learning.

Put that together with smaller numbers of full-time faculty, greater numbers of lecturers and graduate assistants behind the desk at the front of the room, more work for less pay, fewer raises, overcrowded classrooms, necessarily less face-time between professors and students, shorter comments on papers and stories and tests as a result, the proliferation of online courses that sabotage human interaction and Socratic pedagogical models, more emphasis on silly national rankings that privilege quantity over quality, more emphasis on "outcomes assessment" than thinking, and a departmental atmosphere virtually everywhere rife with a sense of being under the gun (which invariably leads to greater tension and petty squabbles), and I wonder how many of us will be able to recognize what higher learning will have become in another five or ten years.

All of which is also to say my relationship to the academy is conflicted at best. The thing that keeps me here now is the extraordinary arena—even in its currently decadent form—of the classroom. It's one that exists nowhere else in our culture, and when a conversation is firing beautifully there—well, for me it gets no better. Still, I'm not at all clear on how long, given the above situation, that environment (or I) will last in any meaningful way.

You suggest that "texts that make us work, make us think and feel in unusual ways, attempt to wake us in the midst of our dreaming, and dream us in the midst of our waking, are more useful" than others that do the opposite. Yet, some think that when this "work" does not come from a direct response to current pressures in the content of fiction, it cannot be political. Are you implying that texts can resist, or at least question, the cultural developments you mention without addressing them directly in their content?

I mean to suggest that texts can critique dominant cultures, not only through their content, but also through their structure, their use of language, their problematics, the demanding processes one must learn to negotiate them. I tend to be fairly uninterested in texts whose politics—whatever those politics may be—are situated primarily and simply in their content and are primarily and simply effortless and obvious rather than involved and nuanced. I'm left blank before a novel like, say, Toni Morrison's *Beloved*, which wears its predictable social conscience on its sleeve, despite some absolutely beautiful language. I remember Marjorie Perloff once asking me, with reference to it, whether there were really still any readers out there who might come into contact with the book who would need convincing that slavery and slavery's specter were bad things. Morrison's novel, to put it differently, is telling us what we already know in ways we already know it. I simply don't find that a particularly appealing reading experience. I'm not suggesting novels invested unsubtly in identity or leftist or conservative or other politics shouldn't be read. I'm just suggesting I'm not going to be their most ideal reader.

I'm interested in the opportunities inherent in any individual sentence written by Ben Marcus's *The Age of Wire and String* or Vi Khi Nao's *A Brief Alphabet of Torture*—writing which seems, at least on the face of it, at least in terms of its content, nearly apolitical much of the time. Such writing's formalistics—different as they will surely be from example to example—are machines to help us wonder. *A Brief Alphabet* challenges us through its narratological, epistemological, and ontological conundrums to contemplate how we narrativize our worlds and why; reminds us that at root the word narration is related to the Proto-Indo-European word *gna*—to know. Every sentence, every paragraph in Gerald Murnane's *A Million Windows* asks us what a sentence or paragraph is, how they task, how language languages, what their relationship is to things, how they are always already manipulated, asks us by each sentence's or paragraph's very presence on the page to consider by whom and to what end. Such writing by its otherness tells us to remember variety and change at an existential level, which strikes me as an immensely significant social act.

Limit Texts, I've called them (varieties, Lydia Davis might say, of disturbance)—those that take various elements of narrativity to their brink so we can never think of them in quite the same ways again. To the brink, and then over. They're the sorts of texts that, once you've taken them down off the shelf, you can't put back up again. By being in the world, they ask us to embrace a politics of thought, freedom, radical skepticism. I imagine which texts comprise such a category will be different for each of us, depending on who we are, and where, and whence we've come. For me, today, they include such weirdly sundry texts as Jen Bervin's *The Desert* and Graham Rawle's *Woman's World*.

When reading Head in Flames, *I found myself wondering about which font of the story attracted me the most on each page, which one seduced me when I did not focus on processing the words only. I thought about what called my attention, and I asked myself: Do I usually look at fonts in prose this way? To me, this is an example of the formalistics you mention. Could you expand on your use of font and pagination in* Head in Flames *or in other novels, and perhaps of other explorations of formalistics in your work?*

Those fonts are emblematic of structuration-as-meaning. Every novel's form is also its politics. "Our satisfaction with the completeness of plot," Fredric Jameson once noted, is "a kind of satisfaction with society as well." One could say much the same about our satisfaction with undemanding style, character construction, subject matter, *et cetera*.

From that perspective, I've been interested in disruptive linguistic and architectonic shapes since *Tonguing the Zeitgeist*, that Avant-Pop novel I wrote in the early nineties about the commodification of the body. In it, Ben Tendo, an unassuming clerk at a porn supplier, Beautiful Mutants, Ltd., is kidnapped by a music corporation, forcibly addicted, implanted with a new voice box, and otherwise manufactured into the Next Big Thing. The book marked a kind of breakthrough for me, a movement into syntactic complexity and energy, as well as into structural perversions (frequent jump cuts, rapid point-of-view shifts, foregrounding detail over scene, deliberately hazing key plot points), which led me away from the relatively conventional shapings I was doing in my first two novels, *Live from Earth* and *Burnt*, and toward textual breaches—toward an understanding, to paraphrase Charles Bernstein, that narrative can be the possibility of possibility.

From the early nineties on, my wife Andi and I also began collaborating on text-image collages. Right now we're working on a series of fake diseases for her ongoing installation *Freak Show*. Once we began working closely together, the page lost its invisibility for me, became a conscious element in authorship. Recently, we collaborated on the entire text-image collage chapter in *Calendar of Regrets*.

Another important moment for me with respect to this idea of structuration-as-meaning occurred when I was working on *Girl Imagined by Chance*. Its first draft, although slanted in content (the young couple creates a make-believe daughter and make-believe existence for her in order to appease our culture of reproduction), was quite conventional in form, which didn't feel at all right to me, although I couldn't have articulated why. Shortly after finishing the first pass, I traveled to Finland on a Fulbright for half a year and rediscovered those stunning pared-down lines, not of northern European literature, but of northern European architecture—the sort imagined by Alvar Aalto, the so-called father of modern Nordic design, himself intrigued by the Cubist and collage impulses in artists like Braque and

Picasso. I worked on *Girl* almost every morning while in Turku, a town about an hour north of Helsinki by train, where Andi and I lived and where I taught at two universities, a Swedish and a Finnish, and by the third month there I noticed the sentences in my rewrite of the novel had changed dramatically, become leaner, more compact, more lyrical. The movement from one to the next worked less by conventional transition than by collage-like juxtaposition. I also became increasingly aware of white space—how the reduced, purified sentences floated in it on the page in ways that struck me as beautiful and somehow sad, cut off from their friends.

I returned to that notion of white space as Nordic formalistics in *Head in Flames*, and, as you noticed, also became interested in how font itself influences how we read, how we think of the text before us, how we (usually unconsciously) process it. I suppose for me there's some weird synesthesia at play. Early on in the writing process, my imagination came to associate a gentle, graceful Times font with Vincent Van Gogh. The brash bold version of that font seemed quintessentially Theo, a type of Michael Moore figure (only more so) in the Netherlands. And a font from an entirely different universe—elementary, brutal, even—felt right for Mohammed: a Courier for the courier delivering a message that the western world doesn't want to hear; one can't see that font, I think, without hearing the loud, unsettling clacks of the manual typewriter.

So the page has become increasingly part of the stage in my writing, affording, I like to think, its own contribution to the dynamics of the text, its own awareness of the author's role in the production of the text's materiality. I can't imagine that having happened without books like Federman's *Double or Nothing* or Theresa Hak Kyung Cha's *Dictee* being in the biosphere first. To know they exist, at least for me, is to be influenced by them.

I notice that you use the words "white space" instead of "blank space," a term often used to describe books like Head in Flames *or* Girl. *I've always found the word "blank" inadequate to talk about the page of such books because it implies that the text is lacking something in its whiteness. I am, however, interested in the notion of white space, and I suspect that, for you, it does not express a void or a lack. Could you say more about how you consider the white space, its materiality, its role?*

That's right. For me white space is never blank space, never void or absence, in my writing. It is invariably something else, even in the most conventional short story or novel, where it functions as a visual announcement that a modification in time, space, or point of view is occurring. In innovative fiction that function widens a good deal, frequently becoming something close to graphic metaphor. In Carole Maso's *Ava* the wash of whiteness on the page suggests the wash of death itself infecting the protagonist. In Mark Danielewski's *House of Leaves*, white space is emblematic of the not-knowing that pervades the novel, the Nothing at the text's and the house's heart. In Beckett's *How It Is*, it functions as a kind of musical notation: the breaths the protagonist takes on his eternal crawl through the mud. And there's that startling splash of it following the final period of the nine-page semantic erasure that "concludes" his *Unnamable*: a torrent of white silence that gestures toward what self and text have become, present absence and absent presence, the trace of all that's there that isn't there.

In *Girl Imagined by Chance*, white space operates in an architectural capacity, as I say, while in *Head in Flames* it operates in several roles at once: as metaphor for the absolute distances separating the voices and visions of Vincent, Theo, and Mohammed, each a kind of artist manifesting an aesthetic position unconditionally inconsistent with the others; as Cubist design principle reminiscent of the one at work in *Girl*; as the silences that refuse to be silenced in our culture, and yet are, and yet aren't, as first Vincent's voice, then Theo's, and finally Mohammed's flicker out of existence during the course of the last third of the book. *Calendar of Regrets* couldn't exist in its present form without my growing consciousness of what is materially present and un-present on every page.

You mentioned your use of photography in Girl, *which is another way to approach textual materiality. Because you've also experimented with visual texts before* Girl, *I wonder if your approach to them might have changed from your earlier projects to your later explorations.*

When Andi and I first started playing around with text-image collages in the nineties, the process involved literally cutting and pasting—creating text-images by scissoring found visuals and gluing them on a page, then adding words, then photocopying or scanning. Very Max Ernst. The process was much more tactile back then, which I confess I miss a little these days.

When Andi moved completely to the computer, all sorts of new prospects opened up, including the illusion of seamlessness in the finished product, which illusion, interestingly, can generate a stronger sense of the uncanny in the reader/viewer—you know, something so perfect that it actually disconcerts. One image in our fake diseases project shows an elderly woman with her mouth sutured shut. Andi digitally manipulated the photograph of sutures she had on her own leg (the result—long story—of a chainsaw accident she suffered several years ago) and, as it were, grafted those onto that woman's face, which was appropriated from, I believe, an old psychiatric textbook. The consequence is so realistic as to be doubly deeply strange. With the photographs in *Girl*, and those in *Calendar*, the manipulations are subtler, but the consequence is the same: a *trompe l'oeil* that amounts to a rupture in habituation. Andi and I also explore, in another chapter in *Calendar*, as I mentioned, the idea of layout, and, in another, I'm exploring words *as* images, single words as having a very real visual component to them.

Living with Andi's remarkable sense of sight for more than 40 years has taught me so much. And I've always been attracted to highly visual writers like Laird Hunt, Guy Davenport, and (oddly, perhaps, considering his blandly suburban plots and characters and forms) John Updike when I was a teenager; always been attracted to page manipulators like Anne Carson and Steve Tomasula; always been attracted to painters, sculptors, new-media artists, filmmakers; always been fascinated by how the purely visual can usually do a lot more work a lot more quickly than can the purely linguistic (think of any four square inches of a polyptych by Bosch, or any dense panel in Gibbons' and Moore's *The Watchmen*, and recall how many narratives are at play there, how many intimations), yet also by how the visual performs in remarkably different ways in different media.

You mention your collaboration with Andi, and you have explored collaboration throughout your career. Our discussion is a different mode of collaboration, one that involves a weaving of ideas through our written exchange. Would you care to comment on your views concerning the interview form?

These are the oddest things for me, these written interviews that take their course over a period of months and yet engender the illusion of unedited spontaneity, improvisation, facility … while in reality taking the form of carefully constructed artifacts—fictions (like memoir, like history), perhaps we could call them, that masquerade as nonfiction, as unmediated structures of communication, even as they meticulously stage voice, character (which should never feel like character), plot, rhythm. Later in life, Nabokov refused to give real-time ones because he was keenly self-conscious about how stuttery and stupid he could sound in them. Even for those he did participate in that impersonated face-to-face ones, Nabokov would, as I recall, sit up in his room at the Montreux Palace Hotel in Switzerland and have the interviewer sit down in the lobby. The interviewer would then write a question on a card, which he would send up. Nabokov would write out his response, which he would send down. Such a process allowed them, as our interview does us, to think in slow motion. I wouldn't have it any other way. Who in the world wants to watch an interviewer and writer think in real time? The consequence, at best, would usually be the same as art speeded up and flattened out: heat rather than light.

I'm grateful for the opportunity here to shape what amounts to a necklace of mini-essays, a collage. Looking back, I hear silence after silence among what we've said that could have been filled with interesting sound, but we've covered some wonderfully productive, suggestive ground. I greatly appreciate it, greatly appreciate your sharp questions, Flore, that have taken us both into spaces we didn't know we were heading toward. What we've generated has underscored the sense that collaboration is the basic mode of most writing, most creation, although our culture usually likes to repress the fact. The only thing we're doing here that most writers aren't is acknowledging the obvious: we're producing something neither of us could have produced alone, and have thereby taken ourselves to destinations we couldn't have imagined before beginning our journey, and most likely not even then. How can one not love that?

WITH MICHAEL LACKEY

Lance, thank you for doing this interview. I really appreciate it. As you know, Georg Lukacs's The Historical Novel, *published in the mid-1930s, is considered one of the most insightful and exhaustive studies of the historical novel. In that work, he argues that the biographical form of the novel is doomed to failure because the focus on "the biography of the hero" leads authors to overlook or misrepresent significant historical events and truths and thus "reveals the historical weakness of the biographical form of the novel." Given the nature of his critique, he would say that* Nietzsche's Kisses *and* Head in Flames *are not just failures—he would argue that they were doomed to failure from the outset because the very form of the biographical novel is limited and even flawed. How would you respond to Lukacs's critique?*

Thank *you*, Michael. Let me begin by challenging a couple of Lukacs's assumptions. He's working with a set that immediately strikes me as quaint. For example, he seems to believe in some kind of transcendental truth: that we can easily define what history or the novel is. Such assumptions reveal a monolithic imagination. Part of what *Nietzsche's Kisses* and *Head in Flames* are doing, part of what historical and biographical novels in general are doing, at least by my lights, is problematizing those assumptions—problematizing our relationship to "truth," "history," and, ultimately, narrative itself: how we tell ourselves, our past, our cultures, and the like.

That is, I might, by way of my critique of Lukac's critique, point out that interpretation is a mode of closure. Our first instinct when we approach a novel is to limit it, totalize it, deaden it into containment. Yet each time we enter the inexhaustibility called a novel, the thing before us becomes a different novel because we're different people who are reading it at different times, in different places, in different contexts, through different frameworks. The inexhaustible, I would argue, is the only productive strategy to deploy when discussing "biography," "history," "truth," and what have you.

Given your claims, would you say that it's problematic to even refer to your novels as "biographical novels?"

Let me think a moment. I suppose it might be accurate to say my biographical novels are the investigation of the impossibility of biographical novels, even as they are examples of them. A fruitful way to get into this may be to discuss science fiction novels for just a minute. Some of us read SF novels with the assumption that they are out to make claims about what the future might look like. We read William Gibson's *Neuromancer* and say: "Oh, he predicted cyberspace accurately, but missed cellphones, and that's a point against him." But that's absurd. Science fiction novels are about something else altogether. They're a continuous lesson about how the future will never be knowable. They teach us again and again that ten minutes from now will be an enigma. In other words, what SF novels do is problematize our notions of prolepsis, futurity. Historical and biographical novels undertake a similar meta-project with respect to the past and identity. They're not about yesterday and/or selfhood. They're about the difficulties of trying to capture yesterday and/or selfhood, about how such spaces are elusive and multiple. If we're paying attention, they draw our attention to something other than what they seem to be drawing our attention to.

Putting aside for the moment some of your quibbles with the designation "the biographical novel," can you explain why there has been an explosion of these kind of novels since the 1980s, and can you offer some sort of explanation? Can you explain why you decided to write such a novel, with the focus on a particular character like Nietzsche?

I'm not so sure the position I'm voicing with respect to "the biographical novel" could be considered "quibbles." I want to suggest something much more fundamental than that. But I have to confess, until I talked with you, I didn't realize that there had been an explosion of these novels since the 1980s. I've been interested for years in novels having to do with pastness, especially when the idea of pastness itself registers as interrogation.

Linda Hutcheon's term, historiographic metafiction, is particularly productive here. Historiographic metafiction refers to a kind of writing practice that's self-conscious about the complexities involved in narrativizing last week—a weird (for lack of a sharper term) postmodern beast that is both trying to tell history and think about how we tell our history simultaneously. Novels like Coover's *The Public Burning*, which is about the events that led up to Julius and Ethel Rosenberg's execution, but which is also about the predicament involved in telling those events. There are parts of that novel that are linguistically explosive, hallucinogenic, in ways that destabilize all the other parts, call attention to their making, lead the reader to question the authenticity of any monologic perspective on history. Couple that impulse, in the case of *Nietzsche's Kisses*, with a much more prosaic one: I've always been interested in Nietzsche, interested knotting the way Nietzsche has come down to us, drawing attention to the many different Nietzsches that history has written. I discovered that the more I investigated this noun, *Nietzsche*, the less I understood it, understood its antecedent—and in really interesting ways. The more you look into the Nietzsche function, let us call it, the less you can say about it from any sort of privileged position. To study that function is to study how to unlearn it. For some reason, that's an enterprise that delights me.

You know, in Nietzsche's Kisses, *one of the things I've noticed is that you alter historical fact. Here I really want to challenge you. I want to ask you if this is legitimate. I mean, is it fair to history? Or the historical figure you represented in your work? I'm going to give you a quick example. You have Nietzsche's sister Elisabeth fire Peter Gast, who was a Jew and one of the first editors of Nietzsche's work. Historically, Elisabeth did fire Gast. But then she rehired him, which you do not mention in the novel, and eventually came to like him, something that you also do not mention. How can you justify your alterations of the historical record, and what kind of impact do you think that has on readers?*

That's a great observation. Let me approach your question through two different optics. The first has to do with a novelist's point of view. There is an aesthetic logic that drives novel writing. Continually present in one's imagination is the relatively limited number of pages with which one has to work. 250? 450? One can only inject so much material into those pages. When you're working with history, when you're working with biographical figures, the result is a remainder. For my purposes, what was interesting wasn't the later relationship of Elisabeth and Peter Gast, but rather that moment when Elisabeth had begun to rewrite her brother, gain control over him by narrativizing him.

This answer leads to the second lens: historiographic metafiction. I wanted a novel that wasn't only about a Nietzsche, or a series of Nietzsches, but also about the difficulties in wanting a novel about such a subject.

Did Gast's Jewishness matter? Did that play a role in making your decision in creating that character or that moment?

I don't think it did. Not at that moment. It's hard, if not hopeless, to remember what I was thinking about during this or that point in the writing process. I can't imagine this isn't the case for most authors. We're all so far away, temporally speaking, thoughtfully speaking, from a book we wrote many bodies ago. Be that as it may, I want to say it was a technical decision

I needed to make, one where Gast, given the novel's focus, had to play a smaller role in the whole, and one where Lisbeth had to manipulate so the reader could focus on how, from very early on, people began to express the Nietzsche they needed to express for very specific socio-cultural purposes—in Lisbeth's case, of course, proto-Nazi ones.

Back to Linda Hutcheon for a minute. She makes a distinction between facts and events. Facts, she says, are discourse determined, while events aren't. The gesture historiographic metafiction performs is to make conspicuous what for most of us remains inconspicuous. Most of us conflate facts and events. But to start expressing an event—something that happened on a specific date at a specific time—is to start transforming it into a constellation of chosen (and discarded, erased, tampered with) facts.

In Nietzsche's Kisses, *you focus on a character who is concerned about the condition of knowledge and who formulates a theory about knowledge. Can you briefly discuss what motivated you to focus specifically on Nietzsche, and in particular his obsession with the condition of knowledge?*

I was raised for my first couple years in the jungles of Venezuela. My dad was helping to set up an oil refinery there. The world into which I came to consciousness thereby took a certain amount of unhinged reality for granted. A snake drowned in our washing machine and flopped out in the sheet in which it had become entangled. Six-foot-long iguanas hung on our screened windows. Thousands of butterflies would ascend out of the grass each spring. These were profoundly surreal images for a kid born in Jersey.

My family and I returned to the States and settled into a quiet suburban existence. During show-and-tell in school on Friday afternoons, I would recount my childhood and be sent to the principal for lying. I'd have to call my mom and have her vouch for me. When I was in my thirties, my sister and I would get together and try reminiscing about our childhood in South America, only for it to become apparent that, whatever event we tried to bring to mind, the facts surrounding it were torqued. We could never figure what really happened to whom. Things I believed had happened to her ultimately turned out to have happened to me and vice versa. It became painfully clear that the past simply wouldn't settle down. That realization has tracked me my whole life.

The theorist in me has from very early on been interested in epistemological questions—certainly from my undergraduate days, when I took my first philosophy and theory courses. I quickly became intrigued, thanks to the poststructuralists, in how we come to know and understand texts and what our relationship is with them. It remains extraordinary to me that all of us sitting here could read the same text, and could try to talk about it, only to learn, again and again, that we were really talking about five different iterations. Twenty. That was one of the things, I believe, that drew me to Nietzsche early on: his notion of perspectivism in relationship to knowledge. One can never simply ask what I know. One must ever ask: "What vantage point do I know it from? How am I framing my understanding of that knowing? How am I ideologizing my knowledge? Am I knowing or simply wanting to know? What does this word *knowing* mean beyond what our gut says it means?"

I want to shift now to a more specific question about the novel. As you point out, Nietzsche's sister married Bernhard Förster, who was a Christian antisemite. Elisabeth and Förster shared a dream of building a utopian community which would be free of Jews. In the late 1880s, they actually established such a community in Paraguay, and they called it "Nueva Germania." Nietzsche despised Förster, and he passionately opposed his utopian community. Nietzsche did this in part because he hated antisemitism, as you make clear in your novel. And yet, Nietzsche's sister, who took charge of the Nietzsche Archive after Nietzsche's mental collapse, revised and even forged some of her brother's texts, thus making them acceptable and even appealing to Hitler and the Nazis. Your novel brilliantly builds up to that scene when Hitler visits the Nietzsche Archive, and Elisabeth presents him with Nietzsche's walking stick. Why, in a novel about Nietzsche, did you shift the focus to Elisabeth, and specifically her meeting with Hitler, and why did you do this in a novel rather than a scholarly study? Put differently, what does the novel allow you to communicate about this history making event that you could not communicate in a traditional biography or a scholarly monograph?

Every genre exists because it can do things other genres can't. So the question behind your question is this, as I hear it: "What can novels do that genres like scholarly monographs (or drama, say, or film) can't do?" One answer is simply language. Novels can do language—beautiful, uproarious language—for extended periods of time; can float language to the surface, delight in its fabrics, not for one page, or 20, but 500. Another answer is that the novel can explore deep consciousness. Film can only try to do so for maybe 90 minutes, maybe 120, and it's going to have to do so from the outside, from an external point of view, because that's its generic nature; one infers psychology from a film rather than inhabiting it. A novel can create the impression of diving fully into the consciousness of another human being, place the reader deep within that consciousness for days, if not weeks. What a dazzling thing.

A scholarly monograph can't do that. Rather, it can form a so-called objective investigation of a problem, can document externally. Now, at the same time, the novel makes genre difficult because it comprehends that the character that it's diving into isn't, in fact, a biological character; it's a paper person, a construction of language. The noun on the page of my novel that says *Nietzsche* doesn't point to Nietzsche. It points, in a very real sense, to Nietzsche's absence. Novels by nature are disruptive zones. They both try to trick you into believing they're exploring a consciousness other than the author's and know that they're not doing so.

A final answer to your questions: a novel can perform thought experiments. So one of the things *Nietzsche's Kisses* is trying to imagine (at the same time understanding such imaginings are futile) is what Nietzsche might have been like, given the Nietzsche that Lance Olsen read and experienced when he was studying "Nietzsche." I did extensive research for *Nietzsche's Kisses*, both in terms of reading various biographies and Nietzsche's work multiple times, and in terms of travelling extensively, following Nietzsche's life journey through Germany and Switzerland and Italy, taking voluminous notes on details along the way, taking photographs and film footage, visiting the Nietzsche Archive, standing in the room in which he died. But I was also trying to move beyond those kinds of events into a series of conditionals about Nietzsche, which is to say the novel comprehends through its very mechanics that Lukacs is wrong. The best we can do is to set up these thought experiments about the relationship of the individual to history and then disrupt both of those terms.

Building on this, you talk about how the novel accesses consciousness. I wonder if consciousness has undergone a transformation in the last 50 years—you know, not necessarily consciousness itself, but our understanding of consciousness—and if that has any relevance to the rise of the biographical novel. Instead of doing the kind of classical, traditional historical novel, which focuses on events, we're now going to center it within consciousness itself. Do you think that this helps account for this transformation, or the rise of the biographic novel? And if so, can you specify what happened to our understanding of consciousness?

What you say feels right: in our age of indeterminacy, that our sense of consciousness has changed dramatically. I wouldn't want to speak for anyone but myself, here, now, but my intuition is that we've moved away from early-twentieth-century (read: modernist) notions of Freudian depth-consciousness. They no longer seem to fit our lived experience. In part, this is because of the troublings poststructuralism launched in the middle of the last century, in part because of the digitization of our culture: the data overload so many of us experience as experience these days, the splintering or multifaceted-ness of our consciousnesses. I'm speaking of that new way of being—you know, sitting at our computers, writing, say, a novel on the screen, but also simultaneously researching on the web, perhaps checking out the news, our email program running in the background, Instagram whining behind that, a dictionary behind that, Facebook behind that, and, for a break, perhaps we flip over to Youtube to check out a video clip, and maybe we're listening to iTunes, and our friends are texting us, and someone in the next room is watching TV, and, well, you get the picture. Pictures.

Compare that to the information intake for someone living in, oh, 1347. Or 1847. And you see what I'm getting at. By necessity, I should think, we process our worlds differently, have a different sense of what we mean when we say thinking and/or feeling. We have the continuous impression of mediation, remediation, unreadability, dispersion, distraction—something closer, perhaps, not to Freudian thought, but Baudrillardian: schizoid selves, switching stations for all the data networks flowing within us and without. So the question for authors is this: how do we write such a state? That is: how do we write our experience of experience, this feeling of living deep within Nietzschean perspectivism?

Such questions don't in any way divorce us from the historical. Rather, they seem a result of the historical. Authors I'm most interested in now are trying to tackle them. When reading a novel like David Foster Wallace's *Infinite Jest*, I can't help being aware how profoundly it couldn't have been written 100 years ago. Or there's this beautiful hypermedial work by David Clark called *88 Constellations for Wittgenstein* that employs audio, nonlinear narraticules, video, images, and text in a failed attempt to understand that philosopher and his thought. Throughout, it's aware of the reader, or the viewer, or the listener, or whatever you want to call this new participant who's trying to navigate this new arena—aware of that participant's presence, aware of trying to activate that presence by making the navigator continually choose how to move through the hypermedial field Clark created. That is to say, one is keenly aware that one is constructing narrative as one proceeds.

That experience points to what you're talking about, Michael. To a much lesser extent, perhaps, *Head in Flames* and *Nietzsche's Kisses* partake in the same kind of project. The latter is structured in groups of three. Each chapter has a first person, a second person, and a third person point of view. The first person constitutes the real time of Nietzsche on his deathbed, his last mad night on earth. The second point-of-view chapters constitute irrational, hallucinatory moments of Nietzsche's semi-consciousness. The third person point-of-view chapters constitute attempts by Nietzsche to narrativize his own life. The structure, then, is insistently polyphonic. The consequence of that is to bracket Lukacs's totalizing systems.

I wonder if this shift to perspectival notions of self, which is to say of consciousness, is paradoxically expressed in the increased interest in biofictions, which ask what constitutes identity now, what may constitute it in a decade, even as they seem to offer a contradictory impression that self, self's consciousness, is more stable than our quotidian existence argues.

Shifting focus again, there has been a tendency among biographical novelists to emphasize the role of religion in shaping major historical events in lives. Here, I'm thinking about Jay Parini's The Last Station, *Bruce Duffy's* Disaster Was My God, *and David Mamet's* Old Religion. *This focus on religion stands in stark contrast to what we see in canonical interpretations of Western intellectual and political history, which tend to emphasize secularization. And here I'm thinking of Hannah Arendt, Benedict Anderson, Adorno, Horkheimer, Charles Taylor ... We know all of these people. Can you explain why there is this emphasis on religion in contemporary biographical novels, and, in particular, can you explain why there is this focus in* Nietzsche's Kisses? *Here I'm thinking again when most of the scholars who talk about the Hitler moment with Elisabeth—when they talk about her transformation of the texts—they always emphasize, "Look, this is a part of the secularization process." Your novel has a different feel, because you underscore the fact that not only is she an antisemite, but she's a Christian antisemite. A lot of people overlook this point. You mention Bernhard Förster's antisemitic petition to Bismark in your novel, but they don't mention the fact that that petition starts with a very clear religious justification for getting rid of Jews. This is something that the scholars don't want to talk about. I think it's interesting that a lot of the biographical novels do mention these kind of religious dimensions to the thinking. Can you explain this discrepancy?*

My sense is that all writing—whether novel, poem, newspaper article, scholarly monograph, whatever—is, at the end of the day, an act of spiritual autobiography that says more about the author than the subject. One of the reasons I decided—and it was, as I recall, a very clear decision on my part—to bring religion to the fore in *Nietzsche's Kisses* is to help me think about how in the United States in the last, say, quarter century, there has been the resurgence of a frightening fundamentalism, a dangerously overstated Christianity that in many ways is reminiscent of Förster's undertakings—religion in the service of repressive politics, a generation of politicians who have weaponized religion. I wanted to use *Nietzsche's Kisses* (and *Head in Flames*) as remindings about how religion is deployed to justify all manner of horrendous acts. These days we only need to think of the MAGA moment. This observation is the opposite of new. Yet it is one our culture is very good at forgetting. Religion (spiritual practices generally) can be used—and usually are—to close down debate, categorize under the guise of "acceptance," kill—both ideas and human beings.

Okay. You know, we want to open up the discussion now to other questions. If any of you have some questions for Lance, please feel free to ask.

Question 1: I sort of have a nascent question. [Laughs.]

[Laughs.] Well, I'll try to come up with a nascent answer.

Question 1: All right. We're in agreement. I have been pondering sort of what you've been talking about: the importance of authorship, specifically in these types of creative, historical narratives, and how you use the term "spiritual autobiography." I was wondering, given the theory of the death of the author with Roland Barthes, how we can liberate the reader from the tyranny of the author who wants to impose his particular perspective. Do you think that that's a new kind of transcendentalism, where we actually can't escape the author's framing? Or do you think that Barthes was actually trying to say something a little different, more Nietzschean, like the death of God, where we claim our identity when we're reading these pieces by imposing these interpretations?

After World War II, generations of authors, instead of coming to writing on their own while working second jobs like Hemingway as a journalist, attended university. By the late sixties, they began to stumble across a new kind of course in English departments: literary theory. There they read and became self-conscious about questions concerning how texts might mean. Those generations, I would argue, our generations, have come to think of writing practices differently because of that. Certainly I have. Exposure to theoretical engagements with textuality harass myths of authorship, put writers in a new position with respect to their own work, ask us to un-think or at least bother certain intuitive responses to our being in the textual world.

The operative word through our interview has been *problematization*, and here we come across it again. Now, if you're a theorist, or you're a literary critic, you get that, and we move on. If you're an author, you live with that bothering every day. Every day we need to ask ourselves, in a very practical way, what our relationship is to our work, how much of what we're doing, or think we're doing, partakes in the very magisterial space of authorship Barthes seeks to overthrow. So the short answer is I honestly don't know, again and again. Which is to say: such a series of questions excites me, makes me want to think deeply about the issues they raise, examine my own practices and goals, forces a self-examination to be perpetually active—which is my definition of the writer, the artist: one who spends a lifetime practicing interest and skepticism, how to attend, practicing not philosophy but thinkfeeling.

So if you look back to how I've tried to engage with Michael's questions, I believe you'll discover that that self-examination with respect to narrativity figures in them all, that that's my larger project, and it's one, I would contend, someone like Hemingway simply didn't get. That self-examination produces a different sort of narrativity, or narrativities, altogether, species I find unbelievably interesting, ones by the likes of David Markson, John Barth, Thalia Field, J. G. Ballard, Milan Kundera, Benjamín Labatut, Stacey Levine, Maggie Nelson, Haruki Murakami, Olga Tokarczuk, Paul Auster, Susan Steinberg, William Gass, José Saramago, David Mitchell, Julian Barnes.

I should emphasize that I'm not convinced that I'm the same person who wrote *Nietzsche's Kisses*, and when I was writing *Nietzsche's Kisses*, I wasn't convinced I was the same person who was writing *Nietzsche's Kisses*. So I'm not sure I want to answer your question as much as agree with the complications inherent in it.

Let me say this another way. I used to know a lot more than I do now, and that makes me very happy. I'm sure (in an unsure way) that's why I'm drawn to writers like Nietzsche, Barthes, Derrida, Cixous, Foucault, why I'm increasingly comfortable with the discomfort they create. This is another reason, I suppose, Lukacs and I don't get along. He knows too much. I love the definitiveness with which he states his case. At the same time I acknowledge that definitiveness strikes me as utterly foreign, enviable, and nonsensical. What I can talk about with absolute assuredness is precisely what I don't know, whereas I think Lukacs really thought he knew what he was talking about. I know I never know what I'm talking about. And I can articulate that not-knowing, as you can tell, for very long periods of time. [Laughs.]

Question 2: I have a very specific question about the text. And maybe, since you're a different person than the person who was writing it, you won't know.

I'd put money on it.

Q2: I am wondering about the conflict of saying that Nietzsche got syphilis from being a medic in the war or from having sex with a prostitute. In this novel, he has sex with the prostitute Ingrid. Ingrid, I thought, was a really interesting character or placeholder for the three or four other times she seems to come up in the novel or her similarities with the girl at the Wagnerian opera in the "Liver" section. So I'm wondering kind of why you chose that scenario. Was it purely aesthetic or is there more to it than that?

Syphilis was for a long time the only answer to what was going on those last few years of Nietzsche's life. Now, apparently, it's less clear. So, for me, Ingrid was an aesthetic choice, a narrative necessity, rather than a person based on historical events. The thing about tertiary syphilis—if what Nietzsche had happens to have been tertiary syphilis—is that it takes your brain out completely. That means, if we're to agree with that diagnosis, this novel couldn't have occurred. One of the assumptions the book makes is that Nietzsche possesses a mind with which to think, hallucinate, narrativize on his last night alive, but that couldn't have been the case if he had had tertiary syphilis. During his final days, given the descriptions that come down to us, he was in something a lot closer to a catatonic state. So the novel's premises are contrary to received knowledge.

ML: What are you doing with the different Ingrids? I think Anne raises a really important question.

Anne, do you have a sense of that? We were talking about this over breakfast today.

Q2: My thought is that Ingrid functioned as an ideal of femininity.

LO: Which one? Which Ingrid? The one that takes place in the Wagner theater?

Q2: Yes.

But not the one in the brothel?

Q2: I think that I was kind of thinking of it as a Gilbert and Gubar thing. I was trying to see if she was kind of the same character and the same placeholder persona, given how she's kind of trans-historical because we don't know when these memories are occurring, and she seems to always be 14, except for the time it's her as an old woman that's bald envisioning Ingrid. That passage? So it kind of seemed like she was all of these at once.

This particular Lance Olsen, the one now producing these speech acts, has almost completely forgotten what he did with Ingrid and why he did it beyond what he has already said—although he seems to remember, or seems to remember seeming to remember, wanting to use Ingrid as a way to study the constellation of Nietzsche's notions of power, his torqued relationship with women (thanks, I think, in good part to his manipulative mother and sister), and his mystery sexuality.

We were speaking earlier this morning about how the novel is shaped musically rather than in more customary ways. Part of that musical structure relies on Wagnerian leitmotifs, recurring musical phrasings associated with particular characters, places, or ideas. If you recall, we were talking about how dogs function in the work, how the image of the dog weaves itself through the text, from the Doberman that's mentioned early on, to Lisbeth and Hitler's banal chitchat about dogs at the Nietzsche Archive in Weimar, to Nietzsche himself birthing a dog (or, to be more accurate, a puppy) in one of his hallucinations, to, in another, rabid dogs bounding through the streets—and, in all cases, those dogs are the metaphoric manifestation of the Nazi will to power and a cluster of associated concerns. I think that I think I was making a similar sort of association between the image of young Ingrid and gender dynamics. But, honestly, I may be making all of this up. I simply don't know. Who does?

WITH ANDREA SCRIMA

Lance, you've written a novel that, in a nod to Ulysses *and* Mrs. Dalloway *(but perhaps also to* Do Androids Dream of Electric Sheep?*), takes place in a single 24-hour period—in this case, June 10, 1927.* My Red Heaven*—which borrows its title from a painting by the exiled German artist Otto Freundlich—is a paean to the Weimar era and a chilling anticipation of the ruinous events that would soon befall Germany and the rest of Europe and the world. What made you choose this particular summer day?*

I was thinking less of Phillip K. Dick (whom I adore, aside from his rushed style) when the idea for the novel surfaced than, as you say, Joyce and Woolf, who I feel are everywhere in *My Red Heaven*. In 2015, I stumbled on Freundlich's abstract Cubist painting at the Pompidou. It was completed in 1933, the year Hitler became chancellor. For some reason, that painting all at once became connotative to me of the cultural energy of the Weimar era. It also gestures toward a collage aesthetic in its collection of apparently disparate forms on a surface that simultaneously unifies them and underscores their multiplicity. I found myself wanting to see what happens when that aesthetic is translated into written narrative.

Each chapter of *My Red Heaven* takes the form of a narraticule set in the consciousness of an historical or imagined figure living, working, and/or simply passing through Berlin's remarkable intellectual and creative possibility precinct during a single day in 1927, as you say. The idea became to create a broad canvas—in many ways Berlin is the novel's disorienting and disoriented protagonist—that explores the resonant complexity of an historical moment.

I chose June because it holds Bloomsday within it, and hence Joyce. And I chose 1927 because it fell nicely in the middle of some of the Weimar Republic's richest hours. The tenth is because it happens to be the birthday of Anita Berber, the cabaret performer whose consciousness guides the first chapter—and hence for simple structural reasons.

Correct me if I'm wrong, but My Red Heaven *also feels like a sideways glance at the current state of affairs in the US.*

So much so. When I conceived of and began writing the novel, I was thinking mostly of other things, the things I've just mentioned, with Trump's early candidacy a sort of hazy joke at the gray edges of our social awareness. (I imagine there were many in Germany who saw Hitler's early days in much the same light.) But as the 2016 election roiled into wreckage, I saw myself refocusing, wanting in part to use *My Red Heaven* as a way to contemplate the parallels between the Weimar years and our own—how a grim populism can contaminate a country so gradually, so insidiously, and yet in the end so completely through a politics of paranoia, xenophobia, pit-bullish nationalism and alpha-male ignorance that most of its essentially decent but unthinking citizens come to understand what's happened only when their democracy has already become something other than democratic around them and in them.

My Red Heaven *trembles with that anxiety: its characters go about their day with no notion of the barbarity about to arrive in their lives in the near future. As readers, we know what's in store for them; it's hard not to want to go back in time and stop the clock. The book abounds with illustrious writers, artists, and thinkers who either went underground, perished, or escaped into exile: among them Hannah Höch, Robert Musil, Otto Dix, Hannah Arendt, Ludwig Mies van der Rohe, and Werner Heisenberg. And, of course, Anita Berber, who appears larger than life in the book's opening scenes. The different forms you adopt throughout the book—prose, newsreel, screenplay, lists, concrete poetry, and a kind of on-the-page art installation—evoke the unprecedented intellectual and artistic innovations of the Weimar years.*

Absolutely. To foreground that bleak irony hovering over the whole, I use the future tense a lot. It underscores the anxiety I hope exists in every line for the reader.

My Red Heaven is also a love letter to modernism. That's why it slant-rhymes with Joyce's collage novel about Dublin, with Woolf's beautiful exploration through her narrator's oceanic consciousness of London, and with various other modernist forms and visions in literature and the other arts, both in Germanic and, more broadly, European and American cultures. I have always found kin with aesthetic and temporal refugees (often geographical, too). Too, I've always found myself much more aligned with European sensibilities than those of my own country.

When critics and novelists consciously engage with earlier work as I often do in my writing, thinking with it, against it, and through it, what they produce is a mode of saying thank you to that work—as well, naturally, as a way of killing their parents. I would never have become the writer I am without all the conflictions and complications we call modernism. For the last I don't know how many years I've taught an undergraduate course about it. Eduardo Galeano has a much better way of phrasing what I'm trying to say than I do: "History never really says goodbye. History says, 'See you later.'"

What fascinates me is the way these characters continually cross paths throughout the narrative: one particularly poignant example is the iridescent blue butterfly that flutters past a zeppelin window—first noticed by the young Billy Wilder, then the sexologist Magnus Hirschfeld—a butterfly that was once Rosa Luxemburg, who "came to conclude that [...] the most revolutionary thing you can do is simply say aloud what is taking place in the vicinity of your life," until it's caught up in a twirling gust of air, comes to rest on a blade of grass, and is then crushed beneath the shoe of the elderly Georg Anton Schäffer, who takes no notice.

I don't know why, but I have always loved books with the rich harmonics (we've returned, I suppose, to Woolf and Joyce, but also to more recent examples like David Mitchell's *Cloud Atlas* or, in another manner altogether, Alyssa Quinn's *Habilis*) of reappearing characters, phrases, images with variations. They feel like they're somehow making sense in a downpour of senselessness. Rosa's role in particular in *My Red Heaven* is that of the artist, the writer, the intellectual: a world witness built to send reports from the subjective and social fronts, who already knows those communiques will almost always end up in some dead letter office. It's the strangest impulse, isn't it? We both have thousands of years of proof that art in its largest sense changes exactly nothing, over and over again, along with the cellular commitment to keep doing it nonetheless. That said, we also each have a lifetime of proof that individual pieces of art change individual human beings all the time—even if only, in most cases, for a few minutes, or a few days, or a week or two.

Lance, you and your wife, Andi, spend time in Berlin each year; the city has become a kind of second home for you. To what degree is My Red Heaven *also a declaration of love to the city's past?*

Andi and I adore Berlin for about 10,000,000 reasons. To a huge degree, *My Red Heaven* functions as a declaration of love to Berlin's past as well as to its present. To Berlin as an idea, too. It's a city especially conducive to *dérive* because it doesn't possess the orienting axes of Paris or New York. Rather it's a gallimaufry space where on a single block the gentrified nineteenth century dwells next to the crumbling eighteenth dwells next to the frayed East German dwells next to the clean Bauhaus dwells next to a McDonalds, a trendy café, an untrendy Indian or Vietnamese or Turkish bistro, a currywurst stand, a chunk of leftover Wall (now graffitied and encrusted with bubble gum), a five-story bunker built by Albert Speer that couldn't be blown up after the war because it was so massive, and was thus transformed (after an earlier iteration as Germany's hottest site for techno raves and gay sadomasochistic festivities) into an art gallery.

I'm struck by how in many ways the entire twentieth century happened in Berlin with a dark vengeance. The US, by contrast, is devoted to repressing its atrocities, its amoral heart, as quickly and thoroughly as possible. It's our inheritance, I assume, from the nineteenth-century doctrine of Manifest Destiny. Americans continue to swear an oath of allegiance to leaving their shit behind them while believing they are bustling ever forward toward righteousness. Berlin—much of Germany—has dedicated itself to perplexing the act of remembering. I understand the difficulties with that gesture, yet I'm buoyed and grateful and absorbed by such serious cultural self-examination.

I've been living in Germany for more than half my life, and my appreciation for the work this country has done to come to terms with its dark history goes deep.

Wayne Koestenbaum talks about hoteling as an existential condition. We hotel when we enter a state of physically not-being-at-home that allows us to read, think, become curious, pay attention. Because of its unnervingly complex history, Berlin by nature hotels Berlin. It has become a mode of hoteling for Andi and me that we've found electrically productive, both aesthetically and existentially.

Ultimately, of course, the beacons of intellectual life that fled Nazi persecution infused America with their creative power and changed the course of history here—Hannah Arendt at the New School for Social Research is one obvious example of the influence of German Jewish thought on post-war American intellectual life—but it strikes me that the Germany we're left with is in some regards an amputee.

What a beautiful way of putting it, Andrea. I see what you're saying, and ask myself—I simply don't know enough to state this with anything like confidence—if there has also been at least to some small degree a partial reversal of that intellectual flow by means of American and other expats who, like yourself, have moved to Berlin to make their lives, reinfusing the culture with a new-found energy while refusing the American night terrors. In any case, unlike Arendt and the others we might have in mind from the Nazi years, many of us in the contemporary move easily, frequently, and relatively rapidly between continents, among myriad intellectual circles, keeping loose affiliation with them all, in a mercurial process that wasn't available in measure to the modernists. Add to that the infinite Borgesian library the internet provides, and it feels to me so many of us are living in a continuous diaspora, a state of endless post-geographical, multicultural, unrooted inbetweenness ever less dependent on family or country to shape ourselves. That grim populism I mentioned earlier is a clear fear-response to the deep-seated feeling that we are all, in some sense, becoming perpetual migrants.

It's hard to fathom just how threatening intellectualism and cosmopolitanism can be to a particular segment of the population; why the gut response is so often racism, nationalism, parochialism, misogyny, antisemitism, and so on. History seems to repeat itself; forces that might have taken a different turn suddenly tip the scale toward calamity. Although John Maynard Keynes lamented that the Treaty of Versailles made no provisions for Europe's economic rehabilitation following the end of WWI and is often said to have predicted the events leading to the next war; and although Luxemburg herself was convinced that if socialism failed, humanity would fall prey to inconceivable barbarity—I've never believed in the inevitability of Nazism. Or let's say: I've never believed in the sense of historical fate promoted by Germanophobes and their deep-seated antipathy, as though the language itself led inevitably to fascism. Because we see this happening now, in a place we call home—where it also never before seemed possible.

I couldn't agree more. Americans love to use that narrative of inevitability with respect to Germany, perhaps, because it makes us feel better about ourselves, gives us a country to blame for the twentieth century, gets our guilt off our shoulders by recasting history as a series of easy fated outcomes. And no country on earth loves basking in its smug self-righteousness more than the US.

But here's the thing in a single image: A couple of days ago I forced myself once again to endure the highlights from a Trump rally, this one in Pennsylvania. He ranted willy-nilly for hours, attacking in the associative course of his hebephrenic garble the media, calling his impeachment a scam, mocking Greta Thunberg for wanting to help slow down our environmental catastrophe, berating Elizabeth Warren for opening "her fresh mouth," and claiming that—I kid you not, this is an exact quote—"last summer at least 19 illegal aliens were charged in connection with grisly homicides, including hacking victims to death and ripping out, in two cases, their hearts."

My deep apprehension is that it's going to get more horrendous than we can currently imagine … and somehow 42 percent of the population either hasn't noticed, doesn't care, or, more horrific still, applauds what's happening because everybody likes a strong daddy figure who can protect us from the heinous Other while making sure the trains run on time. And, well, God help us all.

This brings to mind the darker underlayers of your book. My Red Heaven *is a necromantic evocation of the time between the wars in Weimar Berlin; it brims with motifs that heighten the brevity and hallucinatory nature of life and time: things recede "from present to preterite"; a dying father is remembered with an "elated smile spreading across his wasness"; two condemned prisoners about to be executed on the guillotine are positioned face up "so they can see their futures flying toward them." Some of the sections count backwards in time from a point six years hence, twelve years hence, while in another recurrent image, a portentous manifestation of the future in the guise of a black shadow scrambles across the ground and then flickers out as the respective character notices it and thinks "cloud." The unrelenting pain that is history; the gathering of the dead on the rooftops.*

I sometimes feel, especially here in the US, that each of us is like a fly that's accidentally wandered aboard a 747 in Los Angeles and is now airborne somewhere over the Pacific in the middle of the night, in a typhoon, thinking in its little fly-thoughts that the bit of banana peel it's feasting on in the galley is all time, the whole beneficent universe. That plane, wildly insignificant compared to the turbulent blackness around it, is us; that turbulent blackness, history. Remarkably, many Americans are willfully oblivious of chronology and the myriad forces carrying them along. They honestly think it's all about them and their tiny fly world. By warping temporality, injecting an always ironic and painful awareness of larger futures into *My Red Heaven*—I have Franz Kafka at one point say: "People always live happily ever after until they don't. Every story is also always about night."—I wanted the novel to serve as a 264-page reminder that we all exist as sometimes conscious, sometimes unconscious, yet always doomed historical beings subject, in part, to violences we can, if we really put our minds to it, barely fathom.

Particularly now, as we watch events unfold in the US, it's hard not to wonder if humans aren't subject to the same obscure laws as schools of fish or flocks of birds: moving collectively according to some ineluctable pattern that overrides individual will. Which brings me back to the multi-dimensionality of your book's narrative. Figures from one chapter suddenly turn up in the next, but on the periphery: Werner Heisenberg, whose wallet is stolen at Alexanderplatz, appears as a nondescript man in a "shabby olive tweed jacket" the appearance of whom reminds Nabokov of the "proliferation of proliferations" that writing entails. ("The problem with writing, Vladimir has come to understand, is the part involving writing.") Käthe Kollwitz, working on a lithograph of a mother and child, suddenly gazes out the window and down at a taxi passing by on the street below carrying Mies van der Rohe: "jowly, fleshy nosed, protruding lower lip—perhaps smoking a cigar stub, perhaps picking at his thumbnail." The book brims with polyvalent perspectives; everything seems to be interwoven with the causality of everything else.

You're describing the effects of collage. What's beautiful to me about that form is its emphasis on the plural and incommensurate. Collage not only refuses to privilege one voice—which is to say one vision—over another, but it celebrates profusion as a way of being. It's a mode of juxtaposition that allows visions to clash with, converse with, harmonize with—and even ignore—each other. At its best, this was often at the core of the modernist project. One need only recall Dos Passos's USA trilogy. These are works that invite the reader to pass through a succession of contradictory and ambiguous attitudes about the world, emphasizing how each is both tenable and arbitrary. From one point of view, Heisenberg changed the course of physics in the twentieth century; from another, he was just this unremarkable guy in a shabby olive tweed jacket patting himself down in a train station, figuring out his wallet had just been lifted by a pickpocket.

The form suggests the impossible-to-imagine simultaneity of everything that's happening right this very moment. But it also suggests the inherent conflict in opposing ideologies striving to occupy the same space, doesn't it? Because at some point, something has to give.

I'm reminded here of Jean-François Lyotard's notion of language games, which he appropriated from Wittgenstein and slightly re-imagined in his larger definition of the postmodern as the collapse of metanarratives and the concurrent metastisis of micro-ones. In the absence of big stories, we must become alert to difference, to diversity, to the absolute incompatibility of our beliefs and desires, our ideologies, with those of others. When we converse with someone else, we enter into a network, not of truths, but of language games, aware of the multiplicity of communities of meaning, the innumerable and incommensurable separate systems in which meanings are produced and rules for their circulation created. One might argue that such relativism gives the lie to the possibility of ethics, but for Lyotard injustice comes to mean the imposition of one set of language games on another. Ethical behavior amounts to allowing multiple language games to be played, keeping the conversation going. Murder is unethical precisely because it violently terminates the possibility of language, the possibility of play, the possibility of conversation that is and should be unresolvable. I explore this in depth in my novel *Head in Flames*, where three different world views that can't exist together must exist together. Now I'm not sure I'm fully cozy with Lyotard's position. It's probably too certain of itself by half. Yet I do respond to the perhaps admittedly quixotic idea that opposing ideologies can inhabit the same space without something having to give. Of course, well … do you recall Jean-Martin Charcot's—Freud's mentor's—delightful observation: "Theory is good; but doesn't prevent things from happening"?

That reminds me of a conversation I had with my late father many years ago about theosophy and other esoteric belief systems: "No matter how you look at it, though, if you go outside and walk into oncoming traffic," he said, "you're still going to get hit." I feel we're at a kind of cusp right now, where one system of belief is about to overpower the other—and we're about to get "hit." The years of the Weimar Republic were also a cusp—between a rich cultural and intellectual pluralism and the moment it was abruptly, violently snuffed out—and it's hard not to feel the echoes of our present moment in American history. We see the choice between oligarchy and dictatorship on the one hand and, on the other, the vision of an equitable society gradually escaping our reach—and it looks like we're about to veer off in a very wrong direction. To what extent does the title of the book name this vision of a fairer, more humane socio-economic order: the modestly regulated capitalism currently vilified as "socialism," our very own "red heaven"? Because—and I've scoured the book—among the things that are red are: Anita Berber's hair; her lips, her dress, and the space she occupies when Otto Dix paints her; Adolph Hitler's gums; the wine he dunks a teaspoon of sugar into; the modernist building the Nabokovs live in; money, in the mind of Mies van der Rohe; the face of Ernst Herbeck hanging upside-down from a tree; the shared color of song in a dream he has that night; the scarf and suspenders of a young Black jazz musician playing a banjo; Emil Jannings's bowtie; the Red Army soldiers who start a fire in the wine cellar of the Hotel Adlon; the "fives" in a mathematics professor's dream from last night, "so beautiful, so red"; the colors in Otto Freundlich's geometric painting, which you've described at length; and, of course, the politics that got Rosa Luxemburg murdered.

You're such a magnificent reader, Andrea. Thank you for your care and caring. I wanted there to be—although I'm not sure this comes across—an inherent tension in that title: *My Red Heaven*. On the one hand, I hoped for exactly what you suggest to resonate in it—the possibility, which maybe always seems so close, yet so far, of a fairer, more humane socio-ecology. On the other hand, I wanted there to be the suggestion of a bloody heaven, Hitler's heaven the color of his gums. Structurally, the novel is divided into four sections that start with "Underpainting," then track down Freundlich's painting from the top: "Reds," "Grays: Greens: Whites: Blues," "Blacks." Apparently Freundlich, a utopian, wanted his viewer's eye to travel in the opposite direction, from those blacks suggesting hell, through the midrange suggesting the colors of earth, and finally to those reds suggesting some more perfect realm. But my novel ends with an image that quite literally turns the last page nearly completely black.

Yes, those last several pages, a work of concrete poetry in their own right, are devastating. In a sense, your book mourns for the Germany that might have been—the logical continuation of the revolutionary intellectual and artistic tendencies prevailing during the Weimar era. Are you also mourning for an America that might have been?

The older I get, the more I realize I've been mourning all along for an America that never was. The gap between the ideal and the real here has always been heartbreaking. Under Trump, it was nothing short of annihilating. So we began by talking about *My Red Heaven* as a love song at its core, but it is also an elegy, a lament for the dead who were never alive.

As far as I can tell, most of the characters in your book are real persons whose lives correspond roughly to the fictional events you portray in My Red Heaven. *Walter Benjamin did indeed commit suicide in Portbou, Spain, a day before the small group of émigrés he was with, including the young Hannah Arendt, was allowed to cross the Portuguese border; Emil Jannings starred with Marlene Dietrich in* The Blue Angel. *One notable exception is your serial killer Carl Fischer, who fabricates sausages out of his victims.*

There was a spate of serial killings in Berlin, mostly of prostitutes, during the twenties and thirties, along with the strange phenomenon of so-called murdered-women series of lithographs, paintings, and even films (think *Nosferatu*). Maria Tatar examines this trend in a book called *Lustmord: Sexual Murder in Weimar Germany*. Tatar places these abounding representations of female mutilation and homicide in the context of the gender politics of cultural production of the period, but also as a precursor to Nazism: the growing cultural ability to dismantle, disavow, and ultimately erase victims with an impersonal, machinelike, amoral efficacy. Carl Fischer is an amalgam of several of the serial killers Tatar discusses.

But Fischer also points to another impulse in a novel that doesn't necessarily attempt to realistically (and therefore naively) re-present the past, which can never be re-presented in any meaningful way. I hope I generate enough characters (not only Carl Fischer, but also the pickpocket, sommelier, and myriad ghosts) that never existed, and take enough subtle liberties with the historical record (fiction, as opposed to historical texts and journalism devoted to facts, and hence to surface realities, devotes itself to the five senses and deep consciousness, areas to which history and journalism have virtually no access) that this problem of pastness becomes part of the reading experience.

It certainly did and does, and it's a stirring reminder that history—both the recorded histories of past eras and the history we experience on a day-to-day basis in momentous times—is a malleable narrative we write and rewrite as we try to make sense of it all.

WITH YANNICKE CHUPIN & BRIGITTE FÉLIX

Let us start with this: "I think I've heard of Lance Olsen. I wonder who he was. People in 50 years won't ever say."

LANCE OLSEN: I just finished writing a novel about David Bowie titled *Always Crashing in the Same Car*. It's a prismatic exploration of Bowie through manifold voices and perspectives—the chameleonic musician himself, an academic trying to compose a critical monograph about him, friends, lovers, musicologists, and others who engage with the idea of him. At its core reside questions about how we read others and how we are read by them. In short, in this era of identity politics, it asks: Who is any of us? Read five biographies about Bowie, and you meet five different human beings. Identity—which, from a certain perspective, is to say the past—is nothing if not an anxious, distressed space.

When we first meet a text, whether organic or paginal, our usual instinct is to shut it down, interpret it into regularity, comprehensibility, so we can pretend we have controlled it, a fool's errand. Our instinct seems to be to clear up, dumb down. But, as Bakhtin reminds us, if we pay attention, look and listen, we notice no human being becomes finalizable until they are deceased—and then, it goes without saying, the narratives we create around them continue to be written, unwritten, and rewritten … if they're lucky … if they're remembered at all … for that brief amount of time we mean when we say someone is "remembered" after they are deceased.

We could put it this way: Bowie made his lifework out of researching Heraclitus's philosophy.

And so to your fabulous question, which is really a quote from my critifiction *[[there.]]*: Who is Lance Olsen? The answer is clear: I have absolutely no idea. That guy becomes a little more unfinalizable for me every day. I'm constantly unlearning who I think I am, what I'm about, always feeling a little more numerous at heart. The books I write are ongoing lessons for me into the nature of unanswerability—and I take a certain amount of wild happiness in that.

Though I do believe when I wrote those lines in *[[there.]]*, I was a little more optimistic than I am now. I mean, look at the assumption domiciled within the third sentence: there was a moment, apparently, when I believed our species would survive 50 more years.

ANDI OLSEN: I think we will all be sitting here in 50 years, going: You remember that interview? And Lance will still be writing and we'll actually have more to add to your question. If not, then I think that through your teaching and writing, Lance, there will be people who will carry on versions of you. So things will be passed down, and things will be lost, and people will get things wrong, yet some thread of that bedrock Lance Olsen will have become circulated through others. At least that's what I'd like to think. Of course, once we're gone, the question becomes: Who cares?

In [[there.]], *you describe how you were introduced to the notion of "literary activism" by Larry McCaffery and Lidia Yuknavitch. You insisted on the idea of "getting out the word any way you can, because innovative writing isn't just innovative writing, it's a cultural urgency." Has that cultural urgency been a powerful drive to the writing of your novels since* Theories of Forgetting *and up to now with* My Red Heaven *and* Skin Elegies*?*

LANCE: My first novel, *Live from Earth*, a sweet love story in a magical realist register, was published in 1991. That turned out to be the most normative novel I wrote. A New York publisher, Ballantine, brought it out. I learned a lot from the experience, including that to enter the world of corporate writing is to enter a quasi-literary assembly line, where novels function to maximize profits for masterplot multinationals and thereby minimize narratological risk. I soon came to realize that that wasn't the ecosystem in which I wanted to exist.

Not long after, I met Lidia Yuknavitch and Larry McCaffery at San Diego State University, where they were teaching. I want to say this was about 1996. Both became role models for developing alternative writing/publishing ecosystems. Lidia has wired into her a wondrous way of forming creative communities in order to disseminate work she cares about. Initially she began by bringing out a small journal called *Two Girls Review*. For several years she founded and ran a press: Chiasmus. Larry was sensational in championing new, important innovative novels and novelists in scholarly articles and interviews. He had a finger on the pulse of experimental writing practices, both in the US and abroad.

Long before that, when I was an undergraduate at the University of Wisconsin, I stumbled across Fiction Collective (which in the nineties, for economic reasons, became FC2) while wandering the library stacks one weekend evening, sampling the just-arrived shelf, and I became enamored by its daring aesthetics and praxis. The press had recently been formed—in 1973 and 1974—by a handful of radical writers, among whom were Ron Sukenick, Jonathan Baumbach, and Steve Katz, all unhappy with the world of New York publishing which I just described. They set up what they believed would be a short-lived publishing experiment in which innovative novels and short-story collections would be brought out by innovative writers. What they published opened up countless doors for me.

In 2001, I had the good fortune to become the chair of its board of directors. Over the years, as you know, FC2 has published a plethora of extraordinary authors whose work is synonymous with experimentation, from Raymond Federman to, yes, Lidia Yuknavitch.

Lidia also brought into the conversation the necessity of reaching out to younger writers, inviting them into this alternate dimension. For a few years in the first decade of the new century, we collaborated on the Writers Edge in Portland, Oregon, which was part conference, part series of alternative workshops, and part ongoing conversations about everything from innovative writing/publishing to what we all wanted to do next aesthetically and politically and why, how we might imagine failure (in a Beckettian sense) as motion. Put differently, The Writers Edge was all about helping literary activism leak into the larger world. We felt the cultural urgency in all this become stronger by the week and, needless to say, ever since 2016, when Trump won the White House, and US democracy began its shredding, that feeling has transformed into a critical imperative.

With respect to my own novels, once I left New York publishing, everything in my writing opened up. That's how a novel like *Theories of Forgetting* came about. It thought itself into being through Robert Smithson's *Spiral Jetty*, a visit to which led me to wonder: What would a novel look like that collaborated with it?

Delving further into that question of collaborations and literary communities, can you tell us how your work with FC2 and your long-running creative companionship with writers like Lidia Yuknavitch or Steve Tomasula have oriented your work?

LANCE: I did my M.F.A. at the Iowa Writers Workshop, the oldest and probably the most well-known writers' workshop in the US, between 1978 and 1980. It was founded in 1936 and based on the paradigm of the nineteenth-century French art academy, where students sat at the feet of a master, and the basic mode was critique via a number of unquestioned, unexplored, uninformed assumptions about aesthetics. I didn't know what to expect, arriving as I did just out of college, barely 21, but I was unnerved to find how commercially driven and competitive the subtexts that packed the place were. Editors and agents from New York blustered in regularly, suggesting a business model, while the tenor seemed to indicate that some wannabe authors were going to win and some lose. That atmosphere revealed a strangely myopic vision about what constituted fiction that was nearly devoid of historical/theoretical perspectives, countercurrents, alternative ways of imagining what we were doing and to what purpose. I hope that may have changed over the last few decades. I don't know.

In any case, a diminutive cohort at the Workshop—a metaphor that sends a shiver up my spine, implying as it does that narratives are like kitchen cabinets—at some level sensed this. One in my group, David Shields, and I would attend our institutional "workshop" Tuesdays, then often go out for pepperoni pizza and sundaes afterward or meet during the week to think about and push back against the ocean of uncontested suppositions situating the program, challenge each other to consider what we wanted to be about as writers. That shadow government of support and disputation added up perhaps to the most important education I received during those years. It got me thinking about how writing is institutionalized in the classroom, in publishing, in the culture, how the relations between authors develop and can develop, what "success" might mean in different contexts, and what the theorization of such programs might teach us.

That essential questioning helped frame my later relationships with writers and the publishing/distribution apparatus. How can we sustain each other? How can we oppose, re-envision, re-deploy the pedagogical space? Gentle, caring, fierce, Lidia conceives of writing zones as realms of sustenance and social change. Through her and Larry McCaffery, through entities like FC2 and its board of directors with whom I had the privilege of working for sixteen years, I experienced collectivity and encouragement in transformative ways.

Steve Tomasula came onto my radar a little later. His novel, *VAS*, was game-changing for me, teaching me universes about formal revolution, writing as intense research, about a kind of postgenre enterprise that functions as much as argument as it does as what we once termed fiction. *Theories of Forgetting* would never have been what it turned into without *VAS* and

Danielewski's *House of Leaves* preceding it. All literature, naturally, is a conversation with all other literature across space and time, and I love being conscious of whom I'm speaking to. *Theories of Forgetting* is, among lots and lots of other things, a tribute to both those books.

With my own students, undergraduate and graduate alike, those studying literature and theory and those studying creative writing, I've been dedicated, have been for decades, to exploring ways of moving beyond that Iowa paradigm. I talk about this at length in *Architectures of Possibility: After Innovative Writing*, but the shorthand might be that Barthes conceptualizes the outdated academic space as a magisterial one. You know: the "master" enters the classroom or lecture hall, sits knowingly, the embodiment of "wisdom," at the head of the table, or behind a podium, and delivers Deep Truth. Good god: just shoot me. Unfortunately, that continues to look like most "workshops" and literary seminars, even if many have learned to disguise that Wise Master Reflex slightly in a superabundance of disingenuous ways.

What else might those spaces look like? How else might they function? I call my "workshop" arenas Askings. Students and I try to find the right questions to pose to each other and the text at hand, rather than piling on the "correct" answers, concerning which, cf.: unfinalizability above. We make no distinction between theory and other forms of writing since writing is by its nature a theorization of the world. My goal is to foster a sense of nosiness, close reading, inspiration and motivation and perspiration, query and collaboration, a territory of hovering rather than tethering, and a simple (and complex) interest in the universe and the universe of written texts—a less Euclidean space, as Barthes calls it. A space of opportunities. Polyphony, not monologue. Collectivity rather than hierarchy. And the person whose work is before us—because of the questioning model—becomes the most talkative in the room. After we've asked him or her all the questions we have, she or he asks us about anything he or she might have been wondering about—all sans notions of critique.

That's also the model I wanted to bring to the board of directors at FC2, a model that doesn't rely on sales figures and metaphorical stock markets, but on cooperation and radical vision.

Is FC2 still unique in that?

LANCE: No, thank goodness. By the late eighties and nineties other small, independent presses were emulating FC2 (some consciously, some unconsciously) in response to fewer and fewer engaging alternatives on the New York scene, which had become dominated by a handful of houses. Each indie press evolved its own paradigm, but I dare say most, if not all, wouldn't have done so without FC2 paving the way. Now there are tons of superb alt-presses out there, from The Dorothy Project and Tarpaulin Sky to Deep Vellum and Astrophil. It's fantastic to see such mushrooming. In many respects, the only thing they share with FC2, however, is that they're all looking for new ways of thinking about writing, the bottom line, distribution, and what have you. I do worry that many have a short life span, while others get gobbled up regularly by larger houses. I'm thinking of Soft Skull. I'm thinking of Counterpoint.

How—and this is a question whose answer will remain in a constant state of change—can we bring into the world the eccentric (in its root sense) books we relish? Truth to tell, right now it's actually not that hard. These days most presses support themselves by running contests. If you ask for a few dollars when people submit, you will have enough to bring out four or six books a year that otherwise wouldn't see the light of day.

Is that the case with Dzanc Books?

LANCE: I'm not intimately tied into what goes on behind the curtain there, so I can't answer with certainty, but I believe so. One of the two founders, Steven Gillis, was a lawyer. The other, Dan Wickett, a passionate online book reviewer. In 2006 they committed themselves to setting up and overseeing an unorthodox press. From what I can see, Dzanc's model is quite similar to FC2's, but it further attempts erasing the boundaries between literary and social activism. In addition to bringing out some amazing fiction and nonfiction by authors as diverse and important as Robert Coover, Peter Markus, Robert Lopez, Percival Everett, Nina Shope, Susan Daitch, Joseph McElroy, Lindsey Drager, and Laura van den Berg, it runs the Dzanc Writers-in-Residence Program, which brings authors into elementary and secondary public schools to teach creative writing; the Disquiet International Literary Program, a writing conference in Lisbon; and an intern program for students wanting to engage with independent publishing from the inside out. Steve also has his fingers in various extracurricular social programs.

Not-Knowing *is the title of Barthelme's collection of essays and interviews and the phrase "not-knowing" recurs in your work. In* My Red Heaven, *for instance, a young version of Vladimir Nabokov awakes to the "not-knowing" of writing. That idea is also reminiscent of a sentence by Roland Barthes you often quote, which says that "writing is the question minus the answer." How does "not-knowing" feed your creative energy? Do you yourself wake up to the not-knowing of writing?*

LANCE: When I was in high school, I started coming across Barthelme's stories in *The New Yorker*. That marks my initial encounter with deeply disruptive, evasive stories that refused to quiet down, and it was love at first blight. I didn't possess a language with which to talk about them. That lack intrigued me. I realized as I moved through college and graduate school that my favorite reading instants were those in which I couldn't quite stabilize a text, whether it be one by Stein or Acker, Robbe-Grillet or Saramago. It was those flashes of not-knowing that drew me in, made me feel I was among family.

It's precisely that not-knowing that leads me into my writing each morning. The idea of cranking out some version of the same novel I've written before is shattering. For me, it's all about the sensation of being back on my heels, afloat in unknown seas, coming ashore in what the Germans call *Neuland*—utterly new topography. I still remember with *Theories of Forgetting* waking up each morning with the hope that with that one I might just write a novel nobody would ever want to publish. I like to think I came pretty close.

Which I suppose leads us back to Barthes and that notion about literature being the question without the answer. This is absolutely essential to writing practices that appeal to my heart and my mind. I want to finish reading a novel feeling rudderless. The rest is propaganda. When teaching, I want to present texts to my students that set them into generative lands of ignorance. Texts one can never walk away from thinking: That's it; I've got it; time to move on. One can repress them, pretend one never read them, pretend they don't exist, tiptoe around them and get on with one's life. But think about them a bit, and whole solar systems unfold.

Gertrude Stein is a great way to introduce first-year students to literary experimental texts, with a sentence like "dining is west."

LANCE: Yes! Sentences like that make me outrageously pleased. My favorite from *Tender Buttons* might just be: "Let it strange." Letting it strange as a reading mechanism, a writing mechanism, how we might move through the world of the world and the world of texts in a perpetual state of excitement.

You describe your volume [[there.]] *as a "trash diary," and that term reappears in* Skin Elegies *in the Fukushima section. Can you tell us more about your notions of trash diary and waste aesthetics?*

LANCE: I spent the spring of 2013 as a fellow at the American Academy in Berlin, where I was working on *Theories of Forgetting*. I noticed myself beginning to collect particles of data on the side—quotes, reminiscences, observations, reflections, all kinds of incoming information.

ANDI: One night we would go to experimental theater and see something that just blew our socks off. The next we would attend a concert of *neue Musik*. We'd go to performances, art installations, all kinds of things. You [Lance] would come back, grabbing from here and there, and somehow it all got absorbed into *[[there.]]*. Everything became material because everything was intent on reinventing the idea of art.

LANCE: Totally. And, before long, that collection began to grow and take shape. I started asking myself what this agglomeration might look like if I simply let it become itself, which it did in the form of a critifictional collage-contemplation—I coined the term "trash diary" to describe what I was doing—about what the confluence of questioning, travel, and innovative writing practices might feel like.

Many years after I finished I came across Olga Tokarczuc's *Flights*, which she refers to as a constellation novel. I was thunderstruck by its amalgam of seemingly unrelated narraticules that were connected, not by plot, but by metaphor, image, trope. The result is an activity on the part of writer and reader wherein process supersedes product, forward motion is attained by other means than character development and the rest we expect to purchase in that old rag and bone shop of the heart.

This leads me to recall another, perhaps more distant influence on my work: Kathy Acker. I frequently teach *Blood and Guts in High School* for its exceptional fusion and confusion of transgressive fiction and nonfiction, genres, pla(y)giarized and so-called "authentic" passages, motley discourses, visuals and prose, all shot through with Bataille and Kristeva. At core, Kathy was concerned with what Larry McCaffery, speaking of Donald Barthelme's project, once dubbed an aesthetics of waste—that which cultures must expel or at least repress in order to remain functioning and whole. While my work inhabits a very different cosmos than Kathy's punk productions, mine couldn't be what it is without her project's presence.

Andi, did you also keep your own visual trash diary while you were in Berlin? [[there.]] *reveals how you conceived the project for your film,* Denkmal, *from a collection of photographs that you'd taken every day of the same view of the villa where the Nazis held the Wannsee Conference, during which the Final Solution was laid out.*

ANDI: I've always conceived of my imagination as a sort of garbage disposal. The assemblage sculptures I make are all about taking disparate objects—animal bones, mannequin parts, birdcages—and bringing them together in unexpected juxtapositions. So it's something I naturally gravitate toward. Berlin provided new, fiercely rich terrain.

Denkmal materialized because I was drawn to the beauty off our balcony at the American Academy, which looks out across Lake Wannsee. I started taking photos from there every morning. At some point well into the process, I learned that the Wannsee Conference Center—where, as you say, the Final Solution was set forth—was tucked away in a stand of trees on the far side. You can't actually see it from the balcony, but there it is—the horror of the past inside all that beauty. I was compelled to catalog it. I photographed it mornings, afternoons, and evenings. I didn't know what I would do with those shots, just that I needed to take them, my visual trash diary, deeply aware that had the Second World War gone differently, Lance the intellectual and Andi the Jewish artist would most certainly not be in a position to take in that view. I shot over 3000 stills and whittled those down to something like 1200. And it's from those that I constructed *Denkmal.*

LANCE: You have to understand: to walk into Andi's studio is to see trash aesthetics at work. I'm ostentatiously neurotic, a desperate lover of order in this disorder we refer to as reality. I have a very clean, well-organized desk and computer desktop. Literally if I have a nice view out my window, I pull the heavy shades so I don't get distracted by all the stuff out there. Andi is the magnificent opposite. She possesses an explosive imagination. If I open her computer desktop to look up something, I'm struck down by an anxious wave. Everything is everywhere. Everything is one of those shots from the James Webb telescope.

ANDI: It's like folder, folder, folder …

LANCE: In Andi's studio there's a pile of animal bones here, a collection of doll parts there. False teeth. Glass eyes. It's an extraordinary and extraordinarily stimulating space. The other thing is … I'm thinking of Kienholz …

ANDI: Edward Kienholz. He did these fantastic large-scale installations—rooms you could walk into with scenes comprised of strange beings and various cultural detritus. A bar. A cell in a psychiatric institution. A lonely apartment in New York City. He was the first assemblage artist I think whose work, which I came across in graduate school, spoke to me deeply. Small world, by the way: he moved to northern Idaho, where Lance and I were teaching at the University, and bought—yes, bought—a small town he named, I kid you not, Beyond Hope. We met him shortly after we moved. He was a large man of few words, a kind of avant-garde semi-aphasic Buddha. Ed referred to what he did as tableaux. His work taught me about how one can combine disparate artifacts into gripping if dismaying environments. He used resin to create these cocoons around his figures, employed animal skulls in his sculptures. That kind of thing changed me.

Lance, would you say that your attraction for the Wunderkammer is inspired by Andi's own creative work and imagination?

LANCE: Everything I do is inspired by Andi's work. And, yes, we're the Wunderkammer kids. Andi helped introduce me to the concept—another mode of trash aesthetics, a three-dimensional trash diary, and one that goes back to, apparently, sixteenth-century Italy and England. In many ways my work is the literary manifestation of a Wunderkammer. [To Andi.] One of the things that's so engaging about your Wunderkammers is that they are all sites in which different voices collect, implying different ways of existing in a world without hierarchy.

And so we're back, then, to what Derrida conceives of as the artist/thinker *bricoleur*, where apposition leads to new methods of seeing and feeling. One can, at least from one point of view, conceptualize *Theories of Forgetting* or *Skin Elegies* as Wunderkammers, which by nature embrace anti-teleological visions. One doesn't necessarily have to read either from beginning to end (indeed, the ideas of "beginning" and "end" don't really hold up in the former); both gain meaning through adjacency; there is a sense in both of heterogeneity. One doesn't—one can't—read the Wunderkammer in linear fashion. The eye never quite knows where to fall or how to proceed, and every detail is significant.

Andi's work has this quality of incendiary simultaneity to it. If you look at her assemblages or videos, you'll notice how busy they are, how frenetic, how much is going on in a very limited space or time. They overflow with minutiae—a little plastic ant crawling on the dress of some big sculpture; Adolf Eichmann's manipulated voice chunks in *Denkmal*. It's as if whatever medium she's working in, she's really working in the tradition of the Wunderkammer.

Going back to the trash diary, can you tell us a bit more about Hamari's section in Skin Elegies*?*

LANCE: Three or four years ago Sandeep Bhagwati, a composer based in Berlin and Montreal, asked me to contribute a poem to a sonic memorial he was composing about the Fukushima disaster. I wrote an erasure poem backwards, as it were—one, that is, in which more and more words materialize as the poem takes shape on succeeding pages—based on several first-person accounts of the nuclear accident. That grew into what you read in *Skin Elegies*, which itself, at least in my mind, is a gathering of narratives about emblematic moments that made the second half of the twentieth century and the beginning of the twenty-first incomparably overwhelming.

At the same time, cellphone novels—a popular medium in Japan that allows commuters to read easily on their way to and from work on trains—caught my attention. I studied a good number of them and, in all honestly, found them just awful: threadbare romances and flying dragons, mostly. What I found bewitching, though, was how they looked on the screen. The form turned prose into poetry, estranged the commercial framework of the page. So the first-person accounts about Fukushima—a kind of trash diary of quotes from interviews, news articles, and videos—distilled into one account, written as a cellphone novel (or, more precisely, cellphone memoir) by a more-or-less fictional school teacher in an attempt on my part to ruminate about how the contemporary comes to terms with how we put into language that which can't be put into language. How, through that, we might develop a sense of radical empathy for others involved with us in this ahistorical fiasco we think of as the present.

Many sections in Skin Elegies *are about one moment, which you expand into a fragmented narrative. Is this a way of working on the encounter between narrative prose and poetry?*

LANCE: I've told my creative-writing students for years now, somewhat truthfully, somewhat mischievously, that I used to know what the difference was between prose and poetry, but I've long since forgotten. For the last couple decades I've been finding it ever more arduous to separate the two alleged categories in any meaningful way. So it is with fiction and nonfiction. I'm more drawn to projecting beyond the inherent belief in "borders," which is such a dangerous concept both aesthetically and politically, not to mention in terms of gender, race, physics, or philosophy. Another way of saying this: I like to conjecture what happens to writing and thinking and feeling that pictures itself as both-and.

What we once labeled poetry has an ability to condense or blur time, reconceptualize it, compact language in ways that prose writers haven't tended to do. Yet then one recalls writers like Ben Marcus in *The Age of Wire and String*, or any of Barthelme's or Anne Carson's work, and that facile observation breaks down. Prose writers have usually had an urge toward the chronological, toward prose as transparency, toward rounded characters. I'm curious about how and why we might disrupt such moves, turn reading into a troublesome event from the layout of the page to how we view identity, no longer boxing these concepts into the language of those creative-writing textbooks written in what feels now like 1735.

Too, I'm drawn to timeless moments, moments where temporality doesn't function as we've been taught temporality should—those last few minutes after the Challenger has disintegrated, when the crew apparently remains alive and conscious. That retelling of the Icarus instant in the grammar of technology and spectacle. What happens to a minute when you know it's your last? Asking if those seconds are more fit for poetry or prose seems beside the point, evidence of imagination idling.

What you say about trying to figure out what goes through someone's mind in a dramatically short time span evokes Tobias Wolff's short story "Bullet in the Brain," which first tells how a man called Anders, a literary critic, gets shot in the head during a bank robbery. The second part of the text proceeds to narrate what happens in the man's brain, where the bullet does not travel as fast as the neuronal connections. The second half of the story presents itself as the list of what the man might have on his mind at the exact time of his death, which turns out to be none of the supposedly significant moments of his adult life. Defying the bullet's speed in neuronal temporality, the narrative—as if in slow motion—reaches the core of the man's existence: that seminal childhood memory when for the first time Anders heard another kid speaking with a Southern accent saying "they is" in a phrase that sounded wonderfully incorrect and liberating. At which point the story stops, before the bullet exits Anders's skull, with the resonating "they is."

LANCE: I don't know that story, but I have to tell you: I wish I'd written it. Robert Coover, whom I admire to no end, pulls off the same move, only in reverse, in "Going for a Beer," where he encapsulates a man's whole life in two and a half pages and just a few sentences. That's what's most extravagant about that piece: its denarration of time. That is, "Going for a Beer" predicaments conventional narrative's temporality to capture the experience of life's rush from alpha to omega, that sense of time smear that seems only to accelerate as we get older, that feeling my mother had, dying of cancer, as we sat together in her living room on a rainy day as she looked out the window, contemplating, and said after a long pause: So that was it? That was all? Meaning her last 77 years.

Coover enacts that denarration in several ways. First, he has his story compact what would normally take, say, a full scene—or at least a few robust sentences—to delineate and, as it were, reverse the Newtonian impulse built into received syntax. Listen to the opening line to hear what I mean: "He finds himself sitting in the neighborhood bar drinking a beer at about the same time that he began to think about going there for one." We could talk a lot about those first twenty-six words, how they make the protagonist nameless, and hence into a kind of Everyschlemiel, or how he abruptly discovers himself sitting somewhere, as if waking into a dream ... and not a particularly nice one. We could talk about the generic quality of the setting that reflects the generic quality of his life. But perhaps most remarkable and disorienting is the transposition of sequence: he is at the bar before he considers leaving his digs for it.

Coover deploys what I think of as temporal jumpcuts there—not between scene and scene, per routine writing, but rather within single sentences. So a half page later our protagonist takes out a woman for a nightcap to the same bar as mentioned in that first line, the place where they originally met (note the cliché of the *soi-disant* life our protagonist is living), "where a brawny dude starts hassling her. He intervenes and she turns up at his hospital bed ..." The fight with said brawny dude, the protagonist's subsequent pummeling, and the trip to the hospital are contained, as it were, in the second sentence's conjunction. Or, better, that conjunction marks a story void, a befuddling leap ahead in time, a temporal lurch which causes the reader by necessity to trip and thereby awaken.

We read sentences that look like they should behave, seem to be doing a perfectly good job at acting like respectable sentences, but that in fact generate through their matter-of-fact dislocations a static. Coover further suffuses that shock-structure with a language of doubt. In addition to the six question marks threaded through his piece (a relatively high frequency deployment of said punctuation), note the proliferation of such words and phrases as *he can't remember, he's no longer sure, maybe*, or *so he supposes, wondering, uncertain of what part of town he is in ... or what part of the year.*

Given the sexual shenanigans and doltish masculine violence rendered through Coover's signature energetic hyperbole, one often initially reads "Going for a Beer" in the key of bawdy comedy. But another tone simultaneously and inextricably intertwines with that one. As with so much Kafka (think *Metamorphosis*; think Gregor, bourgeois worker bee, trying to figure out how to disembark from bed so he can get dressed and hurry to work on time [we never want to displease our bosses, do we?]), we are aswim in a night lake of hole-in-the-heart disorientation and sadness.

In some measure, I think that's because "Going for a Beer" can be read, not only as fun denarrational romp, an exercise in formal (and hence social) misbehavior, and/or a concomitantly sober clownish reminder of how every tale ends in that white scramble of death following its final period, how every life scrambles at breakneck speed toward the silence of the white sheet tugged up over its face, but also as an exploration of a consciousness—the protagonist's? the implied author's?—blurring into the bewildering atemporality of early dementia.

Or we might instead want to translate our reading into political terms. Do so, and we can read "Going for a Beer" as a biting critique of how hyperconsumerism doesn't work, again and again. From such a vantage point, "Going for a Beer" mimics capitalism's speed of mass production. It simulates a narrative assembly line stuck on fast forward, which would be one loud slapstick laugh, except for the fact that the nameless widget it chews up and spits out is called a human being.

I recently finished Jenny Erpenbeck's *Not a Novel*, an extraordinary un-memoir in which she reminds us that literature's job is to show "that what we know is never the whole truth, but literature also tells us that the whole truth is waiting for us, if only we could read." Yet the more we read, the more we learn, the more we recognize truth never occurs in the singular outside religion, spirituality, psychotherapy, psychopathology, and other reductionistic, Liliputian modes of thought and being.

That interruption in our certainty about Truth with a capital T, which is to say that interruption in our certainty about stable language and narrativity in which such an Ur-truth could somehow be housed all pristine and speakable, has been one of Coover's primary obsessions since that first book of his I plucked off my campus library shelf, *Pricksongs and Descants*—and one of its stories in particular, "The Babysitter," which has proven to be so many readers' darling. In it, Coover dishevels centered surety primarily by means of splintering both point of view and the line between reality and the other thing. In "Going for a Beer," he does so primarily by means of splintering our most basic assumptions about time's arrow: that we can somehow easily chart and articulate it from start to stop; that's its trajectory will add up to something we can refer to in the end as sense; that its yield will therefore always be cogently, snugly narrativizable, which is to say cogently, snugly livable.

Wrong, Coover's indecorous compositions say, wrong, and wrong.

In your essay "Reading/Writing as Tangle: Metafiction as Motion" you write that "[a]rt willfully slows and complicates writing/ reading, hearing, and/or viewing." Could you say more about that slowing down process in your writing? Andi, would you also care to comment on the variations in speed that we often see in your videos—whether it is slow motion, as in Where the Smiling Ends, *or extremely rapid montage as in* Denkmal *or in some parts of* Theories of Forgetting?

LANCE: I suppose this returns us, in a fashion, to the view of making reading into a difficult event. Espen Aarseth coined the term "ergodic" to describe in some measure what I'm talking about, moving through a text as non-trivial activity—an event whereby we can experience the incredible strangeness of the act we forgot sometime when we were children: deploying bizarre squiggles on a page to empathize with other humans across space and time. What a crazy idea.

Behind that observation floats Viktor Shklovsky's famous essay on the defamiliarization effect in art—the attempt, I would argue, not only to make the reader sense the stoniness of the stone, as he claims, but also to teach her or him at an existential level to become more present in the world by becoming more present in the world of deliberately challenging texts. We usually read Shklovsky in terms of technique (after all, his essay is titled "Art as Technique"), but I would say behind his discussion of technique is a crucial phenomenological contention.

Andi's riveting work in *Where the Smiling Ends* is the embodiment of that, isn't it, Andi: this anthropological undertaking where you see across cultures that, as people stop smiling after their photo is taken, and they move from the public to the private again, there is something forlorn that emerges in their body language: this dropping of the head, this gesture of giving up and turning inward. We didn't pay enough attention to the world until Andi's piece taught us how.

ANDI: What about this at the level of art versus entertainment?

LANCE: Completely. Entertainment, we could say, is all about speed—those movies, you know, where lots of things blow up in the dark, yet you can barely remember whether or not you've actually seen them a week after you've left the theater. My students are keenly, painfully aware that they're members of the Distracted Generation, plugged into the continuous bewilderment of surfaces. Art, however, is all about the opposite: an invitation (an intervention, maybe, is closer to the point, as in the discourse of recovery) to slow down, embrace Heidegger's sense of Dasein.

On the first day of each semester, my students and I take a little time to talk about how one reads hard work, how unplugged focus gives one a very different experience of reading—reading as this act of loving, caring, disquiet, not-being-sure, elation. What do we mean, to put it differently, when we say: *I am reading?*

ANDI: Which is a form of seeing, isn't it. And that kind of seeing is all about a process of putting on the perceptual brakes. So I think of *Where the Smiling Ends* as an investigation into what photography leaves out—that second after the photograph has been snapped, what happens beyond the frame of a picture. That's the alluring story. To get at it, I needed to slow down the video clips that comprise it and really see what happens. I recall you and I, Lance, were sitting in a cafe near the Trevi Fountain in Rome. I said why don't you go ahead and have another cappuccino—I want to wander over there and take some footage of all those people getting their pictures snapped. As I videoed, what I thought I'd been observing, that gesture we've been talking about, became more apparent to me. Then, as I started editing, I was like: *Will you look at that.*

Somewhere I read that people visiting museums spend an average of 30 seconds in front of a masterpiece. You know: been there, done that, time to take a selfie and move on. I've always been committed to providing enough detail that one is tempted to stick around a little, come aboard and take a journey with me.

Paradoxically, there's another way that urges seeing, and that's to infuse a video with a certain kind of unusual speeding up. I'm thinking here of *Denkmal*. I wanted to fit as much information as possible into as few frames as possible, so that the viewer could see seasons changing, weather changing, place itself changing and yet staying the same, time undergoing continuous transformation in a state of historical irony.

Either way, if all goes well, one re-experiences the nature of temporality, the nature of being somewhere. That's what art can do that entertainment can't.

Does this also happen in your writing process, Lance? You said you like to be able to pay attention to the acoustics of your sentences. When you reread a sentence you've just written, do you see or hear things you didn't think would be there?

LANCE: Oh, always. It's the oddest occurrence—editing my work. It feels like somebody else wrote every syllable I'm reading. Each morning I go up into my writing studio and work. I start from where I began the morning before. I write and rewrite a few pages until they feel like I can leave them alone for a while, then push forward with the promise of going back when a first draft is complete. I rework again, both at a global and local level. Each time I move through a passage, a sentence, a phrase, I hear something I didn't hear the last time, see some turn, some image, that surprises and delights me—or disappoints me, chagrins me, demands rejiggering.

That may be another reason some have the sense of slowness and/or condensation when reading my work. I'll write a sentence over and over. Often what I thought was one sentence will grow into a paragraph or page. And, as Andi said about her work, I love texturing my writing with specificity—full-on sensory particulars, the stuff only novels can do with such long lusciousness. When I feel like an area of the text I'm working on is nearing completion, I read it aloud. That invariably leads to another series of astonishments and disappointments.

Could you expatiate a little more on how you created the video for Theories of Forgetting, *Andi?*

ANDI: Lance was far enough along in that novel that we knew the protagonist, Alana, was going to die in a pandemic called The Frost, which causes an increasing sensation of coldness and growing amnesia in its victims. (One could call it, I guess, a bad case of the twenty-first century.) He had written a passage that talks about a so-far non-existent video that Alana had made, ran that passage off, and said let's see what we can come up with around this, okay? The first thing I showed him was a little *too* busy. And that's where that collaborative spirit kicked in. We started going back and forth, forth and back. I wanted to create cascading images of the landscape around Smithson's *Spiral Jetty* that paralleled Alana's increasing psychological disorientation and physical decline. Then, in the second half of the video, the recited narrative from the novel that accompanies those cascading images begins to reimagine itself visually through erasure.

The key was to have the novel extend past its borders into the world by way of a video. Somewhere in that process we decided not to stop there, but rather to put together a video retrospective of Alana's work and show it in actual galleries under the title *There's No Place Like Time*—hence a novel you can walk through that doesn't stop at the usual novelistic prison doors.

There is a pervasive sense of anxiety in Skin Elegies, *which can be linked with this impression of speed and slow motion.* Skin Elegies *is somehow difficult to read at one fell swoop for that reason: it's a book that is "difficult" to experience. You have to take breaks, lifting your eyes up from the page because of the intensity of events described and that pervasive sense of anxiety. Can we connect all this to a phrase in [[there.]] which defines reading as a "mode of pain"? What about your own experience when you write those fragments: do you physically feel that tension? Is it a productive energy into your work or the opposite?*

LANCE: I suppose at the largest level I wanted to apprehend in *Skin Elegies* this cultural agitation we're all feeling in our contemporary Beyond Belief, where, thanks to the climate cataclysm, pandemics, the proliferation of war, surveillance capitalism, and the rest, we as a species are writing ourselves to death. I sought to generate a concomitant sense of instability in my readers, a continuous sense of disconnection and misconnection—perhaps the literary equivalent of Freud's notion of free-floating anxiety. So, yes, I wanted in some sense to make *Skin Elegies* into an anxiety machine.

[To Andi:] It's like *Denkmal*, to the degree that an exercise in pain is a productive reading/seeing mode.

I don't understand why reading should always be a pleasurable undertaking. I know at first that sounds odd. But we all remember times when reading has been the opposite of effortless. It can be hard. It can be bewildering. It can be frustrating and boring and mystifying—all in the same sentence. Barthes talks about a certain kind of reading as bliss, which is absolutely the case, yet I think there's another side to it, a shadow side few speak about, which involves distress, something approaching suffering that can be inextricably bound with that bliss—watching Beckett's *Waiting for Godot*, by way of example, traversing the arduous passages in *Gravity's Rainbow* or *Infinite Jest*, or, in a very different way, Kenneth Goldsmith's *The Weather*, a transcription, during the course of a year, of a minute of each day's weather report from 1010 WINS. From one angle these are trauma texts, not in the sense that they portray trauma, but rather in the sense that there's an element of trauma that comes into the very act of reading them. Often they are easier to talk about, work through, after the fact than while submerged in their inconvenience. Counter-intuitively, the inconvenience is part of the joy of taking on such texts.

Some readers have certainly found *Skin Elegies*'s relentlessness tough going. There's not one sequence that I would describe as an especially happy one. [Laughs.] I get that. The book also leaps among narratives mercilessly. And many readers want, at the end of the day, to locate a wink of solace in the reading process that I'm afraid I'm simply not interested in. Solace strikes me as an overrated concept. *Skin Elegies* is probably one of my most relentless novels because, I would suggest, this is our most relentless world. We need to contemplate what that means, yet many of us want to do the contrary. We want to live in the Disney Channel. Our addiction to New Age absurdities masquerading as Zen wisdom and wacky Pollyanna-ish religiosity aside, solace is not exactly in abundance—unless one has drilled deep into the practice of self-delusion, made bad faith into a theology. I know most people don't want to hear this, but so it goes.

ANDI: The mind upload sequences in *Skin Elegies* are such a perfect metaphor for capturing that anxiety—that sense, as the mind you describe is being uploaded, of digital heebie jeebies.

In My Red Heaven, *there is that other sense of anxiety for the reader which is linked with the several layers of temporality running through the book. Most of the time the readers are immersed into the lively and enjoyable present time of the characters back in 1927. But very regularly a voice just comes out of the contemporary moment and reminds the readers of what will befall these characters in a few years or so.*

LANCE: To ask how we experience time—something none of us can define—is to ask how we experience narrative. As soon as that voice from the future, or from elsewhere, appears, as it sometimes does in *My Red Heaven*, something off-kilter transpires: the present becomes suffused with further texture. Imagine how painful living our lives would be if we knew how they would end, or even what three years from now might look like. It's one thing to show a young man eating a pound of chocolate daily because he's addicted to the stuff, another to allow the reader to realize gradually that that man, whose friends call Adi, will become the Hitler we know only too well.

In *Skin Elegies* something else happens, too, temporally speaking. It's told in a perpetual present tense, except for the intrusions from that future/elsewhere voice. That absolute presentness, I hope, adds to the novel's relentlessness. The reader in many cases already knows what's going to occur (the Challenger waiting on the launch pad is already doomed, and forever, has already come apart and is tumbling in pieces toward the ocean), so a different sort of dramatic irony blossoms. Each narraticule in the novel is part of some larger catastrophe, and one comes to feel it's horrific present, followed by horrific present, followed by another.

The resulting anxiety on the reader's part, I should like to think, forms resistance to formulaic responses about how we are used to telling catastrophes. Humans have a tendency to want to story them in such a way that they ultimately offer reassurance, catharsis, but these times we're living in ... They can't be told that way. Here we're raising the narratological ghost of Christianity again, that narrative need so deep in us we think it's natural to crave redemption. But why? The data doesn't support the assumption.

Here I'm thinking of B. S. Johnson's *The Unfortunates*, a novel in a box about the slow death by cancer of the narrator's friend Tony. The chapters can be shuffled, read in any order, and the outcome is a dismantling of the trauma narrative, which usually works in an arc through said trauma to recuperation, healing, resolution. Johnson's narrative suggests loss and pain are everywhere, all the time; that we can't escape trauma, nor are we always lost in it—yet it's both, simultaneously. The sentences themselves are broken by white space, lack final punctuation, repeat phrases obsessively, trail off in mid-thought. Johnson's is a text, then, about disease that enacts dis-ease, an autrebiography that puts me in mind of works like Maggie Nelson's *The Argonauts* and Carmen Machado's *In the Dream House* that write against the innocences of contemporary memoir, which has ingrained into it a tranquilizing form. And which, naturally, speaks to its current popularity.

ANDI: It's equally important to disrupt how the stories get repeated endlessly in the media cycles and then utterly forgotten. Thinking of the Columbine shooting: hideous as it was, we do nothing in its wake as a country save wait for the next one. We have become habituated to fear and crisis. [To Lance.] I think you wanted to take some of those moments and show different aspects of them and not focus on that thing we always see and know about them.

LANCE: The history behind the history. That's the difference between journalism or an academic history book—both, from a certain vantage point, subsets of fiction—and self-conscious fiction: the latter is engaged in imagining the mind, in deploying all five senses in summoning a world from the inside as well as the outside. The consequence is, all going well, the creation of an intimate—if uneasy—empathy, a humanization—or, if nothing else, the fictive approximation of it. After all, if we can't over the course of a lifetime come to fully understand ourselves (and we most certainly can't), then how in the world can we expect to fully understand another?

While each of the historical junctures I tell in my novels stays very close to the exterior facts—or as close as one can when speaking of a past event, an event that invariably makes yesterday into a narratological obstacle—each also attempts inhabiting those junctures in a fashion only self-conscious fiction can access.

We would like to ask you about the importance of "skin," which is very much present in My Red Heaven. *We're thinking of Anita Berber, for instance, or "the skin that people call Anita Berber." The novel after* My Red Heaven *has this beautiful title,* Skin Elegies, *such a startling association of words. There is also that fragment from Vladimir Nabokov's* Pnin *that you quote in* [[there.]] *that says that "Unless a film of flesh envelops us, we die." We would love to hear you on the notion of epidermic sensations in your novels.*

LANCE: Isn't that wildly beautiful, how Nabokov writes about our skin as something akin to an astronaut's fragile spacesuit? Over the last, what, twenty or thirty years, our social domain has wrestled with the trouble referred to as the body in manifold ways. What is the relationship between those false binaries, mind and body, thought and sensation? Where does the body stop and digital prosthetic begin? In what sense do the bodies we refer to as ours remain a stable site in the face of time's onslaught? How does that help us nuance notions of identity? Temporality itself? As mind upload technologies are conceptualized, do we need to reconceptualize what William Gibson calls "the meat" as we narrativize leaving the body behind entirely—something it looks like we'll probably be able to do within the next fifty years, just in time for the death of the planet—thereby attaining a very unchristian immortality?

We sometimes conceive of our skin—erroneously, I would argue—as the primary site of home. During the pandemic years that changed. Or, rather, our pandemic brought to the fore something that has always been the case (we need only look to horror films for confirmation): our bodies are forever radically other, estranged, sites of dread, memos from the front office that we are all astronauts in fragile spacesuits, strangers to ourselves and others in an unrecognizable land. My students, it turns out, felt that profoundly as they were cut off from others, cut off from serious education, by a welter of screens, made to fear the consequences of their own bodies' actions.

Behind all this dis-ease stands our stubborn aging. Believe as we might, time's arrow flies in only one direction as far as we are concerned: right through our unsteady hearts. This awareness imbues *My Red Heaven*, *Skin Elegies*, and *Always Crashing in the Same Car*, the latter, as I mentioned, about David Bowie's last months—those during which he worked on his acclaimed album *Black Star* while battling liver cancer and the consequences of his sixth heart attack. It's about being on the far shore of youth. I'm flabbergasted that, in our walking-on-eggshell age of self-awareness, even self-flagellation about such incredibly important subjects as gender, race, and disability, we can remain so blind about an equally huge prejudice: ageism. Not a day goes by that I don't hear some mean-spirited joke or another about it that would never be allowed to stand with respect to, say, the LGBTQ+ community.

Bowie was all about ceaselessly reinventing music, reinventing self, but our culture somehow moved on after the eighties and in many respects he became an increasingly marginal figure to most. The question he asked himself during the years that followed was how to come to terms with the idea that one's voice doesn't sound like it did in one's thirties because it's shot through with the effects of drugs, those accruing heart attacks, that eruption of that cancer, which is to say Mr. Blue-Eyed Death himself? And yet how does one not give in to the habitual under those conditions? We walk unceasingly through this blast furnace we name our flesh … and then what? Which is to say, interestingly enough, we inhabit a society permeated by ageism that doesn't know—doesn't care—it's permeated by ageism. Somehow one's life after forty is perceived as historical detritus, benighted, superseded by the very people whose lives, of course, someday will be perceived as historical detritus, benighted, superseded. The irony is palpable, and it's striking how few novels confront these issues in any meaningful way.

Anyway, this obsession with the body, with what we might call the Aesthetics of Disability, are essential to your work, Andi, from Freak Show and your assemblages to your fascination with skin in your video *Written on My Body: The Scar Project*, which documents a number of writers' stories about their physical scars which the world has etched on them.

ANDI: This might be a good time to recall that the working title of *Skin Elegies* was *We Held Hands*. That leitmotiv still runs through the novel—that anchor of human touch. I remember you, Lance—we were having coffee one day, talking about possible titles, and it occurred to you that, because it's such a robust leitmotiv, it couldn't be what this book was called. That would be too obvious, philosophizing with a hammer. "Skin Elegies" became its own little poem instead.

LANCE: When you touch someone, you know, your blood pressure actually goes down, a calmness is wont to enter you, and you all of a sudden feel connected with another human being in a way that no device (at least so far: be still, virtual reality) can duplicate. And yet there is not just one but two spacesuits separating you at that instant, as well. And yet you forget that's the case. And yet to touch someone for the first time is always the beginning of touching them for the last time. So every inch of skin forms the first syllables of an elegy.

ANDI: Even as it constitutes a home chord. The first months of the pandemic, which no one wants to think about anymore, underscored this: that physical separation, those spacesuits, that essential isolation so many felt. It burned us all to the bone.

LANCE: As you say that, I recall my mother's long death by cancer in 1993. Andi and I were fortunate enough—"fortunate enough" is an understatement—to be the only two people in the room at the assisted living center when she changed tenses. How can I describe what a crucial instant it was for the three of us? The human touch we shared felt direct, despite her morphine fog, her semi-consciousness, her undone flesh. My mother responded keenly. She may not have known where she was, but human touch was the language we spoke at the end. We spoke her out of the world, which is to say we loved her away.

Going back to the working title for Skin Elegies, *is there a trace of the idea of "holding hands" as a vital form of connection in the way some sentences from one section are repeated at the beginning of another—"holding hands," so to speak?*

LANCE: What a wonderful insight. Yes: I wanted to weave each disparate narraticule into the next through some kind of unique procedure, and settled on that phrasal hand-holding, which also struck me as a form of music—you know, one set of sounds, or one set of images, echoing another in various ways.

We haven't talked about that component of *Skin Elegies* yet—that idea of musicality as shaping tool. All my work has been tremendously influenced by two musical forms: Bach's fugues and Coltrane's jazz, each of which seems to me a version of sonic perfection. How, I've been asking myself forever, can such structures help us reconsider narrativization? I'm currently reading an excellent collection of essays on narratology in preparation for my graduate seminar on Narrative Theory and Practice: edited by Marina Grishakova and Maria Poulaki, it's titled *Narrative Complexity: Cognition, Embodiment, Evolution.* Last night I finished a marvelous piece by Martin Rosenberg, "Jazz as Narrative: Narrating Cognitive Processes Involved in Jazz Improvisation," that's helping me continue to wonder in deeper ways about these things. Rosenberg talks about how members of an improvising ensemble must work wholly differently from those in a classical string quartet. They must tell their story "in sophisticated harmonic, melodic, and rhythmic contexts, while responding at the same time to other musicians." The result is that several cognitive processes must be going on at the same time. Rosenberg shifts attention in narrativity, then, from the already-written to story-writing as emergent property, which feels much more like what I'm doing most of the time.

But I also want to mention music from a different galaxy altogether by proposing my Theory of First Albums, which goes like this: the first album you buy as a kid often functions at some deep-down level as an act of speculative autobiography. It functions, in other words, as a species of science fiction. That is, it evinces SF's allegedly predictive role by hinting at something about your future: about, perhaps, your tastes to come, certain aesthetic and psychological predilections you possess that not infrequently will shadow you in one guise or another for the rest of your life.

Mine was *Sgt. Pepper's Lonely Hearts Club Band*, which appeared on 2 June 1967. I had never heard anything like it and

I believe something in me altered for good during the roughly forty minutes it took me to listen to it the first time. I learned later that the producer, George Martin, and the Beatles created it over the course of 129 days in that famous Studio Two on Abbey Road, and that while they had spent 585 minutes recording the Beatles's first album, *Please Please Me*, it took them 700 hours to do *Sgt. Pepper*.

Even on initial listen, though, I could intuit the ludic brilliance that went into the thing—how, two cases in point, Lennon insisted that Martin attach a couple of seconds of mischievous fifteen-kilocycle tone to the end of "A Day in the Life" in order to annoy any dogs that happened to be in the neighborhood, or how the group recorded several seconds of hebephrenic babble (which sounds like *never do see any other way*, though I'm not really sure, even now) and then stuck it in the runout groove so that people who bought the record but didn't have an auto-return on their stereo would suddenly hear this caffeinated twaddle looping just when they thought the album was over.

And there was Peter Blake's incredibly self-reflexive cover littered with simulacra of Poe, Brando, Stockhausen, Wilde, and Marx (not to mention, interestingly enough, three SF writers: H. G. Wells, Aldous Huxley, and proto-avant-popster William Burroughs), among many other cultural icons, including a tidy gray-suited 1964 simulation of the Beatles supplied by Madame Tussaud's standing directly to the left of the flesh-and blood 1967 version wearing lime green, electric pink, sky blue, and redcoat red pop military-marching-band regalia.

That cover pointed to a certain density, a certain richness in the project that was borne out again and again by the music itself. Here was a real-time group, after all, that had created an unconsciously Baudrillardian concept album about a nonexistent group (with Ringo as the lead singer, "Billy Shears," no less) that seemed to be playing live before an audience that was in truth simply generated with Martin's help in the London studio.

And here was a record that took chance after Avant-Pop chance with form and content. There were McCartney's orchestral tune-up noises and audience murmurs on the title track, Lennon's surreal lyrics for "Lucy in the Sky with Diamonds," the warped carnival sounds on "Being for the Benefit of Mr. Kite!," Harrison's world-music dreamtime sitar on "Within You Without You," and lots of cut-and-splice and reverse-track procedures, not to mention the intricate development of "A Day in the Life" and that awe-inspiringly resonant final chord thrumming for what seemed like forever at the song's conclusion, which suggested to me through its force and abrupt appearance a key (yes) SF trope: the detonation of a nuclear bomb that brings to startling conclusion this day in the life of London (with distant echoes of that great final montage in *Fail Safe*) that the album as a whole has been about all along: the laughter, the youth angst, the sad departures, the circus, the meter maid, the love, the loneliness, the sex, the spirituality, the generation gap, the drugs, the multiple social registers, all amounting to an Eliotic pastiche that does not so much do the police in different voices as contemporary urban reality itself.

I know all this stuff I'm talking about can sound quite calculated and abstract, but that's only a sliver of what we're really discussing. The other is fanatical intuition and enthusiasm, which is another way of pointing to the author performing as multiplicity.

You talked about the writing moment as the creation of an "existential space of contemplation." Many descriptions seem to aim at plunging the readers into the midst of a world of sensations, a sensory, sometimes very sensual world. In "Reading/writing as a tangle," you explain how experimental reading/writing practices imply that you "thinkfeel" the text. Can you tell us about this phenomenological dimension of your writing, so to speak, being in the midst of the world, in the grain of things and writing about that?

LANCE: One of the greatest pleasures I receive from my writing is trying to put into words—which is to say trying to articulate thought and feeling—the countless experiences of being alive: what this smells like, what that really looks like, what something else sounds or tastes or feels like. At that stratum, all my work seems to me an extended journal about observation. The actual process of writing coaxes me into that room.

The act may seem slightly ironic, naturally, since I pull the curtains in my writing studio and never look out the window while I'm working. But that's an optical illusion. Turning inward turns me outward, gives me the focused opportunity to exist more fully in the world beyond the walls of my house and the walls of my skull. Isn't it odd, how while I write I'm completely separated from every other human being on the planet, yet more connected to the act of being human than ever. This is what I mean by writing as tangle ... in the best sense of the word—with the world, with the self, with others I will never know, with the problematics of existence.

In my creative writing classes, I notice, because of our screen-based globe, my students tend to privilege sight in their writing while concomitantly repressing or at least failing to attend to the other senses. They tend to render scenes as if they were part of a film script. When I point out that short stories and novels don't want to be films, my students display dismay. They seem to believe corporate films are the highest art form. But we all know, as Truman Capote said of Kerouac's *On the Road*, typing isn't writing. Composing veneers isn't fiction. Not paying attention isn't narrative. Skating on surfaces isn't living.

It goes without saying that the thing itself, as Derrida underscores, always escapes. Of course it does, certainly, and much to the chagrin of the phenomenologists, yet that inevitable failure is precisely the motivation for authors and intellectuals, I have to believe.

I recall when Andi and I started dating, we would go to a museum and stand in front of a Monet and try to see what we were seeing. I'd say something dumb like: "I see an icy river in the snowy countryside." And Andi would counter: "But look: there's no white at all used to render winter. It's all shades of blue and gray." Andi helped teach me how to perceive. Seriously perceive. I like to think we've helped each other sharpen all our senses like that through our engagements with art, with writing, with the stuff on the other side of my curtains. I like to think we've helped each other over the course of the last forty-plus years together gather experiential richness—meaning that we've helped each other sharpen our nosiness, what we ask and how.

But the phenomenological engagement is always desperate because we never actually encounter the world, do we. We encounter, rather, our perceptions of the world—the various constructions we've set in place, or, perhaps more to the point, which have been inculcated into us. The thing itself always slips away. That brings up an attendant dimension to my writing: how keenly aware I am that it is motivated by dilemmas rather than solutions. Writing for me isn't solely about contemplation, though it is most certainly that, or at least not the sort of contemplation associated with a meditative state, but also an active investigation into the complications of a thought, a metaphor, a disturbance I sense around me.

We're curious about the titles of the subsections in My Red Heaven*: two phrases united by a kind of colon, which is not exactly a colon.*

LANCE: I talk about this a little bit in *[[there.]]*, both seriously and whimsically: that the English language is bereft as it is, in part, because it contains only fourteen punctuation marks. Fourteen. That may be the saddest sentence I have ever spoken. Punctuation, after all, is the musical notation of the sentence. And we only have fourteen!

So what would happen, I ask myself daily, if we were to invent more punctuation marks, a greater range of ways of expressing? Each section of *[[there.]]* is preceded by four colons. To me those four colons express an introduction to the inexpressible. In *My Red Heaven*, I use the colon in the manner you describe as the sign of metalogic, a skewed micro-poem about what's to follow, two words or phrases separated by a space, a colon, and another space. What appears on either side of that notation is sometimes a vital metaphor, sometimes a principal phrase that sounds beautiful, a pretty image, a jarring one. In other words, one might think of the modified colon in this context as the mark of a clash, which, after all, is a kind of signature for the whole novel. It indicates a larger movement in the text, too: the mark of collage, that juxtaposition of unlike objects or voices.

As you can tell, I'm embarrassingly entranced by punctuation. One of the things I love most about *Tristram Shandy* is its use of the em dash. It's such an underused, underrated mark—and one students are often at a loss to employ or understand correctly. Sterne uses it as a token of hesitation, of connection between two ideas that don't seem to go together, of Locke's associative thought that Sterne examines, celebrates, and lampoons ... and which unwittingly looks forward to William James's assertation in *The Principles of Psychology* that consciousness is a stream, an assertation the modernists took up wholeheartedly. There's something comic about an em dash, too. Ever since reading *Tristram Shandy*, I can't feel them as a fully serious gesture. In *Dreamlives of Debris*, by the way, I consciously quote the em dash as used in *Tristram Shandy*—to some extent as a way to thank Sterne, but also to some extent as a device to introduce a certain breathlessness into prose.

ANDI: And that says nothing about the double bracket ...

LANCE: Oh, my god. Don't get me started. Every use of those is a thank-you letter to Heidegger, who spoke about bracketing concepts that, as it were, can't fully land, that we take for granted without critical reflection. My double brackets are Heidegger's on steroids. What, I ask through the title *[[there.]]*, do we even mean when we use such a pregnant word? Why do we think of it (as that period connotes) as somehow finalized, when it is just the opposite. The operation of bracketing estranges what the brackets try to contain and can't. "There" is such a haunting, haunted word, one that you can never actually believe in in a work of fiction because in a profound way there's never any "there" to be found "there." Fiction is indeed always about what isn't there. And nonfiction: well, it was trendy for three or four days in creative writing courses during the nineties to talk about "a sense of place." But, needless to say, that's the one thing no piece of writing will ever evince except in delusive terms.

Sometimes in Theories of Forgetting *the brackets are open and sometimes don't close.*

LANCE: Visually, I hope, that move creates a jarring effect in the reader. For me writing like that sure did: it signals that the contemplation, the problem, the strangeness will never end.

How do you work with your publishers? How difficult is it to publish novels that are formally and materially experimental? Andi, as a visual artist, are you a part of the dialogue with the publishers about the book cover and general design?

LANCE: I don't know how things work in France, but in America, in New York, in corporate publishing, as I say, which consists of only a small handful of houses now, when you sign your contract, you sign away rights to design and covers. You only own the actual words of your text—and really, economically speaking, only a small percentage of those. This, for me, is emblematic of current Big Publishing, which has very much bought into Big Capitalism.

(Agents, by the way, have essentially taken on the role of gatekeepers for corporate publishers over the last 20 or 25 years in the US. So I haven't used one of those, either, since, I want to say, around 2000.)

From a very early date, I tried to have as much control as possible over my writing by working with smaller, independent presses committed to experimental writing practices. It was exactly the right decision for me. Actually, I think they found me even as I found them. What I mean to say is that writers ferret out their audiences serendipitously, even as their audiences ferret out them. An example: with *My Red Heaven*, given the text was about Berlin in 1927, I wanted the cover to mimic the look of posters in Germany from the Weimar years. Matt Revert—an amazingly talented designer who invented that book's cover—and I spoke, at first through the publisher, Dzanc, and then directly. He was all about it. That way I got to control the novel from cover to cover. That's something that almost never happens in Manhattan.

And you can imagine how nightmarish *Theories of Forgetting* proved to lay out, given its anti-familiar design. I've become increasingly engaged not only in writing novels, you could say, but also in what I think of as genuinely erecting them. I worked quite closely with FC2's great designer, Steve Halle, on *Theories*, and with a novel like *Dreamlives of Debris* I laid out everything myself in InDesign, then sent Dzanc the file. What a sheer delight it is to work at that level. It demands a thoroughly distinct skills set, where the visual supersedes the linguistic.

ANDI: In *Theories of Forgetting* the protagonist's daughter—a performance artist—enters marginalia in pen into the allegedly found manuscript one is reading. Lance wanted a very specific color: that of the Great Salt Lake on a sunny day. Not just any blue, mind you. It took a while to hit on exactly the right one. And Lance didn't want a front cover on the novel, either, since that would suggest a privileged beginning, so he asked the publisher to create identical back covers. FC2 obliged. Bookstores didn't know how to display the novel on their shelves. They thought the novel had been misprinted. [Laughs.]

LANCE: Bookstores would receive copies of *Theories of Forgetting* and ship them back to the warehouse, saying there must have been some sort of printing error—there were two back covers. That Keystone Kops situation was amusing to watch, because on some plane it flagged what the novel was really all about in the final analysis: the act of reading itself; how we make sense of unfamiliar data hurtling in. I suppose that's been my life project. Well, one of them.

I first encountered artists' books in the late nineties, began to look back at their history and their present instantiations. The library at the University of Utah has an extensive collection with more than 80,000 titles. So I take my graduate and undergraduate students over when teaching creative writing or talking about the materiality of textuality to urge them to think about books in a less parochial context. And, it goes without saying, I've been profoundly infected by my own rendezvous with the opportunities artists' books present.

ANDI: Oh, just another example. Lance had also asked that the pages in *Dreamlives of Debris* form a perfect square, connoting that each page was a kind of room in a readerly labyrinth. At first Dzanc said no, that wasn't salable, then they came back a week or two later, having realized what a cool idea it was, and said not to worry, they'd figure it out.

LANCE: At times even independent publishers think they understand what a book should be, what it should look like, so when you give them something that doesn't look like what they expect in some very basic way, they resist.

In children's literature, deviations from the traditional book form are accepted and even encouraged. There is a lot of visual invention in illustrated books for children, for instance.

LANCE: So true. But adult books are treated as a whole other beast. Isn't that odd? And sad, too. I mean, we've been talking in large academic terms. But there's obviously also something incredibly pleasurable—in the sense of childhood wonder—about getting a book that you don't know how to open, don't know how to read, must explore in embodied terms to understand.

We've been taught through enculturation, indoctrination, how to forget all kinds of joy.

Plus I guess I'm a sucker for the little impish impulse: Why not a square book like that? Why not a book with two back covers? Let's play.

When exactly did you start collaborating together in the creation of books? Was it with Girl Imagined by Chance?

ANDI: We've been doing collaborations since the early nineties, I think. "Deathwatch," a small DIY SF graphic comic, I believe, was our first. We exhibited it in a gallery as part of a cyberpunk installation.

LANCE: While the short-story collection *Sewing Shut My Eyes* consists of several of our early text-image collaborations, I guess *Girl Imagined by Chance* was the first *novel* we collaborated on in a fairly extensive way, very carefully thinking through the relationship of text and image. Andi supplied manipulated photographs—the novel was all about simulation—each one of which formed a kind of prologue and occasion for reflection about each chapter. The most complete sense of collaboration, though, remains *There's No Place Like Time.* Often when artists or writers work multimodally, they have a real strength (visuals, say), but aren't particularly strong in some other area (storytelling, say, or language). What's been so special for us is sharing our strengths. It takes all our talents, such as they are, to produce a hybrid novel, catalogue, videos, gallery-space design, and "found" objects in that ever-growing retrospective.

ANDI: We've had such a great time nudging the reader out of the text of *Theories of Forgetting* and into the real world, which isn't quite the real world. How, we've kept asking ourselves, might we explode the binding of a book further?

With collaboration, one plus one always equals three, something greater than the sum of its parts. That's a blast—that process of conversation, creative problem-solving, instinctive searching, and the rest usually takes the form of good-humored, exploratory exchanges between us. We provoke each other, egg each other on, sustain each other, find enchantment in what the other comes up with. The consequence is that there's much less ego involved than many might assume. Brainstorming sessions are the best. We're also quite good editors of each other's work. We have a long history—over 40 years!—and know the conditions in which each of us is working, what we're capable of.

Back to that erasure I mentioned earlier. In the *Theories of Forgetting* video, the one that links from that page in the novel, there's a passage that Lance narrates. That passage is then erased in the video—parts of it drop away to manifest as another story, a poem that has been hidden in the original text. I think we had both recently met Jen Bervin's exquisite book-art project, *The Desert*, and had begun speculating about how we might allow it to influence us. I wanted to be the one to do the erasure of the original text, but the more I tried, the more I was reminded how I'm most definitely not a wordsmith. I passed it off to Lance, and he's all like: "Oh, cool, let's see what I can do." And he goes away for half an hour returns with just what we needed.

Does that mean you never disagree on essential decisions?

ANDI: When Lance has a manuscript ready, I'll read it and I might suggest a cut or an addition. He might do the same with a piece I'm working on. We both know it's never the final word. Sometimes the suggestion floats between us for a while. Sometimes we need to let it sink in. Sometimes we'll say that isn't quite what we have in mind. More often, however, it will lead us into productive territory. Our work always comes out stronger because of those back-and-forths, that openness to creative possibility.

LANCE: I'd simply add it all goes back to that idea of warm-hearted give and take, an attempt to bring out the best in each other and each other's work.

A parable: once upon a time I was working on a long SF novel called *Time Famine*, which appeared in 1996. I passed off the manuscript to Andi and, well, as you can probably guess, there's this long silence while she carefully works through the text. That gets to be unnerving. I'm the kind of guy who wants to accidentally on purpose wander into the room where she's reading every five minutes and ask how things are going. But, anyway, in this case, if not in them all, I controlled myself, waited patiently, and, after going mum several days, finally stuck my head into the kitchen where she was reading—and saw her with a pair of scissors, scotch tape, a magic marker, and parts of my book scattered everywhere. She was cutting up sections of the novel, splicing them into other sections, and … um, that may not have been the most ebullient moment of our relationship. [Laughs.]

Seriously, *Time Famine* turned out to be tremendously better for Andi's efforts. I'm so grateful. I always am.

ANDI: While I clipped and pasted, I kept thinking, what's the worst that can happen? You know, I cut this thing up and put it back together in a different way. Lance runs off another copy … But I could feel his eyes on the back of my neck, just like: "What are you *doing*?"

LANCE: What was worse was that I looked at what she had done after the fact and thought to myself: "Damn, that's good." So I had to both perform anger, and then repentance, and then penitence. [Laughs.] Honestly, though, it was all gratitude all the way down.

ANDI: Back to our collaborative video *Denkmal* for a minute by way of another parable. Originally, I had set it to a Philip Glass piece called *Metamorphosis*. I showed Lance and his response was, well, you'd already made a similar classical acoustic choice with *Where the Smiling Ends*. How about going somewhere else? And that was dead-on. We started thinking about other possibilities and before long drifted into the idea of an aural collage—something we were especially interested in at the time because of the *neue Musik* we were listening to in Berlin. Lance suggested I pull snippets from the transcript of Eichmann's trial in Israel, where he spoke about the infamous meeting at the Wannsee Center. I isolated several phrases, developed it into a sonic piece, and, bam, we had it.

There's No Place Like Time *is still traveling, still being shown. Do you plan to expand it?*

LANCE: Andi's working on a new piece right now. Alana is an amorphous-enough figure that, even after her death, work she's made keeps fruitfully showing up.

ANDI: This one in part has to do with what we were talking about earlier—the unfinalizability of history and identity. I'm using photos of myself, something I haven't done before and don't usually care to do. Invisibility suits me. But here it feels good. I'm working with ones from my childhood, ones taken in the house in which I grew up in Des Moines, Iowa. In 2021 I happened to notice one day on Zillow that that house was for sale. An idea caught me: what if I could gain access to it, to the same spaces in which I was a child, and try to duplicate—or at least approximate—those earlier photos, then somehow overlay them, so the past ghosted the present, and the present ghosted the past, thereby raising into view that great philosophical thought experiment, The Theseus Ship Paradox: if each plank of Theseus's ship has been replaced over time, at what point does that ship become no longer the same ship it was on the day it was built? In what way am I that kid in those photographs, even though I'm not? In what way is that kid a familiar stranger to me?

LANCE: In what way is Alana, who was never in those photographs, in those photographs, and not in those photographs?

So the fiction expands ...

LANCE & ANDI: Hopefully forever until we're ... finalizable, in a manner of speaking.

Do you think there might be other works in the future, other collaborations that would have this opening-to, like a text leading to a video, or maybe an installation?

LANCE: We'll see. Right now we're having a fantastic time mining the gifts Alana has given us. We keep thinking *There's No Place Like Time* might be done, and then ... no ... it keeps augmenting. Unfortunately, the pandemic stopped the live-exhibition version of the show, although much of it is present online at its website: zweifelundzweifel.org. We hope the live part will soon start up again.

ANDI: So far, Alana keeps giving.

We would like to conclude by asking you the same question Katya Fischer asks Alana Olsen at the end of the interview in the catalogue for There's No Place Like Time*: "Is there anything else you'd like to add?"*

LANCE: No. [Laughs.]

Which is what Alana basically said ... but her exact answer is: "No. I've probably said too much already."

LANCE: Oh, we must end with that. It's perfect. Alana always knows just what to say.

ACKNOWLEDGMENTS

I think that I think of this collection as a kind of photo album of my imagination over the last nearly four decades. There are so many people to remember and thank for helping me become myselves.

This list surely simply skips across the surface, and for that I apologize, but to begin: Kathy Acker, Jessica Alexander, The American Academy in Berlin, Ralph Berry, Scott Black, Karen Brennan, Kelly Cherry, Brian Clark, Gene Coleman, Robert Coover, DAAD, Guy Davenport, Douglas Day, Samuel R. Delany, Jeffrey Deshell, Trevor Dodge, Michelle Dotter, Craig Dworkin, Raymond Federman, Joyce Garvin, Molly Gaudry, Steven Gillis, Robert Glick, Eryn Green, David Hamilton, Noy Holland, Harold Jaffe, Aristotle Johns, Daniel Takeshi Krause, Matthew Kirkpatrick, Brooks Landon, Marcie Langley, Ray Levy, John Madera, Rachel Marston, Carole Maso, Larry McCaffery, Susan McCarty, Brian McHale, Michael Mejia, David Memmott, Bradford Morrow, Gurney Norman, Violet Olsen, Joy Passanante, Marjorie Perloff, Karen Power, Doug Rice, Rockefeller Foundation Bellagio Residency fellows, Joanna Ruocco, Davis Schneiderman, Alf Seegert, Katt Schaum, Elisabeth Sheffield, David Shields, Ken Smith, Susan Steinberg, Kathryn Bond Stockton, Ronald Sukenick, Walter Sokel, Melanie Rae Thon, Patricia Troxel, David Foster Wallace, Curtis White, Gary Williams, D. Harlan Wilson, Anthony Winner, Robert Wyatt, Lidia Yuknavitch.

Nor can I thank deeply enough the following venues, in which earlier versions of these pieces appeared in often quite different forms: "Carnage Carnival" was first presented as the keynote address at the 53ème Congrès de l'Association Française d'Études Américaine, Université Bordeaux Montaigne, and first published in *Big Other*; "Renewing the Difficult Imagination" in *Creative Writing: Theory Beyond Practice*; "There's No Place Like Time & Maze Reading" in *Fictionality and Multimodal Narratives*; "Reading/Writing as Tangle: Metafiction as Motion" in *Revue Française d'Études Américaines*; "14 Notes Toward the Musicality of Creative Disjunction" in *Symploke*; "Lessness" in *Conjunctions*; "Literary Autism" *in Modern Language Studies*; "Not-Knowings" in *Vladimir Nabokov et la France*; "The Art of Stupefying Malfunctions" in *Review of Contemporary Fiction*; "Stand by to Crash" in *Critique: Studies in Contemporary Fiction*; "Queen of the Pirates" in *Seattle Weekly*; "Reading Milorad Pavić Reading" in *The Writer's Chronicle*; "Termite Art" in *Review of Contemporary Fiction*; "Ontological Metalepses & the Politics of the Page" in *Steve Tomasula: The Art and Science of New Media Fiction*; the interview with Flore Chevaillier in *Divergent Trajectories: Interviews with Innovative Fiction Writers*; the interview with Michael Lackey and his students in *Truthful Fictions: Conversations with American Biographical Novelists*; the interview with Andrea Scrima in *Brooklyn Rail*; and the interview with Yannicke Chupin & Brigitte Félix in *Transatlantica.*

LANCE OLSEN is author of more than 30 books of and about innovative writing, most recently the novels *Always Crashing in the Same Car: A Novel After David Bowie* (Fiction Collective 2 2023) and *Absolute Away* (Dzanc 2024). His short stories, essays, and reviews have appeared in hundreds of journals and anthologies. A Fulbright Scholar as well as a recipient of the Guggenheim, Berlin Prize, D.A.A.D. Artist-in-Berlin Residency, Rockefeller Foundation Bellagio Center, two-time N.E.A. Fellowship, and Pushcart Prize, he taught experimental narrative theory and practice at the University of Utah.

SHRAPNEL

www.ingramcontent.com/pod-product-compliance
Ingram Content Group UK Ltd.
Pitfield, Milton Keynes, MK11 3LW, UK
UKHW040846100325
4921UKWH00041B/442